Ded... ...ted to
surviv...
Tammy

Through the Valley of Tears

An Incest Survivor's Story of Trauma and Recovery

Through the Valley of Tears

An Incest Survivor's Story of Trauma and Recovery

Tammy Lansaw

XULON PRESS

Xulon Press
2301 Lucien Way #415
Maitland, FL 32751
407.339.4217
www.xulonpress.com

xulon
PRESS

Printed in the United States of America.

ISBN-13: 978-1-54567-026-2.

Table of Contents

Introduction .... *xi*
Dedication .... *xvii*
Acknowledgements .... *xix*
Endorsements .... *xxv*
Foreword .... *xxix*

Chapter One ~ Introduction to My Nightmare* *1
A Household Name, A Household Event *1*
Introduction to My Nightmare *5*
My Personal Perspective *13*
How Could a Good God Allow This? *19*
My Own Personal Journal–Damaged Emotions *33*
Quote by Betsie ten Boom *35*
When the Shepherd Chooses Pain for Our Pathway
Notes *36*

Chapter Two ~ The Trauma That Changed My Life* *39
Symptoms of Sexual Abuse *39*

"O Love That Will Not Let Me Go" by George Matheson 43
About Shame 44
My Own Personal Journal–Restless, Lonely, and Scared 48
The Story of My Trauma 50
My Own Personal Journal–Feeling Rejected 57
My Memories of the Trauma 62
My Own Personal Journal–Anger 69
"The Gift of the Thorn" by J. Danson Smith 73
Notes 74

Chapter Three ~ Emotional Pain and Loneliness 75
The Trauma Becomes More Intense 75
My Own Personal Journal–My War With God 79
Quote by Dave Carder, M.A. 83
My Own Personal Journal–Deep Hurt 84
"The Consoler" by M. P. Ferguson 90
My Own Personal Journal–Nightmare 91
My Own Personal Journal–Feeling Nauseated and Dirty 92
Deep Darkness 93
"Nothing in the House" by Amy Carmichael 98
My Own Personal Journal–Tears, Tears, and more Tears 99
Darkness, Confusion . . . and Then a New Light! 103
My Own Personal Journal–Self-Esteem and the Lack Thereof 131
Health Problems 138

My Own Personal Journal–Despair and Prayer .. 141
Letter of Encouragement from God 144
Notes 147

Chapter Four ~ Healing Words of Life 149
"Upon Your Word I Rest" by Frances Ridley Havergal 149
Healing Words–Introduction 151
Scriptures Applied to the Wounds of Incest 154
Notes 251

Chapter Five ~ Special Psalms to Encourage You 253
Meditations on Psalm 139 255
"Children of The Heavenly Father" by Karolina Wihelmina Sandell-Berg 268
Thoughts from Psalm 25 269
"My Beloved" by Annie Clarke 275
Meditations on Psalm 86 277
The Beauty of Psalm 55 283
Who is God to an Incest Victim? 285
"God is Easy to Live With" by A.W. Tozer 287
"God of the Impossible" by J.H.S. reprinted from Springs in the Valley 291
Notes 293

Chapter Six ~ Getting Through the Recovery Process 295
The Recovery Process 295
Steps to Recovery 308

My Own Personal Journal–Fulfillment, Loss, and My Concept of God 319
Cycles 322
Feelings Caused by Incest 327
Letter to My Dad 331
Quote by Dave Carder, M.A. 339
Survival 340
What is Survival Mode? 341
Survival Mode Overload 343
Symptoms of Survival Mode Overload 351
Things I Have Learned in Review 353
Coping 357
Do I Really Need God To Heal? 361
Notes 366

Chapter 7 ~ A Song of Healing and Praise ***367***
Psalm 40 368
Psalm 40:1 368
Quote by Earl Henslin, Psy.D. 370
Psalm 40:2 371
Psalm 40:3 372
Psalm 40:5 374
Psalm 40:6 376
Psalm 40:11 376
Psalm 40:13-14 377
Letter to my Heavenly Father 379
My Own Personal Journal–Growth and the Acceptance of Self 383
Notes 385

Epilogue 387

Appendices:

I – Bibliography.. 391

II – About the Author... 395

III – Recommended Reading............................... 399

IV – End Notes 403

V – What We Know about Child Sexual Abuse ... 413

VI — Endometriosis Linked to Child Abuse 421

VII – The Use of Forgiveness Therapy with Female
Survivors of Abuse 429

VIII — Scriptures Referenced............................. 455

IX — Index.. 460

Introduction

It has been more than 38 years since I began the process of journaling and counseling, and I am very grateful to say that I would not be where I am today without the love, godly mentoring, and advice of the many individuals who have influenced my life during and since that time. It is to them that I attribute the writing of this book.

Parts of the original manuscript of this book are taken directly from my journals written during my counseling years, when I was going through the darkest time in my tunnel of depression. Other narrative parts were written during those same years for therapeutic reasons, when I thought it would be a good idea to keep a record of what had happened and was continuing to happen.

My first emotional response to the incest was to withdraw into feelings of deep depression. The people who loved me with the kind of love that could reach deep into my wounded soul were mostly Christians.

As a result of God's love for me through them, I soon responded to Him by accepting Jesus as my Savior and the Lord of my life.

When I was going through counseling and facing the trauma of incest, all those dark feelings came rushing up from deep inside me like an exploding volcano. At the same time, my outward circumstances left me empty inside. I had moved away from my hometown and away from all my familiar surroundings and friends. The environment and culture was completely different, and I felt like a fish out of water. I felt like the Lord had taken me away from every comfort and put me into an environment where it felt like I was living with porcupines. It seemed like everywhere I turned, I was getting quilled. I knew the Lord had led me to make the move, but every indication felt like I was in the wrong place. However, in retrospect, I know that He had led me to make the move so I would have no choice but to trust Him at every turn with every step.

At the time it seemed like He had taken a great risk with my life. My depression scale (with zero being the lowest emotional level possible) was below zero. It felt like God had taken such a great gamble with me that I became extremely vulnerable to the temptation to end my life. I will be forever grateful for the way God prepared me for that temptation. Prior to my move to these unfamiliar surroundings and people, I had worked at Western Conservative Baptist Seminary in Portland, Oregon. While there I worked as a faculty secretary with professors who were also pastors who had worked with individuals who had similar problems.

In the course of their teaching, they gave me handouts on the topic of suicide to either transcribe, edit, or make copies for their classes. I was thus educated on the subject of suicide, while the pain of my incest was buried deep inside. One of the first things I learned was that when a person becomes suicidal, they must talk to someone they trust. I will always be grateful for the wisdom and foreknowledge of God in giving me this knowledge before I needed it.

During all this time I learned the truth and knew in my heart that God *never* takes risks with our lives. He knows how we will respond to each thing He brings into our life. Even though *we may think* He is taking risks, what He allows into our lives is no risk at all. It is an *investment*. If there was any risk-taking, the risk was how He sacrificed His own Son to death at the hands of mankind–at my hands and yours—when we couldn't be any worse. But that wasn't really a risk either, as God was completely in control of every part of that event. He knew what would happen, in what order it would happen, how mankind would respond to it, and how it would turn out for His glory and for our redemption.

When I looked at the events of the cross where His Son Jesus died, I realized that God took no risk at all with my life. I was surely depressed. That was to be expected, when you consider the exploding volcano being released inside me. It is true what the Apostle Paul writes:

But God demonstrates His own love toward us, in that while we were yet sinners, Christ died for us.
Romans 5:8

The truth is that our souls are so valuable to God that *He makes an incredible investment in us.* This was what I previously perceived to be an unthinkable risk, because I only saw it from my own perspective. He invested the life of His own dear Son. He invests pain into our lives as well, so that as His priceless treasures, we will become magnificent jewels in His crown, cut and polished to absolute perfection. He does all of this for His glory and for our unspeakable joy, benefit, and fulfillment. This means that we truly are of immeasurable valuable to Him.

In the Old Testament Book of Job, the main character, for which the book is named, suffered greatly losing all his children and all his possessions, wealth, and finally his health. The book contains dialogues between him and his three friends, as they discuss the reason why God brought this suffering into Job's life. In Chapter 10 (verses 12-13), Job has the most encouraging words to say to the Lord. He has just described in detail how God created him in the womb of his mother. Then he says this:

You have granted me life and lovingkindness;
And Your care has preserved my spirit.
Yet these things You have concealed in Your heart;
I know that this is within You . . .

Even in his extreme physical pain and the emotional pain of great loss, Job could see how special he was to the Lord. And it is the same with us. We are precious to Him and He will not let anything hurt us without a divine purpose under His control.

> *But we have this treasure in earthen vessels, so that the surpassing greatness of the power will be of God and not from ourselves;*
>
> *2 Corinthians 4:7*

> *The LORD has today declared you to be His people, a treasured possession, as He promised you, and that you should keep all His commandments;*
>
> *Deuteronomy 26:18*

> *Then those who feared the LORD spoke to*
> *one another,*
> *And the LORD listened and heard them;*
> *So a book of remembrance was written*
> *before Him*
> *For those who fear the LORD*
> *And who meditate on His name.*
>
> *"They shall be Mine," says the LORD of hosts,*
> *"On the day that I make them My jewels.*
> *And I will spare them*
> *As a man spares his own son who serves him."*
>
> *Malachi 3:16-17 NKJV*

Even as we are a priceless treasure to our Lord, when we come know Him personally, He will become a treasure beyond all worth to us. It was that focus that gave me the strength to walk through my Valley of Tears, until it was no longer a place below sea level involving deep depression and tears.

It is my prayer that this book will be a blessing and an encouragement to all who read it, and that it will bring healing and hope to those who are hurting from the secret wounds of abuse carried in their hearts and memories.

It is to those who hurt that I devote this book.

Tammy Lansaw
Battle Ground, WA
2019

This Book is Dedicated to . . .

. . . my dear husband, Vic, who has loved me through all my difficulties as a survivor of this horrible trauma, who has encouraged me so patiently and lovingly through so many years to publish this story and my journals, so that others may be encouraged.

. . . my maternal Grandmother, Amelia Grace Smith Poor, who prayed for me every day during the most difficult years of my depression. Although she could not be with me in person due to her blood pressure, she was faithful with her telephone encouragement and prayers.

All the glory goes to my Lord Jesus, the One who has so magnificently transformed my life through His love, encouragement of the Scriptures, and the prayers of so many faithful friends and family.

Glory to His name!

Acknowledgements . . . and many thanks . . .

I have had so many loving and supportive friends and mentors over the years, that in mentioning all their names, I fear I would still leave out some very important individuals—especially some that I knew at the beginning of my journey. To those anointed individuals, I give my most heartfelt thanks.

Many friends and mentors loved me as it came natural to them. I am especially grateful for Mrs. Sandi Swanson, Mrs. Susan Heath, and Mrs. Wendy Carter—high school classmates who loved me to the cross of my Lord Jesus. They never gave up on me and continued to gently inquire about what was going on in my life, sharing the love of Jesus with me, and inviting me to come to church with them time after time ... after time. Along with them, I will not forget my first youth pastor and his dear wife, John and Judy Worley. They gave me rides to church and mentored me for many years, introducing me to the church where I stayed for ten years.

Moving on from high school, the Lord gave me other friends through my work at Western Conservative Baptist Seminary and my local church. I am very grateful for Dr. Robert Cook, Dr. ~~Robert~~ James Sweeney, Dr. Stanley Ellisen, and Dr. H. Crosby Englizian, who were professors I worked for and with at the Seminary. I shall not forget Mrs. Diane Touhey, Mrs. Linda Livingston, Rev. and Mrs. Loren and Joyce Fischer, and Mrs. Teresa Amey, who were also co-workers at Western; and dear friends and roommates like Miss Joyce Macht and Mrs. Cindy Adams, that I fellowshipped with at my local church.

I will not forget Rev. Jerry Larson and his dear late wife Nancy. Jerry was my first real pastor from the time I was seventeen until I was twenty-seven years old. He was a passionate teacher of God's Word. I learned much about the Scriptures under his capable teaching, as He would teach in an in-depth, verse-by-verse style. He has a true pastor's heart and currently has a strong Friendship Evangelism ministry. I am very proud to continue to call him my friend.

I am also grateful for the special employment opportunities, in which I was able to learn many things about myself, my Heavenly Father, and His Word. I found a number of quality mentors at these places of employment. The first was Western Conservative Baptist Seminary in Portland, Oregon, where I worked from the late 1970s until the early 1980s. While working there I was able to meet and become acquainted with Dr. Gordon Borror, who also served as the Music Minister in my church. Gordon taught me about the awesome character of God, and that everything we do should be done as an act of worship with excellence for the glory of God. He would say that nothing done for the glory of God is ever wasted.

Along with my friendship with Dr. Borror, I also want to give acknowledgement to his late wife Janine, who was my voice teacher for about four years. Janine was a very professional, knowledgeable, and patient teacher. She was also a wonderful listener. I will always be grateful for her insightful instruction during that time in my life.

During this time the Lord gave me a very special roommate, Mrs. Cindy Adams, for whom I am especially grateful. I had already learned to keep some journaling notes when important things happened and when I found a special Scripture that encouraged me, but Cindy was the one who taught me by example to really journal. She even wrote a special "book" about me in a home-made journal book, complete with pictures, and gave it to me for Christmas one year. My journaling took on a new life as a result of Cindy's influence in my life.

The second special employment opportunity which the Lord used in my life was my two-year tenure at Insight for Living, the radio ministry of Charles R. Swindoll, where I enjoyed working while living in Southern California. At "Insight" I transcribed Dr. Swindoll's church sermon messages for his radio broadcast. Listening to Dr. Swindoll five days a week, as I transcribed his messages, my Bible knowledge again skyrocketed. The theme at Insight for Living is also that everything we do must be done with excellence for the glory of God, and this value was further strengthened in my life.

Mrs. Shirley Evans is our neighbor and wonderful friend who lives next door to us. She is the author of a number of Christian fiction novels. She has also given me valuable writing and publishing advice and is also the editor of the first draft of my book.

I will always be grateful for my dear friend Elizabeth Hightower. She is a retired English Professor and she gave me excellent editing advice as well as other tips to help me in my writing. I credit her for the generous time that she offered on this project.

I am also very grateful, in fact I would say, *grateful beyond description*, for my dear husband, Victor, for his tenacity and patience. Over the time we have been together, he has continually encouraged me as to the value of my journals and story. For many years he prompted me to work on turning them into something that could be published for the benefit of others who have also suffered from the wounds of incest. He has never given up on me or this project. Before the final intensive editing, he went through each chapter, line by line, checking for grammatical errors.

I am also deeply grateful for my pastor, Dr. Mike Wilde. He is a true friend and prayer warrior that my husband and I can always count on. He has also been a faithful supporter of this project from the time he first learned about it. He has a faithful admonishment which he frequently repeats: "*Much prayer, much blessing; little prayer, little blessing; no prayer, no blessing!"* I am very grateful for the "much prayer" that has gone into the writing of this book.

I would like to give special thanks to Donella Schmidt, her husband Randy, and their daughter Kara for their work in editing the final manuscript. Their tenacious willingness to go the extra mile to make things clear for me was completely amazing! I could not have produced the book you have before you without their knowledgeable help. I will always be grateful for their work on my behalf.

Then I will not forget the enthusiasm of Steve Lantz when I presented my need for help with the interior photos. He said he loves to use his talents to do what anyone needs to do, and he put that to work on my photos.

I would like to give my heartfelt thanks to Carole Wolaver from the Pottery Lady for Him, for her gracious permission to use the picture of her pottery Hebrew tear bottle pictured on the front of this book and also pictured on page 232. Thank you Carole for your generosity.

Above all, I give my thanks and praise to my Heavenly Father, *the one Father I can always completely trust*, and I give all glory and praise to Him!

Tammy Lansaw
Battle Ground, WA
2019

Endorsements

Tammy approached me some time back and shared her story; giving me a rough copy of what you have in front of you. As I listened, as my heart ached, and as I read her manuscript, stopping at times to wipe away the tears and compose myself, three words came to mind; raw, real and redemptive. No little girl should be subjected to the horrors that she went through. Her story is the raw and unvarnished account of what she endured for so long. Her story is real and it's a sad reality that causes me to wonder how many others are out there who have experienced similar betrayals in their lives? As one well known counselor said, "At times, I wonder if every person in the world, male and female, young and old, have been sexually abused." Finally, Tammy's story is redemptive; she points to where God is in the darkest nights of our soul.

Throughout this book you will see how Tammy experienced some of the worst betrayals and pain in her life, her struggle with God, and the leading of the

Spirit to bring her hope and healing. Can God use the betrayals, the abuse, the pain in our lives for anything other than sorrow? This book shows the path that Tammy took to find that answer. I trust God will use her story to help you discover that truth as well.

Dr. Mike Wilde
Laurelwood Baptist Church
Vancouver, WA
2019

I met Tammy and Vic last year when they purchased the house next door. I had prayed God would lead believers to the neighborhood. The Lord, who never fails, came through again. For I found that not only were they believers, but that we had several things in common. Vic, who had served in Vietnam, was a disabled Vet. My deceased husband served in both WWII and Korea. Tammy was completing this book just as my 10th book was released. Tammy and Vic were also close to the ages of my two sons. The Lord certainly went above and beyond my prayers this time.

Tammy asked if I would read the early version of her book and I offered up a few suggestions. Thank you, Tammy, for trusting me, not only with your writing, but with your heart's desire to help others living with the pain that you have suffered. May God use your words to reach those going through much the same.

Shirlee Evans
Battle Ground, WA
2019

Foreword

I first met Tammy in Southern California on a blind date set up by our chiropractor, of all people. When I knocked on her door we were both surprised to see that we were color coordinated. I was wearing a pink polo shirt and a pair of white slacks. Tammy was wearing a pink blouse with a white skirt.

On the way to the restaurant I kept sneaking peeks at Tammy because she was so pretty. From the very start, Tammy said she had something to tell me and it was important for me to listen. She explained how she doesn't kiss on the first date, she doesn't hold hands on the first date, and she doesn't hug or give pet names on the first date; and most importantly, she loves God with all her heart. She said I had to earn the right for each one of them, and she hoped that I would be okay with this—which I was.

I thought to myself, Wow!! Not only is she pretty on the outside, but very beautiful on the inside too!! Since I loved the Lord as well, it was refreshing to sit across the table with a beautiful woman and just talk, knowing there were certain boundaries I dare not cross.

After many more dates and a year and a half later, I asked her to marry me and to my delight she said, "Yes!" I think the first time we held hands in public it was like I was a schoolboy on a date, going to the junior/senior prom. I was totally twitter pated! I think my heart was trying to jump out of my chest!

As our relationship continued to grow, we would share our past experiences, both good and bad, with each other. She shared about her upbringing, the story of her nightmares, the guilt and shame, and the severe trauma she had endured for so many years.

During the first couple years of being married, I could see that Tammy had a difficult time trusting me. Actually she had a difficult time trusting anyone. One question that would frequently come up was, "What do you mean by that?" I would pray, with her and for her many times over the years, asking God to heal her pain. I understood her difficulties to a point, but I never fully grasped the severity of what she went through. For thirty-two years I have watched Tammy slowly come out of her shell of insecurity and distrust to the point of writing this book you have before you.

I am a very blessed man to have a woman of such courage. Even though she's been through this incredible journey, Tammy still loves the Lord with all her heart, reads His Word every day, prays, and seeks His guidance and direction.

We have three P/P's that we live by. They are: "we are partners in *Prayer*, partners in *Pain,* and partners in *Passion*."

So, in conclusion, I would like to say, "Tammy, I love you ever so much and I am very proud of you." I will close by asking you the reader one question. My question to you is (and please forgive my grammar), "Ain't God been good to me?"

Victor Lansaw
Battle Ground, Washington
2019

Chapter 1

Introduction to My Nightmare

The noblest souls are the most tempted (and tried).
The devil is a sportsman and likes big game.
He makes the deadliest assaults on the richest
natures, the finest minds, the noblest spirits.

~John L. Lawrence, reprinted from Springs in the Valley

A Household Name, A Household Event

"She lived in foster homes until she reached her eleventh birthday and then lived in an orphanage. She married at the age of sixteen. Her early life was very troubled, and she felt unwanted. But she was not really an unwanted orphan. Her mother had been diagnosed with schizophrenia and lived most of her daughter's childhood in and out of a mental hospital. When released from the hospital on weekends, her mother took her to the movies in Hollywood, California. When this beautiful and talented young woman grew up, she became an actress.

"But she still led a very troubled private life, and for that she received much attention. She struggled with substance abuse, depression, and anxiety. She had two highly publicized marriages, both of which ended in divorce. She then passed away in her mid-thirties from an over-dose of barbiturates. Her death was ruled a probable suicide.

"Much was revealed as to the likely cause of her troubled life and sudden death when her personal correspondence was read. It touched on her great fear of displeasing others and of the great traumas of her life: *the numbing pain of rejection and hurt* at the destruction of an idealistic image of true love. And of her early sexual abuse she wrote, *'I will not be punished for it, be whipped, threatened, or not be loved for it . . .'*

"Between her psychiatric sessions, she began recording some of those raked up memories, including a devastating incident of sexual abuse. Described around 1955 in a green Italian notebook, this memory fully emerges. During a 1962 interview she states that in her childhood, perhaps during this hazy period of foster-home existence, or perhaps even earlier, she was sexually molested. In recounting the story, she gave her age at the time of the incident as about the age of eight or nine. According to her, a family friend or perhaps a boarder in her foster home molested — *or raped* — her in his room. For days after this incident she would repeatedly take showers and baths to make herself feel clean and to wash the dirty feeling away. This is indicative of women who have been raped or sexually molested.

"When she told her foster mother what had happened, the woman refused to believe her. She states that the foster mother slapped her, shouting, 'I don't believe you. Don't you dare say such things about that nice man! He is our best boarder.'

"When this young woman was born, the name on her birth certificate was Norma Jean Mortensen. Her mother subsequently divorced her father and changed her daughter's name to match the sir name of her current husband, so she grew up with the name Norma Jean Baker. But when she became an actress in the late nineteen-fifties and early nineteen-sixties, her name became known in every household in America. That name was Marilyn Monroe."

But the truth is, it does not matter how gifted or how talented a person might be or even how beautiful, what their name is, or how privileged they become—the pain and trauma of sexual abuse is no respecter of persons. The unfortunate thing is that it can lead to the same end with *anyone* as it did with Marilyn Monroe.

In Marilyn Monroe's case it led to *a life filled with feelings of being lost, personal shame, depression, and devastatingly overwhelming loneliness and repeated rejection*—no matter how many or what kind of people surrounded her. We're talking about a life of potential promiscuity, drug abuse, and even an early death, regardless of how much that person is adored or idolized, what their life represents, or how wealthy they are. Many victims are fortunate enough to be led down a different path, but nevertheless, it is not unusual for this kind of tormented person to have a life with a background containing a very destructive force in it, whether they are a man or a woman. So as Marilyn Monroe became a household name, so incest has become a household event. But this event happens behind closed doors and has become the untold family secret.

"The sexual abuse inflicted on Marilyn Monroe shouldn't seem surprising. From the mid-nineteenth century to the present, the rate of sexual abuse of girls has remained constant at twenty percent. In other words, one in five girls is molested today, as in the past. The perpetrators are usually the male heads of the households in which the girls live, and they come from all social classes and ethnic groups. Like rape in general, sexual abuse of girls is not a crime perpetrated only by strangers or by violent lower-class men.

"The impact of sexual abuse on girls can be profound. The victim can experience the assault as a penetration of the self that causes shame, self-hatred, and guilt. In other words, abused girls may blame themselves for the crime committed against them. They may regard themselves and other women with contempt, and they may develop an aversion to sex. Or they may degrade themselves through prostitution or 'sex addiction,' the drive for continual sex and the inability to resist seduction. . . . They may become obsessed with being perfect or develop a sadomasochism in which they identify with powerful individuals and then try to destroy them. A low self-image can exist along-side megalomania. [1] Such symptoms can appear immediately after the attack, later in life, or episodically." [2]

Introduction to My Nightmare

This book was terribly difficult to write. It was difficult because the topic of incest is a very personal one that hit directly home for me. But why would I want to write a book on this topic if it's so difficult? I have a couple of reasons. First, because sexual abuse is an epidemic in our nation which tears apart the homes and lives of many young men and women.

Some individuals often respond to this trauma by becoming promiscuous, being led away from home and family or career. Their confused emotions can also lead to illegal drug abuse. It's also common for a person with these developmental issues to be led into human trafficking and into a life of prostitution.

Another reason it was difficult for me to write about incest is because of my personal background. I am not writing from statistics or research or academics or from what I heard happened to someone I know. I am writing because I am an incest *survivor.* Incest reared its ugly head and tore my home apart before I even had a chance to grow up. For many years I was a victim, and now I am a survivor—most of the time.

I will tell you that being a survivor doesn't erase all the memories and scars. No, they are there to stay. A victim or survivor can do many things to try to forget or suppress those memories, but they have a way of coming back in the form of nightmares, insecurities, post-traumatic stress disorder, (otherwise known as PTSD), and health issues. With regard to PTSD, I do not wish to minimize the suffering of those who have experienced the horrors of the battlefield, having gone into the military to defend our nation only to come home suffering from this very trying disorder. PTSD, like incest, presents itself with an invisible disability accompanied primarily by invisible symptoms. However, millions suffer from incest, as a result of just trying to grow up in a safe environment. They have some memories that still haunt and hurt after many years and decades. Many of them are healing, and some may feel that they are almost healed, until someone comes along and says or does something that bumps into those scars by way of a reminder invoking a memory. Then today becomes yesterday all over again and the process starts all over again.

This is the primary reason I decided to write this book. I believe that my experience would be of great help to others going through the recovery process. I have greatly benefitted from the practice of journaling and the counseling process as well as from what I have learned through continued research. Therefore, I am confident this book will help current victims and survivors *to know that you are not alone as you sort through all your crushed and confused emotions, your depression, and your suppressed memories. You can be assured that you* ***can*** *recover and live a productive life.*

Like most victims and survivors, my trauma of incest started when I was young and extremely vulnerable. I was eleven years old and very naïve about sex and everything in the adult world. In most ways I *was* a little girl and I wanted to stay that way. I did want to grow up, while still hanging on to childish things. This is the nature of adolescence. I still liked to play with dolls. I *loved* to sew. My teeth were very crooked, and I had just started wearing braces to straighten them.

My father had also begun to change. He had been in an auto accident earlier that year. He had sustained a whiplash and a head injury in the accident, and he was in a lot of pain. As a result, he had been on several different types of medications for pain, which he had become addicted to. So the doctor gradually took him off those meds. In order to replace the effect of the prescriptions, he began drinking. The change in his behavior also came on kind of gradually, and he was not pleasant to be around. He was beginning to display more erratic behavior and was angry at nothing or just about everything most of the time. To avoid this change in behavior, I tried to remain invisible when he was around, and I avoided him as much as possible. It was frightening to be close to him, because I never knew what version of my father I was going to get. He yelled very frequently at very loud volumes. I was very intimidated by him.

Then it happened. My father, who had been changing in his attitudes and actions toward everyone also changed in a particular way toward me. It was at this time that he committed the unthinkable. He did something I never would have thought or could have imagined he would do. How could I? His behavior was completely unexpected. I was a child and had no way of anticipating him coming into my room and giving me his "special attention." It wasn't long before that special attention turned from something "special" to something very wrong. He began coming into my room at night and sexually molesting me. It traumatized me, and it changed my life forever. I could never be the same.

Incest turned me inside out emotionally and put me into a turmoil that was never ending—or so it seemed. It was an intimate and personal trauma. For a long time, it was every night. I do not recall how long that consistency continued. But the incest and its consequences seemed to go on forever and seemed like it would never go away.

Incest defined my life for many years. First there was the *traumatic sexual abuse*, then there was the *secret*, then there was the *depression*, *withdrawal*, *suppression*, *isolation,* and *thoughts of suicide.* During that time I experienced a loneliness so deep I couldn't describe it—except it made the depression so intense that I didn't want to live anymore. I didn't know where to turn or who to talk to. I had my first suicidal thoughts when I was fifteen, the second time when I was twenty-nine, and the third when I was thirty. I just couldn't bear the depth of the emptiness and the deep loss of dignity and self-respect.

The worst part was that I couldn't talk to anyone about the incest when it happened. Or I didn't think

I could. I knew I couldn't talk to my mother. I thought that either she wouldn't believe me, or she would be angry with me and blame me. I knew that I couldn't talk to any of my siblings. I thought they either wouldn't believe me, or I thought they would ridicule and laugh at me. What sibling of an eleven-year-old is going to believe such a thing about their sister? It would be too embarrassing if people knew, and of course my dad would deny it. Besides, I was so ashamed. I thought that it made me the bad girl. I felt dirty and ugly inside and out. My life had become one big secret. I just wanted to hide.

All this secrecy boiled down to one of the first symptoms of incest, the *in*ability to trust anyone. I didn't think I could talk to anyone because I couldn't trust anyone. It didn't matter who they were, I didn't trust them. But I *was* able to fake it. I was able to go about my teenage life as if nothing was wrong, and that is what I did, trying to fool everyone. I think I became quite good at the play-acting game, pretending that everything was okay. But it only made my hurt deeper, my loneliness more profound, and my depression darker. And for a long time, no one caught on.

This trauma, father-daughter incest, would have been just as traumatic had it been with another family member, such as another adult male—an uncle, grandparent, brother, or even a family friend or a neighbor. But for me, it was my father—someone I had to live with, be in submission to, show respect for, and certainly obey. Oh! What a horrible experience and an even worse thing if I were to have to talk about it openly. When the incest was taking place night after night, I knew I could not escape it. Besides not being able to escape the nightly routine, I was set on a course that I thought I was completely powerless to change.

When my father finally stopped the nightly visits, the nightmares that followed would continue and seemed to last forever. The trauma that it caused, however, lasted for years. I just kept reliving the incest. It kept going over and over in my head until it made me sick. Then I rejected it and pretty much rejected myself, withdrawing into a deeper depression. Even though I wanted it to stop, I withdrew emotionally and sunk into a state of emptiness. On the inside I was numb, but on the outside, I still had to respond as the daughter and sister.

When I was going through counseling and the healing process a number of years later, I would have done almost anything for the opportunity to read or hear the story of what another incest survivor had done that had helped her or him to find some answers. I wanted to know what others in my situation had done to obtain some emotional stability. My counselor did refer one book to me that I thought was very good. This book was so good that it opened my eyes about myself in many ways. The book she referred to me was *Your Inner Child of the Past* by W. Hugh Missildine, M.D.[3] It helped me to understand that so many of the things that were affecting me as a young adult were related back to my young childhood. Further, the problems I had in many of my relationships were there to a great degree, because of the relationship I had with my father and also because of the relationship my father had with my mother. That part I found to be quite complicated. But I found this book to be very helpful. Once I read it all the way through, I wanted to read it again and again.

Books had always been my constant companions and a great comfort to me during those times. I sought more help from them, and, as a consequence, I was always trying to find other books that would help me. But unfortunately, there was not much on the market at that time, and it was not easy to find literature on this subject that was of much help. It was before the days of the internet, but I searched the bookstores. This was one of the only avenues I was aware of for resources on emotional healing other than counseling and/or group therapy. I tried to be as proactive in my recovery process as possible with the resources that were available to me. So along with my counseling, I journaled and read everything I could find.

The incest and the mental and emotional abuse I suffered could have been more or less than what any other victim might experience. In my opinion, from my own experience and from my research, I would say that every victim of abuse responds in their own way, depending on each person's temperament, personality, age, gender, physical and mental development, and a variety of other social issues. From what I have read, I would also say that *my abuse* was in the middle range that many suffer, *and my response* to the trauma was severe. My response was also physical. I developed physical health disorders in my teenage years that either stumped or were shrugged off by my parents and our family doctors. I also responded emotionally with secrecy and by withdrawing into a deep depression. For the most part, I believe that my parents and family were unaware of my depression because I did my best to hide it. They did know of my illnesses but did not understand them. I gradually became suicidal, and by the time I was in my late twenties, I required antidepressant medication to pull me out of it. The focus of this book is not so much on the severity of my symptoms, but on how I was able to recover from them and how you can experience the same kind of recovery.

As my father was the perpetrator of my abuse, in one way or another he was also abusive toward everyone who lived at our address and even some who did not live with us. He tended to treat everyone who came in contact with our family with a complete lack of respect, unless he wanted something from them. However, as you continue to read, you will notice that I am only telling my own personal story. I cannot speak for anyone else.

But in another sense, it is not just my own story. It is the story of hundreds of thousands of girls and boys, women, and men in this country. I am reminded that there is such a large percentage of our population who are tragically abused in this way, and the numbers keep climbing.[4] The statistics are alarming. One in five girls and one in twenty boys are a victim of child sexual abuse. Twenty percent of adult females recall childhood sexual assault and 5-10% adult males recall incidences of childhood sexual abuse. These statistics are of epidemic proportions and they are climbing. These victims need the hope that this kind of book is intended to offer. It is my hope and prayer that my personal experience with this specific type of traumatic abuse and the suggestions in this book will be of help to those who need it.

My Personal Perspective

When I was very young, I knew instinctively that I could call upon the Lord Jesus, my Creator God, in a time of crisis. I knew Him as my Heavenly Father. I had an intellectual relationship with Him. When those times of crisis came, I could call on Him at any time, and I knew instinctively that I could trust Him when I couldn't trust anyone else.

The home I grew up in was not exactly a Christian home. We celebrated Christmas and Easter. My parents didn't go to church, but they did want us to have a basic knowledge of the Bible, so they sent us to what they believed was a non-denominational Bible Church. They didn't go with us or even take us. An elderly couple from this little church picked us up every Sunday and brought us home again. As I recall, we did learn the Bible.

Every Sunday after church we ate our Sunday dinner, then we had a "family quiet time." This was a time when everyone was required to find something to read. We could read anything we wanted to, but we had to read silently. It could be something we brought home from church, our homework from school, library books, or the cartoons from the Sunday paper. I believe the idea was to help us value and enjoy reading. I remember I used to enjoy reading the papers that I brought home from Sunday School, and I would read my Bible along with the lesson for the day. I used to wish my Sunday School papers were more substantial, because I really enjoyed reading them and looking at the pictures that went along with the lessons. I had a hunger to know more.

But after the incest occurred, I found myself questioning, "How could I trust in a God who would allow this terrible, unthinkable thing to happen?" It wasn't until my depression led to thoughts of suicide that I turned to Him in desperation. I became very confused both spiritually and emotionally.

I was on a course of denial, pain, and destruction. This course was set off by being violated by my father, someone I should have been able to trust and feel safe with. It happened when I was extremely vulnerable in a place where I should have felt safer than anywhere—*my own home!!* This was *unthinkable!* These thoughts continued until I was in such a depression that I couldn't get out of it on my own.

I tried everything to get out of this state of emotional chaos. Starting in high school right after the incest stopped, I began to focus more on my appearance. When it came time for the braces to come off my teeth, I had my picture taken. Everyone said I looked beautiful. I had long, golden blond hair. I received compliments on it every day. If a day went by and I did not receive a compliment about my hair, I thought something was wrong with me. I felt worthless and ugly. Even though I wasn't very tall, I wanted to be a fashion model when I grew up. After discussing this for a while, my mother sent me to a Finishing School. I believe she did this, because it was something I really wanted and because I seemed to be so withdrawn. It is possible she sensed that I was struggling emotionally with something related to adolescence or something related to my dad's erratic behavior. She never mentioned it, but perhaps she thought it might help with my self-esteem and help bring me out of my shell. The Finishing School was something I enjoyed very much. But when I came home with new make-up or a new hair style, my dad criticized it. It seemed he didn't want me to explore my new interests or to experiment with my new looks. I was very hurt. It seemed like he couldn't stop hurting me.

I joined the junior varsity high school gymnastics team and worked out very hard for one year. I had a very encouraging and supportive gymnastics coach who recognized my hard work. She made sure that I received a Junior Varsity Letter for my effort, even though I never had the opportunity to compete. I also played the flute in the high school band. I went on to try every wholesome thing I could think of that I enjoyed, in which I could prove to myself that I was worthy to be accepted.

Due to my mother's instruction and Home Economics classes at school, I became an accomplished seamstress and made all of my own clothes throughout high school. But *none of this* was enough to bolster my self-esteem or to adequately lift my spirits.

Then God, in His wisdom, reached out to me through some high school classmates. Due to their influence, I learned that God loved me with a love that was so incredible that it could in no way compare with human love. It was more intense and more alive and purer than any human love I had ever encountered. I learned that I could have a personal relationship—more like a friendship—with God through His Son, the Lord Jesus. That relationship would be a crucial part of my healing as I walked through this sad Valley of Tears. I had never thought of God as a Person who wanted to know me, and I had never believed that it was possible to be in a personal relationship with Him. In my mind, He was always Someone to fear, somewhat like my father. Now I was learning that *He* was pursuing a relationship with *me!* I never knew that He was a relational Person, and He was pursuing me! But when I learned this, I responded to this information by pouring my heart out to Him. I spoke to Him with complete honesty, telling Him how much I hated my life and wanted to have it end, giving Him all the pain and grief I felt at that moment.

This was the first step I took toward God. I responded to His invitation, by opening the door of my broken soul to Him and allowing Him to come in and take the burden of my pain. When I did this, He washed me clean with the blood of His cross, allowing me to be born again to a new life or the beginning of a new life. I knew that it was much more than giving a mental acknowledgement to what I had been taught. *It was allowing His Spirit to enter my soul, so He could affect real change*.

I write all this to emphasize that I believe God had His hand on my life from early childhood. *I am therefore writing from a Christian perspective*. That perspective played a vital role in my healing process. It also played a huge role in my journaling, meditation, prayer, and healing. I would have lost all hope, if it had not been for the influence that my Christian friends and mentors had and the role God Himself played in my life. I really looked forward to writing things down like this and gave it a high priority in my life. It was like I had a calling on my life and I felt compelled to keep a record of what was happening with my chaotic emotions.

I remember it like it was yesterday. It was about four years after the incest began that some classmates at my high school reached out to me. It must have been obvious to them that I was lost and struggling, and they invited me to church. It took going to church off and on for about nine months, before I surrendered my defenses and invited the Lord Jesus to come into my life. I learned that Jesus says,

> *Behold, I stand at the door and knock; if anyone hears My voice and opens the door, I will come in to him, and I will dine with him, and he with Me.*
> *Revelation 3:20*

So that's what I did. I invited Jesus to come into my life. I prayed a simple little prayer, professing my faith in Him. I told Him that I believed that He died for me and shed His blood for me and was also raised from the dead for me. Then I asked Him to be my Savior from sin and the Lord of my life. I thanked Him for the forgiveness of my sins and thanked Him for dying on the cross for me, so that I could spend eternity in heaven with Him.

After I prayed, a huge weight of depressive pain and confusion fell to the floor and sweet peace flooded my soul. I said, "a huge weight of pain and confusion fell to the floor," but it wasn't the entire weight that had to be shed. It was just the first installment of what the Lord would do in my life. I had also learned another verse in the Bible that said,

> *Therefore, if anyone is in Christ, he is a new creature; the old things passed away; behold, new things have come.* *2 Corinthians 5:17*

When I first read this, I thought it meant I would be changed instantly and forever and the old pain would be gone forever. But I soon learned that change is gradual, even with God, spiritual growth, and healing. I would go through many times of depression, loneliness, and confusion. During those times I wondered if God, or anyone else, cared if I would thrive or even if I would survive. But He—that is, God—cared for me more than I could ever imagine. There were times when the Lord would give me one special verse of Scripture. I would call them my "*Verses of Survival.*" He would use them so mightily in my life. One by one and by the power of His Spirit, I came out of a deep emotional rut. It gave me the assurance that there was indeed a light at the end of my deep dark tunnel. Sometimes I would share a very encouraging *"Verse of Survival"* with my best friend at work, and she would just smile and say, "Sweetie, this is how I know you are going to make it through this."

So that is the perspective I pass on to you, and from which I will be writing. God is the Great Physician and the Gentle Shepherd, who gently cares for his wounded lambs, of which I am one. He had His hand on me from the very beginning, and He never let go. As my Good Shepherd, He gently carried me close to His heart when I was broken and bruised. He will carry you as well, until you are able to run and skip with all the other sheep and lambs of His flock.

How Could A Good God Allow This?

You may ask—as I certainly did during my moments of doubt and grief—how a good God could allow such a thing to happen to a child, someone who is innocent, who feels safe in her home, and who trusts her parents. Then while in that state of trust, one of her parents, without hardly a second thought, comes in at night and commits an unthinkable act of betrayal. How could I reconcile this with a God who proclaims His goodness, holiness, and purity?

When I met Jesus at the cross and envisioned His blood running down to His feet, I knew He was dying for me, for *my sins.* I knew I had to forgive this man (my own flesh and blood biological father) for what he did to me. But even in forgiving him, I again had to ask the hard question, "How could my Heavenly Father have allowed this horrible thing to happen?" He certainly could have prevented it, being the all-powerful God of all creation. And how could I trust my father, or any man, or even the God who says He loves me and proclaims His goodness, purity, compassion, and mercy?

The only reasonable answer I can share with you came with time and solid biblical teaching. I learned that God created mankind, each man and each woman, in His own image. In doing so He gave each one of us a free will. He did not want us to be robots, who would serve and obey Him automatically with no thought or emotion involved. He gave me a free will, and what did I do with it? I contributed to His death on the cross with my sins, as did every person since the beginning of time. My biological father chose to use his free will to do that terrible thing to me, repeatedly. His accident, head injury, medications, alcoholism, or Bipolar Disorder had nothing to do with it. He chose to commit that act out of the evil that was in his heart. But all the time *my Heavenly Father was with me*, caring for me as any good father would, loving me, and protecting me from even further damage and pain. Believe me, it could have been a whole lot worse.

One day, as I was trying to find a way to trust God as *my Heavenly Father,* He gave me this most encouraging thought. He showed me that when my biological father was doing this detestable thing to me, my *Savior*, the Lord Jesus, who died the most painful of all deaths*, was sitting in the room with me, right beside me.* He was there with me, *suffering right along with me as if He were being violated in the most shameful way—because He had been!*

In fact, His death was even more shameful than the betrayal that I was suffering! I could see Him in my heart, with tears running down His cheek *because He knew* the anguish I was going through at the same moment it was happening. He knew the terrible pain it was going to cause me throughout my lifetime. He knew what it would mean to give me the oil of joy for the spirit of heaviness and beauty for the ashes I was living in (Isaiah 61:1-3 NKJV). But at this moment, it was all heaviness and ashes. In His perfect will, He never meant for me to be broken by incest and abuse. At the same time, He knew before I was conceived that it would happen, and He had a perfect plan for restoration.

As I looked further into the Scriptures, God's love letter to me, I learned some amazing things about why God allows these terrible things to happen, while *He seems* to look idly by. We think He doesn't care; but the truth is, *He has a wonderful purpose in everything that happens to us—even the bad stuff.* He does care, even more than we can imagine or put into words. The first part of my answer came when I read John 9:1-3 which says:

> *As He (JESUS) passed by, He saw a man blind from birth. And His disciples asked Him, saying, "Rabbi, who sinned, this man or his parents, that he would be born blind?"*
>
> *Jesus answered, "It was neither that this man sinned, nor his parents; but it was so that the works of God might be displayed in him."*

That suggests to me that a person can suffer unjustly, and God will allow it for a high and holy purpose. The purpose for that man's blindness was so Jesus could heal him, and God would receive the glory. But my situation was a little bit different. I know that what happened to me happened because of the sin of my father. My father committed the sin of incest, not once, not twice, but multiple times over at least two years that I can recall. I do not remember how many times, but it was enough to cause trauma and great fear as you will read in the coming pages. The Bible makes it very clear that incest is a sin in the eyes of God. In the Book of Leviticus 18:6 it states:

> *None of you shall approach any blood relative of his to uncover nakedness; I am the LORD.*

The following verses 7-18 describe what a blood relative is in the eyes of God. They are your father, mother, sister, daughter, half-sister, son's daughter, daughter's daughter, father's wife's daughter, father's sister, mother's sister, father's brother, daughter-in-law, brother's wife, a woman and her daughter, her son's daughter, or her daughter's daughter. It also states that you shall not marry a woman and her sister while she is alive as a rival. The Bible identifies a married couple as one flesh. This means that if a woman is violated, her husband is violated as well. Therefore, in-laws are considered blood relatives because they are married to sons and daughters. I believe it is safe to say that it is prohibited, under God's law of decency, to violate anyone with incest. The Lord has made it very clear that this form of immorality is completely unacceptable in His eyes. In fact, He can't stand it! Ezekiel 22 states the following, beginning at verse 10:

> 10 *In you they have uncovered their fathers' nakedness; in you they have humbled her who was . . . in her menstrual impurity.*
>
> 11 *And one has committed abomination with his neighbor's wife, and another has lewdly defiled his daughter-in-law. And another in you has humbled his sister, his father's daughter. . .*
>
> 25 *There is a conspiracy of her prophets in her midst, like a roaring lion tearing the prey. They have devoured lives; they have taken treasure and*

> *precious things; they have made many widows in the midst of her.*
>
> *26 Her priests have done violence to My law and have profaned My holy things; they have made no distinction between the holy and the profane, and they have not taught the difference between the unclean and the clean; . . . and I am profaned among them.*
>
> *30 And I searched for a man among them who should build up the wall and stand in the gap before Me for the land, that I should not destroy it; but I found no one.*
>
> *31 Thus I have poured out My indignation on them; . . .*

To say that God hates incest is a vast understatement. To say that incest destroys the treasure things that God meant to be precious is also quite obvious.

As I continued in my Bible study, I found another Bible story that taught me how my Lord relates to our pain. It was of great help to me. This is a story of a human tragedy, quite personal to Jesus, one that He could have easily prevented but deliberately chose to allow for His own good purpose. He had some very close friends, a small family of siblings, Mary, Martha, and Lazarus, who lived just outside of Jerusalem in a little village called Bethany. During the Lord's ministry, Lazarus became very ill. The sisters sent a message to Jesus, telling him about Lazarus,

> *"Lord, Your dear friend is very sick."*
>
> John 11:3 NLT

What did Jesus do in response to that message? Instead of rushing off to Bethany to lay hands on Lazarus to heal him, He stayed where He was for another two days. And He told His disciples:

> *"This sickness is not to end in death, but for the glory of God, so that the Son of God may be glorified by it."* John 11:4

When Jesus and His disciples finally arrived in Bethany, Lazarus had died and had been in the tomb *for four days*. Many friends and mourners had come to give comfort to the sisters. John 11:32-44 sets the scene:

> *Therefore, when Mary came where Jesus was, she saw Him, and fell at His feet, saying to Him, "Lord, if You had been here, my brother would not have died."*
>
> *When Jesus therefore saw her weeping, and the Jews who came with her, also weeping, He was deeply moved in spirit, and was troubled, and said,*
>
> *"Where have you laid him?" They said to Him, "Lord, come and see."*
>
> *Jesus wept.* [5]

So the Jews were saying, "See how He loved him!" But some of them said, "Could not this man, who opened the eyes of the blind man, have kept this man also from dying?"

So, Jesus, again being deeply moved within, came to the tomb. Now it was a cave, and a stone was lying against it. Jesus said,

"Remove the stone."

Martha, the sister of the deceased, said to Him, "Lord, by this time there will be a stench, for he has been dead four days."

Jesus said to her, "Did I not say to you that if you believe, you will see the glory of God?"

So they removed the stone.

Then Jesus raised His eyes, and said,

"Father, I thank You that You have heard Me. I knew that You always hear Me; but because of the people standing around I said it, so that they may believe that You sent Me."

When He had said these things, He cried out with a loud voice,

"LAZARUS, COME FORTH!"

The man who had died came forth, bound hand and foot with grave wrappings; and his face was wrapped around with a cloth. Jesus said to them,

"Unbind him, and let him go."

This is probably the most incredible miracle of Jesus' earthly ministry. This man, Lazarus, had been in the tomb for four days. He was really dead and there is no human way to explain it away. His body was beginning to decay just like any other corpse would that had been in the grave for that period of time. This was not a resuscitation as some would conjecture, as was evidenced by the odor coming from Lazarus' corpse.

Another interesting point is that Jesus did not simply cry out in a loud voice, "*COME FORTH!*" For if He had done so, all the corpses in the tombs of that area would have come back from the dead and proceeded to walk out of their tombs! No, He identified which dead person He wished to come back from the dead and walk out of his tomb. It was the corpse of *Lazarus* that He was commanding to come out of that tomb. They were truly seeing the glory of God!

Imagine! This was a case where God allowed a serious human tragedy to bring about something beyond the miraculous—another level above the miracles they had previously seen Jesus perform. They had witnessed the blind receiving their sight, the deaf receiving their hearing, the lame walking, the evil spirits being cast out, the sick being healed, and various other miracles over natural creation—all of which were amazing in themselves. But raising the dead? This was something that God used to really get the people's attention and to show them once again that Jesus was (*and is*) His Son, *fully God* and *fully Man*.

This was just weeks before Jesus' own death and resurrection. Imagine how this must have felt for Jesus, knowing His own death and resurrection were just right around the corner and knowing what purpose God had for Him in this. We cannot compare this with our own tragedies, but we can say, without hesitation and without exception, that God has a purpose for the painful situations and tragedies that He allows to happen in our lives.

Jesus suffered *pain with a purpose,* when He suffered for our redemption from sin. He gives us an example that we must follow. As His followers, we must continue in that process to suffer *pain with a purpose* to continue our redemption from the wounds inflicted on us. This is how we grow spiritually in our relationship with Him. As those on the road to recovery from the wounding of incest, we must purposely and deliberately take His nail-scarred hand and lean on Him for strength, as we continue to face our fears. We must also deal with the negative memories and the associated emotions that will surface.

Now here is an important thing to know. We cannot do this in our own strength. Suffering this kind of *pain* in a redemptive way (or in a way that will help us to grow in our relationship with God) can only be done as we lean on Him, live in Him, and trust Him to do the work in us that only He can do. As He Himself says so clearly:

> *"I am the vine, you are the branches.*
> *He who abides in Me, and I in him,*
> *bears much fruit;* ***for without Me you***
> ***can do nothing."*** *John 15:5* NKJV

As I continued to think on this and was researching what other victims and survivors felt, I came across the testimony of another survivor's testimony, who expresses her feelings so well that I decided it must be shared. It is the testimony of Emily Razzi, as printed on the Our Daily Bread website, under the topic "When Life Hurts."

"In my brief 22 years of living, I have known brokenness in too many ways: sexual abuse, anxiety, depression, bullying, anorexia, and suicidal thoughts. Some of it was inflicted on me, some self-inflicted and some of it was a result of not living in line with the Word of God and understanding the Father's abundant love.

"Centuries ago, in a garden, man was deceived by one lie from the serpent: God isn't who He says He is. Once the lie was believed, disobedience came into the picture. Eventually, shame wrapped us in a garment of fig leaves, breaking our relationship with the One who gave us our very breath.

"But in that heart wrenching and incredibly frustrating story, God still brought forth beauty, by showing us His redemptive love and giving us glimpses of goodness and beauty in this world. I love the beauty of His creation. The artistic side of me adores being outside, enjoying nature and looking for ways to create. This is one of the many ways I see myself "made in His image." I love taking leaves, pinecones, sticks, flowers—you name it—and turning them into beautiful crafts.

"I remember hearing the crunch beneath my feet last fall as I walked on broken leaves. Some leaves had holes from the effects of nature, whereas others were stepped on, torn apart, and left in the dust. Brokenness is to be expected in a sinful world. People are broken and remain so when they do not come to God and trust Him to create beauty.

"Looking down, I longed to bring beauty out of that lifeless foliage. I think that's how God sees us. He sees possibility and hope in a way that only He can. He sees beauty emerging from every gaping hole and frayed edge that we desperately try to hide. This is a beauty that He desires for us and delights in giving to us—but first, we must be willing.

The Past Catches Up

"The same fall I trekked through these broken leaves, my past of being sexually abused was brought back through nightmares. I started having flashbacks. Lies surrounded me and grew louder each day. 'It's your fault. You are disgusting. You'll never be good enough.' The darkness filled my heart, even though I wasn't even at fault; I was the victim. I knew there was another layer to this that I needed to deal with. So I left my Bible college and headed back home to receive help for my trauma from the sexual abuse.

"How do we see beauty and hope in such tragedy, especially in one that occurs through no fault of your own? And more importantly, how do you run to a Father when you feel He could have, but didn't, save you in your hour of affliction?

"The first time I understood the hope in this tragedy was through a common form of psychotherapy used to help people unpack their abuse encounter called Eye Movement Desensitization and Reprocessing (EMDR). My therapist at the time used that technique with me, intertwined with inner healing.

"We asked the Holy Spirit to come and bring me back to the memory and to show me where God was during the act. A vision of the Spirit of God holding me and crying with me came to mind and at that moment, I knew that God had never left me. His Word stands true when He says I will never leave you nor forsake you.

"I also came to understand how even the truth of being a victim can become an unhealthy lifestyle. Victimization was so comfortable for me; it was like a warm blanket on a cool autumn day. Yes, what happened to me was cruel and unjust, but the Father never called us to a victim lifestyle. That pain and trauma was taken from you and me and nailed to the cross so that we don't have to relive it over and over again. My prayer is that you'll choose to live in that victory instead of being bundled up in that heavy, tattered victim blanket. Cast it aside, step outside and smell the fresh air that is His victory over sin and death.

"As humans, we think beauty is only found when the broken season is over, like the rainbow at the end of the storm. And although that may be true at times, it's not always the case. I found beauty in grieving my tragedy of being abused. This summer, my pastors took me to a conference where we prayed for deliverance specifically from the lies that were rooted in my abuse. At the end of the prayer, the person leading me through asked the Holy Spirit to show me where He was in that situation and where He was bringing me now.

"I saw the Father literally breaking down the four walls of the room I was abused in and turning it into a beautiful garden. The Father was holding me at the very age I was abused at and singing over me, '*Baby it's okay, you're safe here with Me, no one can touch you now, I am doing a new thing. I am clothing you in My love, you are safe here with Me.*" I'll never forget it. The Father knows His children. He knows exactly what speaks to their aching hearts, and in that moment, He knew I needed the safety of my favorite place—the outdoors, a garden enveloped by His love.

"Going through these life-changing encounters with the Father made me realize that we are wrapped in the Father's embrace and presence wherever we go. This has brought me to a deeper understanding of His love and has helped me whenever my flesh wants to believe the lies. I now see every little act as a sign of His wondrous love for us: from the light beaming in from the window to wake me up, to the prompting of the Holy Spirit during prayer and worship. His beauty is all around us." [6]

My Own Personal Journal . . .
Damaged Emotions

Late Twenties . . .

Oh, God, I'm hurting, and my emotions are drained.
My resources are so very limited.
I feel so weak and small.
Oh, Lord, I am tired, even moving is a real effort.

I'm tired of feeling that my pain
is so ugly that no one wants to be near it,
or near me when I'm hurting.
My pain and depression make me want
to run away and hide, and I feel so alone.
I need to be more aware of Your presence
with me, and to be flooded with Your
love and purity.

If I were more aware of You, of Your closeness
and Your beauty and love for me, perhaps then I
wouldn't feel so dirty and unworthy.
I wouldn't feel so undesirable to both You and
the people who surround me.

I need to be reassured that You don't despise
my pain and that You feel it with me.
Please help me to remember that You are
the "Man of Sorrows and acquainted
with grief" ~ both Yours and now mine.

Please help me to never forget Who You are, even
when I feel this way.
Help me to remember that You are carrying me in

Your everlasting arms, close to Your heart.

Please keep me mindful that You do not expect anything superficial from me, even when I am writhing in pain.

Please keep me mindful that You know my heart and my pain, and that I am made from dust.
Help me to never forget that You will never take chances with me, that You know exactly what You're doing in my life—even when it seems like everything is falling apart in my life and all around me.

Please fill me with the peace of Your presence. Make me aware that I am always in Your arms giving me security that You will never change and that I am accepted in the Beloved—Your forever family.

~Your Chosen Daughter ~

"There is no pit so deep, that God is not deeper still."

Betsie ten Boom [7]

When the Shepherd Chooses Pain for Our Pathway

"Oh, this is bitter work for Him and us—bitter for us to go, but equally bitter for Him to cause us pain; yet it must be done. It would not be conducive to our true welfare to stay always in one happy and comfortable lot. He therefore puts us forth. The fold is deserted, that the sheep may wander over the bracing mountain slope. . . .

"Take heart! it could not be better to stay when He determines other; and if the loving hand of our Lord puts us forth, it must be well. Oh, in His name, to green pastures and still waters and mountain heights! He goes before you. Whatever awaits us is encountered first by Him. Faith's eye can always discern His majestic presence in front; and when that cannot be seen, it is dangerous to move forward. Bind this comfort to your heart, that *the Savior has tried for Himself all the experiences through which He asks you to pass; and He would not ask you to pass through them unless He was sure that they were not too difficult for your feet, or too trying for your strength.* *(Italics added by author).*

"This is the blessed life—not anxious to see far in front, nor careful about the next step, not eager to choose the path, nor weighted with the heavy responsibilities of the future, but quietly following behind the Shepherd, *one step at a time.*" —*J. Danson Smith*

"The Oriental shepherd was always *ahead* of his sheep. He was down *in front.* He is in the tomorrows. It is tomorrow that fills men with dread. *God is there already.* All the tomorrows of our life have to pass Him before they can get to us." *–F. B. Meyer – (Italics added by Author of quote).*

"God is in every tomorrow;
    Therefore, I live for today,
Certain of finding at sunrise,
    Guidance and strength for the way;
Power for each moment of weakness,
    Hope for each moment of pain,
Comfort for every sorrow,
    Sunshine and joy after rain. [8]

Notes . . .

Chapter 2

The Trauma That Changed My Life

Beyond this vale of tears there is a life above.

~ James Montgomery, British Hymnwriter and Poet

Symptoms of Sexual Abuse

Incest creates a trauma with many symptoms. It is sexual abuse in its cruelest form. Many of the symptoms of this trauma co-exist with each other. For example, loneliness is the constant companion of the incest victim. This is because the victim, male or female—must keep this painful part of their life a secret. They cannot share this most painful secret with anyone. This leads to *suppression of their deepest hurt feelings*. This takes a lot of energy. In fact, just keeping the secret can take so much effort it can be exhausting. An incest victim can live with loneliness for so long that it becomes a way of life. These victims suppress their need to survive, and after a while, loneliness feels *almost normal* for them. But deep inside, they are still *hurting and terribly depressed, and this leads to anger and sometimes rage.* On top of this, although they may be surrounded by family and friends (like Marilyn Monroe), they still feel very *lost* and *alone.* Even though their conscious mind is protected by the act of suppression, they are still hurting at the deepest level. Loneliness drains the life out of them, and suppression does it so effectively it's as if they had been emotionally anesthetized. Even though they may be unaware of what's happening deep inside by the process of suppression, the damage that's being done is extensive and overwhelming. But, thankfully, it's not irreparable or too much for their gentle and powerful Creator to heal.

Suppression and *withdrawal* are also related symptoms. In my case, when I was becoming increasingly depressed, I was also gradually becoming more withdrawn and suppressing my thoughts and feelings regarding the incest. I had to suppress the feelings of the incest, because I had to keep them secret from everyone. I thought, "*What would people think of me if they ever found out?*" That would be a heavy burden to bear for a person of any age, but it was especially difficult for a young teen living in a family setting. These thoughts, of course, very gradually led to all these symptoms.

In some ways it was like leading a double life. But it wasn't an intentional double life, because the pain in my soul was so suppressed that I could hardly feel it. Right after the incest I had to act like nothing unusual or abnormal had happened between my father and me. Then from my late teens until my mid-twenties, I was hardly aware of the feelings that the incest was stirring up within me or what it had done to me psychologically. I could talk about it with a few trusted friends. But it was like there was a wall of anesthesia surrounding my broken heart, as if the pain I *should have been feeling* was extremely minimal as compared to what it became later.

I was part of a wonderful church and I became involved in the music ministry. Singing gave me so much joy, that the depression was almost non-existent. I was somewhat withdrawn, but it was not a serious withdrawal or depression. During that entire time, my emotions seemed to be separated from the truth of what had happened. I was freer from the abuse than at any other time in my life, because I had so much joy and purpose in the ministry. The real emotional symptoms of incest did not reappear until my late twenties, when a young man said something to me, suggesting that I had been abused. The young man reminded me of the abuse. In the particular way that he reminded me of it (which I will elaborate on later in this book), opened the floodgates of emotions and memories in my broken heart. I could no longer maintain the suppression.

All of these symptoms work in tandem with each other in a mysterious way that I cannot explain. I just know that they do. This is why I feel so strongly that a person who has been abused must seek help to recover from the trauma of this terrible experience; and the sooner this help is obtained, the better. I am convinced from my experience that it is never a good thing to walk through this Valley of Tears alone.

Much of what I have described is what I experienced as an incest victim, and it is what I experienced internally and externally. What we feel internally eventually comes out in our outward behavior.

If you are a parent and this terrible trauma has happened to your child, I will say that it is imperative that you seek out a counselor for her or him, whichever the case may be. It is vital that your child, regardless of his or her age, receive counseling and/or group therapy as soon as possible. It will seriously impact their life for good, if they are allowed to talk through their emotions, or destroy their future, if they do not have the opportunity for this vital talk therapy.

O Love That Will Not Let Me Go

O Love that will not let me go,
I rest my weary soul in Thee;
I give Thee back the life I owe,
That in Thine ocean depths its flow
  May richer, fuller be.

O Light that follows all my way.
I yield my flickering torch to Thee;
My heart restores its borrowed ray,
That in Thy sunshine's blaze its day
  May brighter, fairer be.

O Joy, that seekest me through pain,
I cannot close my heart to Thee;
I trace the rainbow through the rain,
And feel the promise is not vain
  That morn shall tearless be.

O Cross that liftest up my head,
I dare not ask to fly from Thee;
I lay in dust life's glory dead,
And from the ground there blossoms red
  Life that shall endless be.

George Matheson
1842-1906
Public Domain[1]

About Shame

The preceding poem forms the words of my favorite hymn/worship song "O Love That Will Not Let Me Go." It reminds me of what the Bible says about how the Lord never leaves His children and the fact that He lives in us; that is, He indwells His children and will never leave us.

This song reminds me of the relationship between me in my pain and my God who is *intimately acquainted* with all my ways (Psalm 139:3). He feels everything I do and experiences all my pain, as if it were His own. When I say that He is "intimately acquainted with all my ways," I mean that He knows me better than anyone else ever could. He is closer to me than the air I breathe; He knows every thought I think before it enters my mind. He knows what I will do and why I do it in every situation. He understands my desires and wants and motives. He loves me for who I am and why I am. His understanding of me is very difficult to describe. I could write pages about it, and I possibly will in another chapter. But this song gives a hint of how He understands my pain and gives me great joy in spite of it. When I realized that the Lord Jesus could relate to my trauma in a very personal way, it gave me great encouragement.

The Roman Empire was the environment and culture where Jesus was born and raised and lived His earthly life. That being true, it was also the civil authority under which He was arrested and tried at an extremely illegal trial. They had a type of mock trial for the Lord Jesus, because it was likely the only way they could bring a guilty verdict against this man, who had lived His public and private life in such an innocent and perfect manner. Crucifixion was the death penalty of the empire under which they executed thousands upon thousands of non-citizens and slaves. Roman citizens were beheaded, as in the case of the Apostle Paul. They used crucifixion for slaves, Jews, and other non-citizens because it was the most brutal, shameful, and painful way to die. It was also used as a public example to all in attendance to help those watching avoid the crimes their victims were being executed for. It was their attempt to restrict crime to the very limit in their kingdom. This punishment for crimes against the state was very severe and cruel for the criminal—especially for the Jews.

Jewish criminals, which included Jesus, were executed where people could observe and mock them. Some had family and friends there who grieved their loss, but mostly they were mocked by their enemies. We see many pictures of the crucifixion which show Jesus crucified wearing nothing but a loin cloth. That is a polite rendering of the event. However, the truth of the event is that they even took away the loin cloth. This was a sign of Roman mockery of Jewish modesty and disrespect for their value of dressing according to Jewish law, which called for moral decency and propriety.

Try to imagine the idea of Jesus being crucified naked. In Genesis 2:25 when God created humankind, before sin entered the world through the deception of Satan, Adam and Eve were naked and they were not ashamed. However, after sin entered the world, they were immediately ashamed and sought to cover themselves. They did this because they had sinned and they thought it would please God to cover themselves with the only thing they could find—fig leaves. This act of covering themselves was not the same as the Jewish custom (which came later), but a human practice that came with our first parents. It was carried down by birth to the Jewish Fathers, then to the Jewish people according to the Mosaic Law. It was then adopted by those who continued to follow God's commands by keeping their nakedness covered. However, to bring the ultimate shame on their Jewish criminals, the Romans executed them naked and in public.

An incest victim does not feel the same shame that Jesus felt taking the shame and penalty for the sins of the whole world—past, present, and future. But our Heavenly Father completely understands the deep shame that an incest victim feels, having their nakedness uncovered by someone they thought they should have been able to trust to protect them and to respect their modesty.

This song "O Love That Will Not Let Me Go" gave me great comfort, while I was going through counseling and going through the process of mentally and emotionally living through the shame of those awful nights when my father uncovered me until I was naked and forced himself on me, and the days that followed when I was forced (in a different way) to live a "normal way" as his daughter—days which were never normal again. I was comforted to know that my Lord knew what naked shame was all about.

During those counseling years when I felt like an abused child again, my understanding Lord assured me that I can always bring my fear to Him, because He is the Great Healer, the Man of Sorrows, Who is acquainted with my grief (Isaiah 53:3-5). He is also my great High Priest, Who can sympathize with all my weakness and pain (Hebrews 4:15). He held me by the hand during those times, and at other times He simply carried me in His arms, as my Good and Gentle Shepherd. Along with this, God used Psalm 139 (see Chapter 5) to speak His great comfort to me, assuring me that He knew all about my pain, He understood what would happen before I was even created, and He would be with me through it all.

My Own Personal Journal. . . Restless, Lonely, and Scared

Early Thirties, Before Marriage . . .

Loneliness . . . It's like a giant that overwhelms and destroys. It feels like I'm about five inches high and everyone else towers high above me. They don't see me and they frequently step on me. Their voices are so faint that I can't hear what they are saying. I'm alone, different, and separated.

I'm feeling restless and lonely. I'm emotionally tired of all the changes in my life, and I'm so tired of being alone. I'm tired of feeling detached and disconnected . . .

I'm tired of not belonging anywhere . . . to anyone.

I have no parents. My father has passed away, and my mother is far away geographically and emotionally disconnected. No one is really committed to me. I'm much too young for this. It seems like it's been a very long time since I've had parents who were actively connected and committed to me. I feel like an orphan.

I just don't want to be alone anymore. I want to be with *someone who respects me*, whether it is family or friends or a special loved one.

I resemble a pelican of the wilderness;
I have become like an owl of the waste
places.
I lie awake,
I have become like a lonely bird on a
housetop.

Psalm 102:6-7

That is how I feel.

I'm tired of being and feeling misunderstood. I want to be known and understood and accepted. But it seems impossible.

I don't like meeting new people. It scares me. I'm so afraid of being misjudged, misunderstood, and rejected. There seems to be a barrier of so much to explain, so much that most people would never understand.

Sometimes life doesn't seem worth it. I struggle and struggle to grow and my deepest emotional needs never seem to be met. It's very difficult. I feel like I am drifting in a life raft on an ocean all by myself, with no land in sight. I don't want to struggle to grow anymore. I just want to be loved and appreciated.

Loneliness makes me want to die. It feels like there is no one in existence who knows how I feel, or who could reach me if they did know. Being in a crowd of people makes me feel worse. There is an emptiness inside me that nothing can fill. I feel separated from life. It feels somewhat like death must feel.

I feel insignificant, wasted, and broken beyond repair. The people I know don't seem to understand and God seems far away. God is silent. If He is working in my life, He is working in silence. He must know how lonely I feel and how much I need validation. Why is He so silent?

The Story of My Trauma

This is the part of the story that has been so difficult to write. This chapter, along with Chapter Three, will get into the raw emotion of my story. This is the part that I wanted to just forget about and pretend that it never happened. But I couldn't do that. It kept showing up in my life in one way or another. As I was growing up and grew from my teen years into my twenties, I became very withdrawn and insecure. I felt that I was under a lot of pressure from my family to date (especially through the last years of high school) and then incredible pressure to marry (in my early twenties). I had seen my mother go through one marriage after another. My father was her second husband, and at the time of my counseling, she was married to her *fifth* husband. Because of this, I desperately wanted God's choice for me—and nothing less, regardless of what my family wanted. I wanted this because I wanted to be spared of all the heartache that my mother had put herself and the family through. I wanted God's best because I was His born-again daughter and I wanted my life to bring glory to Him. So I would tell my family that I had made a commitment to the Lord that *I would not take anything less than His best when it came to marriage and in many other areas of my life*—but especially that one. That is what I really wanted. They didn't understand or accept my wishes and kept applying the pressure.

During high school I hardly dated at all and I didn't even attend my Junior or Senior Prom, although I would have loved to have gone. As it was, no one asked me to the proms. As disappointed as I was about this, I think it disappointed my mother even more. Then as I moved into my early twenties, the same thing continued to happen with my dating relationships. I had several male friends at church, but none of them seemed to want to date me. If I had a date, it was always just a one-time event. As one friend described it, men would waltz into my life and then they would waltz right back out, with rarely a second date.

During those years, like most young women, I wanted to date. I looked forward to marriage and a family, but it just wasn't happening. I didn't want to wait until I was in my late twenties or early thirties to get married. I wanted to have children. I would make friends at church and sometimes at my job at the graduate seminary where I worked, but the interest was rarely mutual. I would often feel rejected. Or the individual was interested in keeping the relationship only on a platonic level. Occasionally, the wrong kind of person was interested in forging a serious relationship with me.

I realize that this happens to a lot of young people who have not been abused, who are simply late bloomers. But as for me, it was something different. It kept happening to me *repeatedly* because I was extremely insecure. This was a symptom of the trauma, but I did not recognize it. I became extremely sensitive to rejection. I went to wedding after wedding, and I was beginning to take mental notes as to what kind of wedding I wanted to have, if ever I had one.

While I was in my mid-twenties, there was a young man that I became acquainted with, and we began getting to know each other on a very casual basis. Besides being a student at the seminary where I worked, he also attended my church. One time we were at a gathering at his home (along with other singles), and he praised me for my "gentle spirit." That meant a great deal to me, because it was a biblical character quality I valued and wanted to cultivate in my life. Not too long after that, he invited me to attend a concert with him and I was so honored! I could hardly contain my excitement. This man that I so admired had asked me out! I was thrilled and we had a *great* time. Or at least *I* thought we did. Unfortunately, I think he was just checking me out, because he never asked me out for a second date. He never pursued the opportunity to get to know me better. I later learned that he never asked me out again, because he thought I was too shy and withdrawn and did not have the self-confidence to verbally pray out loud with him. I was *devastated*, and I felt deeply rejected. I knew how to pray out loud, but it seemed that he wasn't very patient. He only went out with me once. When I learned why he had rejected me, I knew I could have grown in the areas for which I was being rejected. I went through this for several years. I was finally forced to face the real reason for what was happening with my "love life." It was much more than being shy and withdrawn; it was God working in my life that had prevented me from having any meaningful relationships with a man. The Lord knew I needed to face some things that a special relationship would have distracted me from.

When I was in my late twenties, it hit me right between the eyes. I had a date with another young man who I was just getting to know. In the middle of our conversation he made a statement I couldn't avoid. He came right out and made this blunt remark, "You were sexually abused by your father when you were younger." He didn't "*suggest*" that it "*might*" be true, he proclaimed it as a *statement of fact*. Now this statement had nothing to do with the conversation we were having. We did not know each other all that well; we were mere acquaintances. I don't know how he knew that my father had abused me, but I felt like I had been caught in the act. I was so unprepared for his statement of truth about me, that I couldn't deny it. I felt exposed and embarrassed. I began to wonder, even if he so accurately discerned this about me, how could he dare to be so bold as to make such a statement? I felt like he had just undressed me with his eyes or like I must have had a "mark" on my forehead, identifying me as one who had been violated. That was the negative result about his revelation, and it put me in a tailspin of depression for months. The positive result of my date's revelation was that it was made very clear to me that my social life had suffered, because of insecurities that were related to the scars left by the trauma of incest. The suppressed memories that I had buried and tried so hard to forget were now beginning to surface at an alarming rate.

Not too long after that date and his strong statement about my life, I received a phone call from one of the seminary professors for whom I had been working, a man named Dr. H. Crosby Englizian. I had great admiration for this particular professor and he had become a special friend to me. He reached out to me because he had great sensitivity for the single women on campus. He approached me when I first began working for him and told me that he understood that I was fatherless. He said that if I didn't mind, he would like to be a "stand-in" as a father figure, while we were both part of the seminary family. It began with my meeting him for breaks and getting to know him on a very casual basis. Then I had dinner with both he and his wife in their home, and I invited them both for dinner at my apartment. It was a little strange because he was a man in the same age-range as my father. But that was where the similarities ended. He was very different from my father. He was educated and what I would call a distinguished and very godly gentleman. When I first began getting to know him, I was a little scared of him, because I didn't know how to receive some of his statements. I didn't know how to relate to a respectful man like him. He had a unique personality. There were times that I just didn't understand him, because he seemed to be a little harsh on the outside. But over time, I learned that he had a very tender heart for people that he cared about. My misunderstanding of his personality was due to my insecurity and because I didn't understand his sense of humor. This was a new thing for me, trusting a man with anything, including the surface things in my life.

When Dr. Englizian called me at my office, he commented that he had observed me from the viewpoint of his office, as I was walking across the campus. He said that it appeared to him that I looked "troubled." He suggested that perhaps I might want to come and talk to him about what the trouble was. So, I made an appointment with him and told him about what my father had done to me. As he heard my sad story of the betrayal of trust by my biological father, Dr. Englizian became the one who was deeply troubled by the thought that *any father who was blessed by God to have a daughter would do such a thing to her.* He said, "Fathers are charged with the job of protecting and nurturing their daughters, and for a father to violate his daughter in such a way is a reprehensible violation of that trust." I greatly admired his respectful attitude about fathers and daughters and wished with all my heart I had grown up with such a father. "But," he countered, "*as much as your father did not deserve forgiveness, you must, you absolutely MUST FORGIVE HIM!*" Then he explained his emphasis. "You must be obedient to the Lord in this matter, no matter what evil your father did to you or for how long he persisted with that evil." He also suggested that my despondency and depression was likely due to my lack of forgiveness toward my father. He said that as I forgive my father, my anger toward him will subside and melt away. He added that it was *for my sake* that I needed to forgive him. He said my emotional, spiritual, and physical well-being was completely dependent on my obedience to the Lord in this matter. He repeated his statement and said, "*You must, yes, you absolutely must forgive your father.*" He then prayed for me and assured me of his continued prayers for me in this matter.

I knew that, based on the affection he had for me, along with the urgency and the admonishment in his voice, *he was very serious in what he said.* I also believed that he was correct in what he was telling me. It was also apparent that I was in deep trouble, because of the great efforts I had made in forgiving my father during the first five years that I was a Christian.[2.] I prayed that the Lord would give me greater desire and power to forgive my father the second time than I had the first time. I was afraid that facing the pain of the incest this second time might make it more difficult to forgive him than it had been the first time, and that had me very concerned.

My Own Personal Journal. . . Feeling Rejected

Early Thirties . . .

I've been in counseling for some time now, remembering and reliving that terrible ordeal with my father. It has made me emotionally exhausted. I'm feeling anxiety and dread, much like I felt just after the incest and in the years following the incest before dad died. It's a feeling that something bad is going to happen and I keep *imagining* and *fearing the feeling of abandonment. Could this be Post-Traumatic Stress Disorder?*

I'm feeling very lonely and depressed. It seems like, from what I've read and experienced, loneliness and fear of abandonment are symptoms of incest. Why? And after so many years, why do I still feel that?

One reason, I think, is <u>*the Fear Of Rejection*</u>. If people knew (I mean really knew), what I was going through, even fifteen years after the initial trauma, then it's possible that I would be misunderstood, judged, and unloved. When I experienced incest, I was terrified of people knowing. I felt dirty and evil, and I feared exposure. I had new desires and I felt guilty; I felt that I had to bear all that on my own. I desperately needed acceptance and approval. And I now have those raw feelings again.

Another reason is that <u>*I Felt Like A Misfit*</u>. I felt like I was emotionally deformed or <u>*Contaminated*</u>. I was afraid of the rejection that exposure would bring. I thought I was not good enough to be accepted or to fit in. With dad, everything was on a performance basis and I was *never* good enough. I still feel that way in many situations.

Another aspect of this was the fear of what it would do to the family. I feared that dad would deny it (*which he did*), mom would divorce dad (*which she did*) and hate me (*which in time, our relationship changed and we grew apart never to be close again*), and our home would be severely disrupted (*which it definitely was—although it was from much more than the incest*). I thought I would be blamed.

I felt responsible to carry it all on my own to protect myself and others. This was a huge burden for a teen (or anyone) to carry.

When the incest happened, *I was an innocent child.* I thought my father was a person who was all powerful *in my world* and someone who could always be trusted. Before the incest, it had never dawned on me to not trust my father. Without thinking about the idea, I was sure that my father was my protector. At first, I knew there was something strange and very wrong about what he was doing. But it was so confusing because he was my father; and my father was the authority in our home. Even if he was wrong, there were severe consequences for disobedience and I didn't know what to do! I was not in a position to judge the right and wrong of what he was doing, and as I recall those terrible nights, I don't think these thoughts really crossed my mind. I just wanted him to stop and prayed that he would. And even if I had known for sure that he was wrong, I couldn't do anything about it. But there was one thing I was very sure of: I knew that I didn't like what he was doing. If I questioned my father, that would make me a disobedient and rebellious (bad) child. It was very confusing and it felt dirty and immoral. I just didn't know what to do about it or if there was anything that I could do. He was my father, a man that you just didn't disobey or deny his wishes. And at this time in his life, he was an angry man and I was afraid to disobey him.

Mistrust. Because of the incest, *I learned that I could not trust anyone*. I went from being a trusting child to one who could not and did not trust anyone. The incest happened, in the seeming security of my bedroom at night, when I should have been comfortable and protected. If I couldn't feel safe and secure in the privacy of my own bed at night, how could I feel safe anywhere? If my father, one of the few persons that I should have been able to trust and feel safe with, violated me and gave me such confusing and conflicting desires and emotions, *who could I trust?*

I Felt Forced To Be Secretive. If other family members found out what had happened, I thought it would be the end of the world for me, my dignity, and my self-respect. Therefore, I felt that I had to keep it a secret, which forced me to be inhibited and shy, leading to loneliness. I also had to keep it a secret, because I was so afraid of my father and what he would say or do if I revealed *his* secret. You see, *it wasn't just my secret*; it was also *our* secret. What if he was hiding behind what he knew was my fear and insecurity? What if he knew how scared I was to say anything to anyone? What if he was afraid that I would reveal his ugly secret? I had *so many* fears.

I never thought it through this clearly, but these thoughts are the best I can do at reconstructing my thought and emotional process. Keeping the secret was the only way for me to keep my sanity.

It wasn't a feeling of *being safe* (like I felt before the incest occurred) but of *feeling safer,* if my secret were never revealed to anyone at all. Maybe dealing with these emotions all these years has accentuated the loneliness. Even though there are literally millions of women who today feel the same things I felt, who can relate to my experience and loneliness, what I am describing is mine and mine alone. They cannot share it because it wasn't their experience.

What about *Abandonment?* It is related to loneliness. If I really let someone get to know me intimately, pretty soon (the fear is) they will drift away. They will not like me. I greatly feared losing the people I trusted. Then I would be completely alone again.

During this time, one of my favorite books was a biography about J. Hudson Taylor, founder of the Inland China Mission, titled *Hudson Taylor's Spiritual Secret.* This book really inspired me, because of Mr. Taylor's great faith and commitment to the calling God had on his life. There is a quote by Mr. Taylor from this book that I never forgot and actually had on my refrigerator where it stayed for a number of years:

> *It doesn't matter, really, how great the pressure is, it only matters where the pressure lies. See that*

> *it never comes between you and the Lord—then, the greater the pressure, the more it presses you to His heart.*

I was brutally honest in my journals. But at the same time, I was clinging desperately to the Lord for all the strength I could gain from Him. He was and is my only real source of strength and courage, as I faced all the fears and other emotions described in this book.

My Memories of the Trauma

Even though the actual act of incest happened when I was in the tender years of puberty and lasted for two years that I can remember (an eternity for me), the effects of it lasted for many years after that. It followed me all the way through high school and all through my twenties. The words that you read here are a true story of a long process that was forced on me by that trauma. It was a trauma that kept repeating itself in my memories and nightmares, along with depression and insecurity. It was a trauma that somehow wouldn't die. And it was a trauma that, without facing it, without proper treatment, and without the proper healing process, would remain acute and never end.

All of this took a very long time to recover from. Truthfully, I wasn't always aware that I was traumatized, and that's what I was struggling with. It began when I was eleven years old. I was only in the end of my twenties, when I realized that I had been depressed for a very long time. I began to search for a way to recover from the depression and to find new meaning and wholeness for my life.

As I remember it, I had developed into a young woman at an early age. Mentally and emotionally I was a struggling adolescent with a mixture of little girl and pre-adult female thoughts and perspectives. I was very naïve about sex—as most adolescents are, and I didn't really understand it or myself enough to desire it. But I did desire to be accepted and I did want approval, which I translated into love. I also learned that sex and love are two very different things. I was a lonely child in a large family. It might be hard to understand how one could be so lonely in a large family. But believe me, it's very easy.

I didn't feel understood or accepted in any setting. In fact, most of the time when I dropped my guard and was just being myself, I often felt misunderstood and ridiculed by others. Perhaps I was more emotionally sensitive than I appeared to be, and maybe people didn't know how much they were hurting me. Perhaps it just appeared that I was simply an overly sensitive adolescent.

Before the incest, I had a relatively normal childhood. I always felt a deep need for acceptance and affection. I lived in an environment of ridicule among my siblings, and I always felt frustrated with my parents. I was a much wanted first daughter. There had only been boys born in my family for a whole generation. Consequently, my parents were delighted that I was a girl, and I was quite spoiled as a very young child. Early in life, I got my way quite a lot; but I was not spoiled with the feeling of being secure. I had a lot of nice toys and cute clothes which my mother made, but I didn't feel secure.

As I grew, I remember always wanting acceptance. I wanted to be liked and loved and to give love and have it well received. But I didn't feel like I fit in, even with my siblings. My favorite childhood fantasy was to grow up, get married, and have children. I spent the bulk of my childhood hours "playing house," pretending to have children, and being a mother with my many beautiful dolls.

As a child, I had a problem with anger. My parents struggled with trying to control the way I expressed it, and I remember being punished for the way I chose to vocalize it. I grew up with the idea that anger is bad and ugly. When other people expressed anger, it scared and intimidated me. I also remember hearing the ridicule about "Tammy's Irish temper." This ridicule made me feel ugly and unattractive, like I would never be a beautiful person. Although most of my expressions of uncontrolled anger had been suppressed after the incest, the ridicule regarding it continued all the way into adulthood.

I don't know why I had so much anger in my early childhood. It could be that I needed attention and the only way to get it was to scream for it. My mother used to say, that I was a "spoiled brat", all the way into adulthood. I have no doubt of the truth of that. But hearing her say that didn't give me much of a feeling that I was accepted, liked, or attractive. I grew up believing my parents loved me, because they always told me so. But I didn't always feel loved or good enough to be acceptable or liked.

I soon learned that compliance worked better than expressing my anger outright. I learned that if I behaved in a pleasing way, I would feel more approval. I didn't really feel accepted, but it felt better than the anger, guilt, and parental disapproval. The compliance later led to withdrawal and depression, and my real feelings soon became too submerged to recognize.

In her younger years, my mother was a beautiful woman, and I wanted to be just like her. I didn't know much about inward beauty, other than a few things that my mother told me. She would say, "Pretty is as pretty does." From that I surmised that my behavior must come from within, and that it was just as important to my beauty as my outward appearance. I thought that beautiful and glamorous women were well-respected, and I thought that it was because of their outward presentation of beauty and gracefulness. I presumed that if I were to be well-respected, it had to come from something I had within that could be outwardly expressed. I didn't feel respected as a child, and so that was something I wanted to attain as an adult. Therefore, I wanted to grow up to be a beautiful, well-respected woman. You see, I thought, if a woman was to be respected, that would be her greatest asset, and she would not be ridiculed. She would find acceptance along with her outward beauty. That is what beauty meant to me as a child. And I dreamed about it. I was very sure that if I had inner beauty, I would be respected; and somehow I would become beautiful on the outside, just like I believed my mother was.

When the incest occurred, I had an emerging woman's body. But inside I was still a little girl. I was a little girl who didn't understand sex and wasn't ready to understand it. Oh, I knew the mechanics of where babies came from, and I basically knew the function of my own body. But I didn't really understand sex. I didn't have a clue about the relational and emotional aspects of sex or about the concept that it could be pleasurable. It had never occurred to me. I had never imagined sex in the context of a loving relationship. The way my parents spoke about it in adult conversations made it sound dirty and not pleasurable. I always became embarrassed when they joked about it in my presence, and then they ridiculed me for blushing.

From observing my parents (especially my dad), sex was also something to fear. He seemed to be an aggressive animal and my mom always seemed to be the prey. Sex appeared to me to be unknown, not understood, and rather gross. And from the perspective of childhood innocence, that was understandable by his behavior. I wasn't ready to see the value and desirability of sex. It was never referred to as "making love."

When I was eleven years old and before the incest, my dad was in a car accident and sustained a whiplash injury. In our later family discussions, we concluded that he didn't just have a simple whiplash but also a head injury. These injuries caused him a great deal of pain. As a result, he was put on several medications:

first pain medication, then muscle relaxants, followed by tranquilizers. All this medication was meant to help him sleep, so he could work the next day. By the time he was taking the tranquilizers, both my mother and his doctor became concerned that he was becoming addicted to the increasing strength of the medication. When the doctor began weaning him off the tranquilizers, my parents began fighting over the strength of the medications and the fact that he was becoming addicted. This conflict led to alcohol becoming my father's drug of choice. All this happened over the course of about a year. My father worked swing shift, so we had to be quiet during the day. Our activities were often interrupted by him yelling for drugs or for us to be quiet so he could sleep.

I write this because this head injury was the beginning of major changes in my father's behavior that had a direct effect on me. First and most important to my story, besides becoming a chemical addict, he also became a sexual addict. He developed Bipolar Disorder,[3] and his other abnormal behaviors gradually became known. In fact, we didn't even know he suffered from Bipolar Disorder until I was sixteen years old. We might have known sooner, but he refused to go to the doctor for tests. He gradually stopped being the man I knew as my childhood father. His normal way of relating to us was completely different, and his attitudes and expectations seemed to change overnight. In fact, it seemed that *everything* about his personality and demeanor had changed.

It was about a year after my dad's accident and fight over medications that my childhood innocence was cut short. At age eleven I still had several years of justified innocent growing up to do, but the incest deprived me of that. All at once I knew about sex—from traumatic experience. There was no pleasure in it for me. It was very frightening, ugly, strange, painful, and so *very confusing*.

My mother had been taking in Day Care children to supplement our income during my elementary years, and it seemed like her attention was divided between the additional children and all her own children. She had five children of her own at that time, and there were always at least 3-4 more that she took in. Then when I began seventh grade, she started taking night classes and went to work outside the home. I felt somewhat neglected and abandoned, and I eventually began to withdraw. It seemed like no one really knew me—not really. They knew the cute little blond-haired girl who liked to wear dresses, sew, do needlework, and play house. But they didn't really know who I was inside. They didn't know the person who desired love and had a lot of questions and desires about life and the future. For that matter, I didn't really know myself that well. My parents were basically happy with me, if I didn't throw temper fits, brought home good grades, and did what I was told. But who I was on the inside desperately wanted approval, especially from my parents. And for me, approval meant love. I wanted to grow up and to become a woman, so that I could experience love and have a family of my own. But my deep adolescent needs seemed to go unnoticed. Now that incest had been thrust upon me, sex completely *horrified* me. I just wasn't ready for it. I'm not sure I was even ready for the whole menstrual cycle and emotional changes, which for me were very painful. As it turned out, I also developed endometriosis. At that time not much was known about it in the medical field. I was simply told that pain and cramps are "normal." I had no one to talk to who understood the heavy bleeding, the huge blood clots, and any other problems that developed like the hormonal imbalances, which made me feel that I was different from everyone else and accentuated my loneliness all the more.

I had to ask myself, "How do I get genuine approval? How do I survive all these changes, to say nothing about the trauma. Is all this normal? Is growing up supposed to be so painful? What is love anyway? Is sex love? Does being touched sexually mean that you're being loved?" I didn't know, and I was *very* confused.

My Own Personal Journal . . . Anger

Early Thirties . . .

Anger is related to loneliness. My inner child is very hurt and *very angry.* She is also very frustrated, because to that child, anger is sinful and ugly. So I am depressed and feel misunderstood.

I seem to be angry at everything. I'm angry at being violated by my biological father. I'm angry because I couldn't trust anyone enough to tell them about the abuse, so they could respond to my emotional needs at the time I was abused. I'm angry because I had to respect and obey my dad after the abuse and had to stay with my family and bear the burden of the secret. I'm angry because of the conflicting feelings created by the incest and my inability to trust men, for fear of being violated again or being used by men and becoming abandoned all over again. I'm angry because my innocence was ripped away from me, and now I feel rejection, due to the pain I'm feeling now from people who don't understand and don't care. I'm also angry because I'm still single and alone and feel unloved. I'm also angry because I'm unable to express my anger and to get my feelings out and over with.

The following is how one woman dealt with her anger after being raped. She wrote a letter to the perpetrator describing some of her feelings. This is part of the letter she wrote to him:

"It's as if when I was abused, I was thrown into a deep, dark pit. I emerged naked. Piece by piece, I was able to retrieve my clothing. Sometimes I had to walk great distances to find the pieces, but I did find them. The first item I had to recover was control over my own life. Then I found strength, self-confidence, dignity, and hope. I'm even discovering my own sexuality. I have found peace with my God. Yet, there was nothing I could put on that could make me feel like a complete woman—a part of me was naked. Inside of me, it felt like a hole, a hole that could never be filled . . . a vital part of me . . . stolen. Will I never be a whole woman?

"Why do I feel like in that part of me called woman there is a vast emptiness? I can look like a woman, I can act like a woman, I can do everything a woman does, but I can't feel like a woman. Every other grown female seems like so much more of a woman. Sometimes I even get jealous of other women. They are whole, but I've been robbed. I look in the mirror, but I'm not all there. There's something missing. I can't explain it to anyone else. I don't understand it myself, but it's missing . . . gone . . . stolen. Will I never find it? Must I always live with this hole inside of me? Can I never be a woman?" [4]

The above quote is from a book titled *Raped* by Deborah Roberts. When I read this I was so amazed at how well she put my feelings into words, just the way I have been feeling them. As I continued to read her story, it had a happy conclusion. The Lord allowed her to heal with a pregnancy and a healthy baby. But

I did not have that kind of a joyful conclusion. I did have the joy of being loved by a wonderful, understanding, tenderhearted man a number of years later, but with no babies of my own. I had to trust the Lord that He had other ways of healing in store for me. He always knows best and I believe He made the best choice for me.

The Gift of The Thorn

Strange gift indeed!—a thorn to prick,
To pierce into the very quick;
To cause a perpetual sense of pain;
Strange gift!—and yet, 'twas given for gain.

Unwelcome, yet it came to stay;
Nor could it even be prayed away.
It came to fill its God-planned place,
A life-enriching means of grace.

God's grace-thorns—oh, what forms they take;
What piercing, smarting pain they make!
And yet, each one in love is sent,
And always just for blessing meant.

And so, whatever your thorn may be,
From God accept it willingly;
But reckon Christ—His life—the power
To keep, in your most trying hour.

And sure—your life will richer grow;
He grace sufficient will bestow;
And in Heaven a morn your joy will be
That, by His thorn, He strengthened thee.

J. Danson Smith [5]

Notes . . .

Chapter 3

Emotional Pain and Loneliness

My soul weeps because of grief;
Strengthen me according to Your word.

~Psalm 119:28

The Trauma Becomes More Intense

I remember the abuse occurring over at least two years. When the abuse started it was initial touching. [1] When it began, my dad came into my room at night. This was very unusual behavior for him. Since I felt neglected, this "special attention" was welcome at first. He was gentle and quiet—very different from his daytime appearance which was loud and overbearing. This happened for a while because I can remember different settings in the bedroom. When it all began, my bed was in the middle of the room and near the window, which provided a little bit of natural light. My dad would come in and sit on my bed and watch me sleep. Before he left, he would make sure I was covered up.

After a few visits, I noticed that, as my dad was covering me up with the blankets, he was also touching my breasts. The next stage came when he began to *un*cover me. He himself had purchased a little pink nylon night gown for me, and I wore it to bed all the time. I loved it. It made me feel feminine and grown up. I did not see any connection between the night gown and his nighttime visits. But after a while, I remember, when my dad would come in to see me, he would push it up around my neck. It became obvious to me that he wanted to see my breasts and touch them. At this point I began to feel very uncomfortable, and I was becoming confused. I had a feeling this activity wasn't quite right, but I was easily sucked in by this new attention and my desire to be loved. However, I wasn't sure this was love. It didn't feel right. *Not at all. This was my daddy. But what exactly was my daddy doing?*

Being touched felt good, but in a twisted sort of way. I was hungry for love and, to me, this attention felt like love. But at the same time, it didn't feel right. I had been taught by my parents, especially by my mother, that I should *never* let *anyone* touch certain parts of my body. She said it was bad, dirty, and naughty. So when my dad touched me, I couldn't understand what he was doing. I had been taught that allowing anyone to touch me that way was just wrong. Why then was he doing this to me—something that he and my mom had said was *dirty* and *bad?* So now how could I trust my parents to teach me right from wrong? I was getting "special attention," when I knew it was wrong. But on the other hand I had been feeling somewhat neglected when I had a deep hunger for love and attention. *But this was not the way I hoped that hunger would be satisfied.* I wasn't exactly sure how my hunger for love should be satisfied. This was very confusing.

When those nighttime visits began, my daytime perception of my dad became more difficult. My whole life had certainly changed after those dark hours. During the day he was still my dad and I had to respect and obey him. He was an authoritarian and a disciplinarian, and a lot of our relatives often said that he was too strict. Dad was very proud of his kids. We made him look good. We had to. We were always well-behaved in public, always said "please" and "thank-you", and (in public) we always looked our best. We put on the appearance of a well-dressed, well-behaved, successful American family.

But it was not so on the home front. I think everyone in the family was being wounded in one way or another by my dad's strange behavior. The more we grew into our teen years, the more restrictive and demanding dad seemed to be about our adolescent behavior and activities, and the more distant he seemed to be relationally. I was afraid to be close to him. That would be like being exposed, close, and vulnerable to an all-controlling, insensitive power. He was much older than my mother, and as we grew into the teen years, he did not understand our interests or the changes we were going through that were brought on by adolescence. When we would discuss our frustrations with dad, we concluded that he was never a teenager, that he just skipped the teenage years, and that he went straight from childhood to adulthood. He even told us that was the case. He would tell us that he worked straight through his adolescence years and so should we.

Mom seemed more distant as well. She also suffered due to my dad's strange behavior. My parents were having frequent bedroom fights and dad was drinking *a lot.* As both parents became more distant, I withdrew into my own fantasy world, looking for love, approval, security, safety, and comfort.

I wanted to take this to God, but I had a problem there as well. Although I wanted Him to deliver me from the prison my father had me in, I could not seem to trust Him either. I thought He was probably too much like my father. With God, I was between a rock and a hard place. I wanted to trust Him, but I was afraid of Him as well.

My Own Personal Journal . . . My War With God

Late Teens to Early Twenties

My head and my emotions are at war. I feel like God is against me. I am having a hard time separating dad's character from what I know of God's, and I am responding to God, with the same feelings of defensiveness and hostility as I had toward dad. I also feel that God has the same attitudes toward me. My emotions say that:

- *God has a condemning attitude toward me.*
- *He expects a holy performance from me.*
- *He is a cruel power.*
- *My inadequate emotions, expressions, and behavior are considered sin, and He rejects them.*
- *He does not accept my failures and shortcomings. He sees me as a failure.*
- *He does not want to answer my prayers and has no intention of answering them. This is especially true of prayers regarding my needs and wants.*
- *He gives me trials and pain to punish me, and to show me how weak and inadequate I am.*
- *He sets me up with hope, in order to hurt and to disappoint me.*
- *He is strong in holiness and judgment, and short on love, mercy, grace, and compassion.*

- *I am one of God's under-privileged and unloved children.*
- *To be loved means being hurt and abused.*

(I later learned that my thoughts about God needed to be changed, and they were changed—very radically changed. This is what really changed my life).

My negative concept of God is a *symptom* of a deeper wound. And wounds have to be healed at the source before symptoms will go away. Therefore the hurtful experiences have to be dealt with first.

The *facts* are that God is ever present and He is timeless. He was present when I was hurt, and He is present now. It did not give Him joy or satisfaction to see me hurt. Instead, it metaphorically brought tears to His eyes and turned His stomach. He was and is not powerless to stop the pain, but, out of respect for the free will that He gave to each of us, He did not interfere with my father's actions, except to let him reap what he had sown. He is not offended by my negative feelings toward Him, but, instead, He understands them. He is willing and interested in hearing all about them. God is very intelligent and infinitely wise. He does understand what and why it's happening.

There is no magic formula to experiencing the love and benevolence of God at the heart of my emotions. The hurts must be healed at the source, and, regardless of how I feel, God must be given the freedom to be exactly what and Who He is.

Another very important thing to remember is why I feel the way I do. When I was being hurt, I was not a Christian. I was afraid of God and saw Him as my enemy—just like my dad was. Therefore it makes perfect sense that, while I was overwhelmed with the hurts and emotions of those past experiences, my hurtful feelings about God would naturally be a part of that. I'm feeling the exact same emotions about God as I felt when I went through the hurts of the original experience. Maybe that in itself is healing.

In dealing with the past, I need to experience more of my anger—the same anger that caused my initial depression. My parents (especially my father) have hurt me deeply. They robbed me of my childhood. They destroyed my innocence. They rubbed mud on my uniqueness and self-worth and put the blame on me. They were and are jealous of me to the point where I felt hated. They denied me the privilege of becoming my own unique person.

Why should I have to submissively accept that kind of treatment as okay and normal? It is not normal—it is sick and hurtful and damaging. Their behavior toward me has always been totally unacceptable and, in spite of the fact that they were my parents, I have the right (and responsibility toward myself) to be angry. I need to be angry and not feel guilty about it.

My anger should not be focused toward God but toward my parents' actions against me. It's okay to hate abuse. It's not okay to hate the abuser. There is a huge difference.

* * * * * *

Now that I am in counseling and reading a book that my counselor gave to me, I have some other thoughts about all this. The book is *Your Inner Child of the Past*. As aforementioned in my book, this book has been very helpful to me. Dr. Missildine speaks about how we adopt the feelings and attitudes that our parents have, attitudes and speech that are prevalent in our homes as we grow up. [2]

After reading about this, I went back in my mind and thought about some of the hurtful things that my dad would say to me:

"You'll never marry anyone as wonderful as me."

"No one will ever love you as much as I do."

"You need a husband with an iron hand to keep you under control." *(And I thought, "You mean 'an iron hand to keep me <u>inhibited</u>.'")*

"If you're sick as an adult, it will be 'survival of the fittest' and you won't make it." (*I thought, "I will be considered <u>worthless</u>.")*

It's as if something inside me not only bought this line of thinking, but also wouldn't allow anything else to be true.

". . . it is common for multiple siblings raised in the same family system to perceive that family very differently. Your brother or sister might have such a different view of your family that you wonder if he or she is remembering the same group of people that you do!"

Dave Carder, M.A.
Secrets of Your Family Tree[3]

My Own Personal Journal . . . Deep Hurt

Mid-Twenties

I feel numb today. I want to cry, and I want to vomit. I'm so lonely. I feel like I'm dying inside.

Mom called today. She was drunk. She still has a problem as a mother freeing me to be an independent-thinking adult. I'm sure her attitude is part of the reason I don't feel like a whole woman. I need my mother to accept my growth into womanhood, but she can't get past the thinking that I am still a helpless little girl—at least in our relationship. Even though I am now in my mid-twenties, she still sees me as the thirteen-year-old wounded child. I've been to a couple of Al-Anon meetings, and the one thing I gained from those meetings was that I must not identify emotionally with my alcoholic parents, with their behavior, their attitudes, their habits and addictions, or with any kind of verbal pressure they may exert over me. That is very easy to say, and very difficult to do. When I find myself thinking the way they do, I must change my thought pattern immediately. That will break the cycle. Otherwise, I will pick up their addictive behavior without even realizing it.

As this conversation continued, she tried to "guilt" me when I stood up for my own rights and feelings. She then started to cry. This is her classic manipulative behavior. But I called her on it and told her that I won't accept any more guilt trips from her. I am an adult and my feelings and needs are important. She didn't like it, *but she stopped crying immediately.*

Although I was successful in this situation of handling my mother, I still feel guilty and lonely. Now that the call has ended, I'm sure she is angry with me and telling the other family members that I care for no one except myself.

Perhaps that is true at this moment. It is not generally the case. I am usually a people-pleaser and I will agonize over what people think of me. But not in this case, and not anymore. My family is going to have to understand that I am changing. They also may not fully understand all the reasons. But they don't need to.

Additionally, my family may not understand the way I am changing, or that the path I am on will continue to change and that I will become more independent. I'm afraid I'm going to have to face some misunderstanding and rejection. That kind of rejection is inevitable and there is not much I can do about that.

However, *I do know that God is working in my life.* I am quite confident of that. However, in spite of feeling confident that God is working, *I still feel spiritually and emotionally numb. And I still feel somewhat emotionally out of sorts.* But today I read Joyce Landorf's[4] book, *Irregular People*, and it also encouraged me to believe that God is at work in my life. *I'm also deeply depressed. I feel like I'm bleeding and dying inside.*

If you look at it as having a dream for your life, and then the dream dies, it is called "death of a dream." Then, if you're fortunate, you'll experience "resurrection of that dream." Emotionally, I am at the point where the dream has died, right before the resurrection. In the natural world, the seed has to die before it can yield new life (see John 12:24). As true as this may be, I just know that I'm at a low enough point now that, if the Lord doesn't do a miraculous work in me, there will be no recovery and no healing; therefore, I will have no hope and no resurrection of any of my dreams. The healing and hope aspect has always been out of my hands, and it definitely is now. It's up to God as it always has been.

Mrs. Landorf describes in her book, *Irregular People,* how a person (her father) had hurt her deeply over many years—all her life actually (See quote in Chapter 6 and End Note Chapter 6, #4). When the hurt had reached its peak, she developed TMJ, a painful dysfunctional condition that affects the jaw joint.[5] Her illness was a direct result of her emotional pain. The application for me is that I've been sick a lot in my life, especially over the past five years. As the symptoms of my medical condition (Endometriosis) have changed as time has progressed, I believe it is also a direct result of my emotional pain. I have read many articles that attribute Endometriosis to sexual abuse during adolescence (See Appendix VI). [6]

But regardless of the cause, I have to get this emotional pain into perspective. It is debilitating. I have to get rid of the feeling that I am marked for life by the incest. I can't run away from it. I *must recover* – from the inside out. *The loneliness I feel is paralyzing.*

It would be a very brave thing to go through this alone, but I don't think I want to be that brave. I don't want to be a hero or a martyr of family abuse. I just want to be well and whole . . . *and loved.* But what will it take?

Why am I alone? Why in God's name am I so alone??

My dad stole life and wholeness from me. *He didn't know* that he was shaping (or misshaping) my self-image as a woman. He was very intelligent, but he was also ignorant about what he was doing. He may have had a high IQ, but he wasn't very wise in terms of understanding the way people work, especially his own children. *He didn't know* he was destroying my self-esteem and self-confidence. *But he did.* What he stole from me was the ability to give and enjoy life. And that has caused me intense pain, deeper than I can describe.

At times it feels like he ***destroyed*** me. However, the destruction was not permanent. *Thank God it wasn't permanent!* But how do I get my life back to the way it is supposed to be?

OH LORD, IT ALL SEEMS SO IMPOSSIBLE!

I look in the mirror and I see a broken woman. I see the eyes of a wounded soul staring back at me. I can hardly recognize her. Could that wounded woman possibly be me?

How can I possibly feel the joy of the Lord again? I don't even remember what that feels like.

Meanwhile, *I hurt. I hurt with incredible loneliness and a feeling of deep loss.* I am built to give but have nothing to give to anyone.

What is worse, I have no one to give to. That is so strange to me. I want to give in a close relationship and I can't. First of all, I'm not currently in a close relationship. Second, I have nothing to give. My memories of my friends and lovely church services that I enjoyed being part of in Milwaukie, Oregon, just a few short years ago fade away. I wish I could forget how happy I was, before all these memories came rushing back to the surface of my mind.

I have this *deep and overwhelming feeling of emptiness.* It's like a deep loneliness. It's another way of saying it. It seems like a multi-faceted pain. There could be many ways of describing it and right now I don't know of a better way. I don't know if it is loneliness, emptiness, depression, or insecurity from the trauma. *But I do know that the Lord knows* exactly what it is, and I am so grateful that I do not need to try to describe it to Him.

Oh, I feel so alone! I do need His assurance and understanding! I am so grateful that He is here with me, because I need His presence and love. Even though I cannot feel His presence, I know He is here and He doesn't expect a performance in return. His love is mercy and compassion, and it is completely *un*conditional. It's the kind that will never give up on me. It's the kind that will stay with me to the bitter (or sweet) end. I honestly do not know how I would survive emotionally, without knowing that I can count on Him.

Oh God, *please*, *please* *rescue and heal me. Please fill me with Your tender mercies and Your unconditional love!!*

(The preceding Journal Entry was a time of deep anguish and many, many tears. As I was crying out to the Lord, He showed me this poem.)

The Consoler

With His healing hand on a broken heart,
And the other on a Star,
Our Wonderful God views the miles apart,
And they seem not very far.

O it makes us cry—then laugh—then sing,
Tho' 'tis all beyond our ken;
He binds up wounds on that poor crushed thing,
And He makes it whole again.

Was there something from that healed new heart,
Made the Psalmist think of stars –
That bright as the sun the lightening's dart,
Sped away past biological bars?

In a low place sobbing by death's lone cart,
Then a flight on whirlwinds cars;
One verse is about a poor broken heart,
And the next among the stars.

There is hope and help for our sighs and tears,
For the wound that stings and smarts;
Our God is at home with the rolling spheres,
And at home with broken hearts.

— M. P. Ferguson [7]

My Own Personal Journal of Pain and Recovery . . . Nightmare

Late Twenties

I had another nightmare last night. I was being sexually abused and attacked. I don't know who was attacking me, but it was two men. I woke up pushing at them as hard as possible and trying to make them stop.

When is this nightmare going to end?? When will all the nightmares and bad dreams and fears stop harassing me? When will sex be something that will be a good life experience for me? Will it ever be something good? Why does something that was intended to be a blessing have to be turned into a curse for me? Why does it have to be something that makes me feel worthless and helpless?

Why?
Why does facing this trauma have to be so
PAINFUL ? ? ?

I had many similar nightmares, in the years after the incest and during the counseling years, when the memories of the incest resurfaced and continued to stay right there in my conscious mind.

My Own Personal Journal of Pain and Recovery . . . Feeling Nauseated and Dirty

Late Twenties

I am physically and emotionally exhausted. I wanted to cry all day. I feel nauseated, guilty, dirty, and ugly. I'm a virgin, other than the purity that my dad stole from me, but I do not feel pure like a virgin should. I feel polluted. I'm in a state of intense loneliness, as if no one is with me and no one can understand.

I want to hide. I visualized my childhood bedroom. I was laying on my bed on the bottom bunk in the dark, but I wanted to hide in the closet. I have memories and thoughts of withdrawal, of daydreaming and fantasizing about being loved, and of being special and important to someone. I figured that was the only way I would experience it. But that's not good enough now. I need to be with a real person and have real interaction.

I feel hopelessness. I thought about statements made by my dad that made me feel that being loved was beyond my reach. My dad's statements of my worth always had an underlying sexual meaning.

The only part of me that seemed to be of any consequence to my dad was my body. The things he said to and about me made me feel that he could not see me as a whole person. Therefore, I felt and acted like I wasn't a real person, only a messed up object of someone else's pleasure. My concept of what it meant to be a woman was that my only worth was sexual.

Had I been born with a misshapen or disfigured body, I would have had no worth at all. Every woman my dad met and saw on the street or who came into our home was evaluated by my dad in sexual terms—she seemed to have no other worth. Being a woman meant that I was to be someone else's plaything and nothing more.

Physically I have been affected by a loss of appetite and have had trouble sleeping.

I felt intense loneliness last weekend and the need to talk to and be with someone who would be interested in what I'm going through. What am I supposed to do when I'm feeling this way, and no one is available? At times I would like to be able to just push it all away and find a way to just be "normal," whatever that is.

Deep Darkness

I was thirteen years old now and dad's visits to my room continued and the touching became more sexual and more involved. My room was different now. My bed was now in the corner away from the center of the room and the window. Because of that, my room seemed darker. He would come in and kneel by my bed and touch me. But he didn't stop there.

One night I remember very clearly. It was typical of many frightening nights to follow. I was becoming more afraid of him and more *un*comfortable and confused than before. It had been at least two years from the first visit. He had been drinking, and knowing what he was about to do made me feel very vulnerable. *The smell of alcohol on his breath was nauseating and detestable!! It was a horrible, repulsive smell! I was so afraid of what he was about to do.* I knew from his odor and his demeanor that his intention was not going to be good for me, and I was *terrified.*

How do I get rid of this animal? How do I tell my daddy to stop doing this to me? I knew in my heart this was wrong. I was so afraid of what was happening that *I froze and tried to pretend that I wasn't even there. I tried to detach my mind and emotions from feeling what was happening to my body.* But it didn't work, and he didn't stop.

Oh, God, what would it take to make this beast go away and leave me alone?? But I was so afraid. I was afraid that, if I were to resist, I would be in trouble for rebelling against him. You did not say "No" to this man. I was afraid of the consequences of rebellion. Besides, who would believe me?

I didn't know God personally, but He seemed to be the only One I could talk to. I knew that He was already aware of what was happening anyway. My next thought was that I might as well talk to Him about it. I knew that at least God would keep my secret. If I were to tell my mom, I feared that she would either not believe me or hate me, because she would feel that I had crossed an invisible line (actually my dad had). I feared that she, subsequently, would divorce my dad. It could possibly tear up my home and it would be all my fault. If she didn't believe me, she could repeat my story and *everyone would see me as a filthy, dirty person, because that is what this whole scenario was—dirty. I thought I would be the one who would be labeled as a dirty, evil child.* But what kind of child would think up such sick things? However, the truth was: *I didn't think this up; my dad did.* And now it was stamped indelibly on my subconscious. What father is sexually interested in his daughter? *That is sick!* To me it was unheard of. At least I had never heard of it. *Oh! I was absolutely sure that no one would ever believe me. I wasn't even sure anyone would listen to me. It must be kept a secret.*

My dad could manipulate his way into or out of anything. He was able to use his intelligence in all the wrong ways and seemed to have the gift of intimidation. Just by raising his voice and using carefully chosen words and phrases, he could threaten anyone. He would be justified, and I would be to blame.

The sad thing about that first night is that it wasn't only one night. He kept repeating his attempts to become intimate with me. But that first night was incredibly traumatic. I felt like I was being *knifed in the heart of my emotions, deep into my soul.* That night my dad stole my innocence. He raped my childhood emotions. He put a deep wound into my soul and it is still there. He stole my childhood purity and zest for life. He took everything inside me that was fresh and clean and threw it in the mud—and all that was left was a wounded, terrified child and a woman's body that seemed to be frozen in place. The scared child could not enjoy the woman's body that was developing. She could not enjoy becoming a woman. To her, the body and womanhood represented filth.

I will say one thing about all those future attempts. I resisted them with every possible movement I could and every ounce of strength I had. But I didn't dare speak a word of defiance to him. I even prayed that He would stop. I knew that God was already aware of what was happening anyway. As a result, my dad did not get any further with me than he did the first time. But the trauma was always overwhelming. That was the thing about the incest. No matter how far it went, it was always traumatic—each time was as upsetting as the first. Perhaps it was because he was my dad and he wasn't supposed to be there with me. Or maybe it was because I wasn't old enough or emotionally ready for sex, and I hung on to my integrity of being a little girl. Perhaps it was God speaking to my heart, in a language I could understand, assuring me that my dad was breaking the rules. But each time he came in to touch me was another trauma to my soul.

The dreams about growing up to be a beautiful woman and being loved were shattered. I knew if I ever became a beautiful woman, men *would* look at me. But they wouldn't be looking at the woman or the person. They would be looking at a woman's body. They would see all the physical aspects of a woman from a carnal point of view. But there were some things that would be missing, that they would never see. They wouldn't see creativity, intelligence, and joy for living. They wouldn't see someone who loved beauty and desired excellence. They wouldn't see someone who loved life, music, people, and relationships. They may never look into my eyes and see a person. They would look at me and all they would see is the potential for a sexual encounter. (Or so I thought at that time.)

I was sure that men were like that, because my dad was like that. So, to maintain my sanity, I came up with an idea. My new idea was not really new, because women have been doing it for centuries. My idea was that love is not real but sex is. For a while I thought, "*If I can get men to love me sexually, maybe I'll feel loved. I'll use men to feel loved. But I'll never marry, and I'll never trust a man. Trust is for little girls and babies!! I'll never trust anyone—especially a man!!!*"

But at that time, I was still only thirteen years old, and there was never any opportunity to use a man to feel loved. Now instead of being the little girl who had been "daddy's girl" (or so I thought), *I had learned to hate my dad.* He represented the ugliest, most repulsive thing in the world to me. He was always drunk, always had alcohol on his breath, always exposing himself at home and in the back yard, and always talking about things from a sexual, carnal point of view. I hated sex and, at the same time, I was somewhat curious about it. I wanted love and I hated the fact that sex had to be part of that. I hated that it seemed to be the only avenue to having a family of my own in the future.

Was I angry? *You bet I was angry!*

Nothing in the House

My servant, Lord, has nothing in the house.
Not even one small pot of common oil
For he who never cometh but to spoil
That ruthless strong man armed, whom
men call *Pain*.

I thought that I had courage in the house
And patience to be quiet and endure
And sometimes happy songs, now I am sure
Your servant truly has not anything
And see, my songbird has a broken wing.

"My servant, I have come into the house ~
I who know *Pain's* extremity so well
That there can never be the need to tell
His power to make the flesh and spirit quail.
Have I not felt the scourge, the thorns, the nail?

"And I, His conqueror, am in the house.
Let not your heart be troubled, do not fear.
Why should you, child of Mine, if I am here?
My touch will heal your songbird's broken wing
And he shall have a braver song to sing." [8]

Amy Carmichael

My Own Personal Journal . . . Tears, Tears, and More Tears

Counseling Years ~ Late Twenties

Tears, tears, and more tears. I keep crying and I can't seem to stop. This Valley of Tears is more like a deep, long desert, and I feel like I'm dying of thirst. I'm thirsty both emotionally and spiritually.

I'm so despondent, that I can hardly function. I feel like I'm bleeding and dying inside. There seems to be no reason to go on.

What has my biological father taken from me? Why did he have to tamper with the process of my growing up? Now there seems to be something missing inside of me. What is missing is something like hope. It feels like self-worth is also missing, and believing that it will all get better. Sometimes it's more and more difficult to believe.

No one can love me; no one can know me. It feels like I'm dead inside. I don't want to smile . . . I don't even want to breathe. It hurts too much.

It has something to do with being a woman. It has to do with the feminine, sexual side of me. I don't know what it is or what to call it, but I don't feel good about myself. I feel misshapen, deformed, and undesirable, like an empty shell. I look okay on the outside and could probably make a lot of people think that everything is okay on the inside, but it's not. I don't feel whole.

I feel like an adult who is playing pretend. I can wear the clothes and the makeup, but, inside, I'm still just a little girl. I feel like I don't have the right to be a woman. It's like I never had the chance to grow up because my childhood was stolen from me.

What did my dad steal from me? Was it the right to grow up? Why did he have to tamper with the right I had to become a woman deep inside? Why did he have to try to rush things? He may not have known what he was doing, but he may as well have taken my life.

That is how powerful the hurt and damage is. If only he had left me alone to grow up the way I was supposed to.

I want to cry, but I don't have enough tears to express all my grief. I feel like I have been emotionally deformed all my life, and I just now looked in the mirror and into my soul, through my hurting eyes, and realized it. I have to say that it REALLY hurts!

When I was suicidal, a friend told me that, as a Christian, I had no business even having thoughts like that. He told me I had agonized over this pain long enough, and I should just accept what happened so long ago and simply move on. I was told that these things happen, and I should stop feeling sorry for myself and be grateful for the good things the Lord has done for me. He was trying to tell me how I should feel. When I asked him how much he knew about incest, he said that he had read a couple of articles.

Really?!? "A couple of articles?!" WOW! This friend was in the ministry and I had known him for a number of years.

My next question was, "How in the world could he possibly know how I should feel?" How dare he tell me what I should feel, when he had so little knowledge of it, had not been through my trauma, and could in no way feel the echo of my emptiness and trauma?

It hurts to share something so personal from the depth of my soul, with someone who cannot accept it, will not understand my pain, or even try to comprehend how incest impacts my life. And this was not the first time that it happened.

This has happened several times for me and it hurts just as bad each time. It hurts to see someone walk away and treat me with rejection because of ignorance or insensitivity. It hurts to have someone tell me how I should respond or compare my pain with someone else's. I am who I am, and I feel the way I feel. Perhaps they simply don't wish to get close to my pain or identify with it. Or perhaps it is far too painful for them to get close. But I do not have that choice. Regardless of how depressed I get, I won't apologize for my feelings and moods. Maybe there is something missing inside of me, but I won't fake my feelings and responses. I won't pretend to have hope, when I don't. I won't put on an emotional performance for another person. I can't and I won't. I flat refuse to, because even I, in my despairing condition, know that I will not heal, if I pretend that the pain is not there. When it comes down to it, I simply do not have a choice.

Sometimes I think it is best to only share my most fragile feelings with my educated and trained counselor. Sometimes trusted friends are really not trusted friends at all. I'm going to have to be a lot more careful.

* * * * * *

Some years after this incident, I was reading a very good book on this subject and was reminded, that my God will give me all the time I need to recover and that I should also give myself the grace to heal in a timely manner. The book I read was Secrets of Your Family Tree, [9] *and this particular quote is by Earl Henslin, Psy.D. I found this to be very comforting and reassuring:*

"We need to remember that dealing with dysfunctional family issues (like incest) <u>will take time</u>—<u>time with God, time for yourself</u>, <u>time with your spouse</u>, <u>time for the children</u>, and <u>time for support groups</u> or <u>supportive relationships</u>. <u>Time to be together</u>.

"Time takes on another dimension when we are dealing with issues we must face personally. Some hurts, angers, and traumas will not go away immediately. A woman or man who was the victim of incest as a child must deal not only with the hurt, anger, and betrayal connected with the molestation but <u>must also totally restructure the image he has of himself as a person</u>. He or she needs to resolve issues of sexuality, trust, and shame—<u>in short, he or she must relearn how to deal with life in general</u>. Likewise, grief over the loss of a parent or child—or of anyone close

to you—will not go away in twenty-four hours. The stages of grief a person must experience will take time to resolve.

"As Christians it is easy to shame ourselves for taking too much time to get over things. After all, isn't it a lack of faith on my part if I am not able to give my grief to God and be healed? No, healing deep hurt takes time. It is not something that can be rushed, no matter how hard we push ourselves. Not even our well-meaning Christian friends who chide us for taking a healthy amount of time to be okay can shorten that duration" (Underscore by book author).

Darkness, Confusion . . . and Then a New Light!

I was very confused. I didn't really know what love was, and I didn't understand sex. I was confused about my body and emotions, and I definitely didn't understand men. And there was no one to talk to. I felt that no one would ever be able to love or understand me. My dad even told me no one would ever love me or want to marry me. That felt like the ultimate rejection, and that was a knife in the heart of my soul. It was insult, on top of injury, to have the one who injured me say a thing like that to me.

On top of that, I felt that if anyone ever found out about the contemptable episodes with my dad, they would despise me for sure. I was becoming more convinced than ever that love was a sugar-coated myth and trust was for the naive. I was sure I was worthless—or so I felt. I knew that what I had been through caused these feelings, but I didn't really understand all the psychological and physiological implications of how it was affecting me.

However, there were also times when I wondered if it was my fault that all this happened. It wasn't my fault, but I had these feelings because of the guilt I felt—in a strange and twisted sense, because my dad had put me in my mother's place. I felt dirty and those feelings always brought on some kind of guilt. Besides, he should have been with my mother, not with me. It's easy to see how confused I became.

I was ignorant about a lot of things. I didn't understand why my father behaved as he did toward me, and I was completely in the dark about his motives—whatever they were at the time. However, I was correct about some things. One of those things was that I knew the incest was not my idea. I did not approach my father in any way; in fact, I avoided him because of his unbecoming and angry behavior. He came to me with his sexual behavior that I totally did not understand at that time.

Right after my father passed away, about two years after the incest became known and about eighteen months after I became a Christian, I was told by someone that my hurt feelings and resentment toward my father were inappropriate for someone who claimed to be a follower of the Lord Jesus. This person insisted that I should have been more loving and forgiving toward him. It was even suggested to me that, in some third world countries, incest was a natural part of the tribal culture. I was deeply hurt by this person's statement, knowing that it wasn't God's way, whether or not some heathen third world tribal culture did practice it—which I doubted. If that was true, those tribal third world cultures were operating under the influence of God's enemy, Satan.

At this time in my life, I just didn't feel normal. I didn't feel liked or desirable. Boys didn't like me the way they liked other girls. I was shy and scared. I wanted to open up and to be friendly, but I couldn't. One of my male relatives even made fun of me, because I didn't date or act like *"normal"* girls. This person even told my mother that she shouldn't allow me to do things *"normal"* teenagers do, because I wasn't *"normal."* To him *"normal"* meant having a personality and behavior that was outgoing and more forward with boys. He meant that I should be more flirtatious and involved in teenage activities. That just didn't work for my wounded personality.

I wanted my personality to be more contemporary and friendly (or at least more relaxed and outgoing), but I couldn't be that way, because, for me, it felt wrong. Besides, I wanted to be a "good girl." I wanted to please my mother and be good. My mother always taught me to save myself for marriage, and I was always determined to do that. Being afraid of sex because of the incest, I wanted to behave in a way that felt safe and pure. Fortunately, for me, the Lord Jesus intervened in my life, before I had a chance to live out my fantasies of using men to get what I perceived love to be.

After I met the Lord Jesus, my life was radically transformed by His power. My ideas about love, sex, and men changed radically. One thing that helped to bring about that change was to observe how Christian men at church treated their wives. I observed them very carefully every week and noticed how they, without exception, treated them with great respect. It was very different from what I saw with my parents and many of my relatives. I was still in search of love, and, to a great degree, I found it in God Himself and in other Christians.

Before I knew the Lord Jesus, I thought God was very much like my dad. My biological father was demanding, ruthless, insensitive, and judgmental. He had his own definition of love, and I figured that God did as well. I couldn't understand how I could ever be comforted by God. In fact, when I first began attending church, I made it very clear to myself and to others that I wasn't there to become "spiritual" or "religious." I didn't want to know God. I wanted friends. I wanted people to love me just the way I was.

During my high school years, my parents had been very strict about my social life. I was not allowed to attend very many social events at school or church, unless I literally begged, and then the answer was usually "No." If an event was on a "school night" the answer was an automatic "No," regardless of how wholesome or well-chaperoned it was. I remember an eighth grade activity that I really wanted to attend and received a lot of invitations to. I went to a middle school that was brand new, and my class was one of the first classes to attend that school. Every Wednesday night there was an all school roller skating event that was very well chaperoned by the school. I wanted to attend this social event, in the worst way, so I could get to know some of the students and make new friends. But I wasn't allowed to go, because it was a school night. I repeatedly asked my parents if I could go, but the answer was always "No."

I can remember my first answered prayer (other than my prayer that Jesus would come into my life). That prayer was that my parents would allow me to join the choir at church. I wanted friends and social involvement. This was about four years after my requests to go to the roller skating events. Singing in the choir at church was very important to me. I had been influenced by certain people in my life, and now their love was becoming more and more vital to me. Now I wanted to know them more personally. I wanted to know their character and interests and what they were like. But I didn't think I could know God that way. I didn't think God *could* be known in a personal, relational way. Oh, how wrong I was! I later learned that not only could I know God personally, but I could know His beautiful approachable character as well.

I learned over time that the God I came to believe in is, in fact, a God who *comforts* His loved ones. I hung on to Scripture verses that spoke of His comfort, such as:

I, even I, am He who
comforts you.
Isaiah 51:12 NKJV

By the time I was fourteen years old, the family was talking openly of dad's problems—in his absence, of course. My mom and some of my siblings said he was mentally ill. The concept of mental illness became a household topic of conversation. We tried to figure out what happened to dad and why it happened.

Along with incest—which I still had not told anyone about—there were other dysfunctional sexual behaviors. What we perceived as mental problems, we later learned was Bipolar Disorder (back then, known as manic depressive disorder). At this time my mother began using me for a sounding board, telling me about some of dad's abnormal sexual behavior with her. I don't remember any of the details of what she told me, but I do remember becoming quite upset with what she told me. Then she would apologize and say, "Honey, I'm so sorry. I shouldn't be telling you these things." She was right, she shouldn't have. At this age, I already had a very warped idea, of what a marriage relationship was supposed to be like and what men were supposed to be like in relationship to their families. So hearing about some of their problems didn't help at all. *I wondered what was wrong with my parents and why they felt compelled to expose me to the sexual part of their life, before I was grown up and ready for it? Didn't they know that children are supposed to grow up gradually, before they learn about these things? Didn't they know that sex was supposed to be a beautiful thing between husband and wife only? What was wrong with them? Why did they force it on me at such a tender age?*

It was during this time that the Lord began reaching out to me in a new way. He had been knocking on my heart's door for a while, but now He was gently urging me to respond. It was during my sophomore year of high school that something special began to happen. I was 15 years old now, and my broken heart was beginning to respond almost in desperation. I needed a special kind of love, and it seemed that the only way I was going to receive it was through the Lord Jesus and His people. He had begun to do a lot of loud knocking at the door of my life, but I wasn't ready to trust in Him or to really respond to Him in any way.

The actual physical incest was over. Dad was no longer visiting me in the night. But I was suffering greatly from its effects and from the entire family situation. I had a classmate, whose locker was next to mine, with whom I shared significant portions of my dysfunctional home experiences. She had been a runaway from several foster homes, and during that year she wanted to run away again. My friend didn't like her foster home, and she made running away from home sound like a viable option for someone who was unhappy. Fortunately, I did not see that I had that option as it would have opened a whole world of new problems for me. I was also afraid to speak to a counselor at school, which I knew could be an option for me. But I didn't want to be put into the State Foster Care System. I had heard nightmare stories about what happens to children and teens in Foster Care. I didn't want to be a ward of the Court. I knew that, if I did that, I could have been jumping out of the frying pan and into the fire, so to speak.

My options were limited, and it came back to my dad being in control. He knew everything about my life that mattered, including where I could possibly live. At least he knew everything I knew about this and a lot more. I knew that if I ran away, he would find me, and all hell would break loose in my world. I was so afraid of him, that I couldn't break loose of his control over my mind and my emotions. If he said I was ugly, then *I was ugly*. I believed him. The mind games he would play affected me, both on the conscious level and deeper down where the real emotions were. I believed and feared every word he said.

One of his favorite mind games, that greatly affected me, was when he said that my physical illness was all in my head. It sounded harmless enough, but it scared me to death. The emotional pain, resulting from the incest, worked its way out through my health, and I was frequently ill. My dad would say,

> "You can heal yourself with your mind—I do it when I feel sick all the time. And if you don't heal yourself this way, your brain and mind will make you weak and deficient."

I believed him and it scared me. It made me feel that he was all-powerful (like God), and I was weak with a mental deficiency.

When I was sick he would say,

> ". . . in your future it will be 'survival of the fittest.' So, if you can't be strong, you will be swept away with the weak and disabled. *There will be no place for you in the future world you will live in.*"

To me, it was another way of telling me that I would be considered worthless. The message that reached my subconscious was, "You *are* worthless! You'll *never* amount to anything!!" If the incest wasn't enough to destroy my worth, his words finished me off emotionally. It made me feel that I had no hope for my future life, so I might as well not make plans for my future career or family life. All during that school year when I was 15 years old, I contemplated suicide or tried to figure out a way of escaping the dysfunction I was experiencing at home.

I thought that, if I couldn't run away, suicide would be the only other escape. But I didn't really want to die. I thought I was too young to die. I still wanted to live. But given my circumstances, I didn't know what other option I had. There were some classmates, who I really admired, that I wanted to model my life after. They were my age and seemed to have their lives all together. They appeared to always be happy, and they seemed to succeed at everything they did. But being like them seemed very unlikely. It seemed, to me, like their lives were everything I wanted to be. Again, I felt no hope of being a person of value and my worth plummeted. I knew I couldn't run away. I had nowhere to go that my dad would not drag me back from. As I contemplated these thoughts, my emotions were on a roller coaster ride. I wanted to live and somehow become like my role models. When I was with them I felt happy and hopeful. When I was at home surrounded by the dysfunction and reminders of what my dad did, I wanted the easiest escape route—whatever that might be.

As a result, I was back to the idea that suicide was my only option. The only question was how and when? There were weapons in the house I could use, if I could figure out how they worked. I was also on medication for a childhood neurological disorder. I could use the medication, if I took the entire bottle when the prescription was first refilled. Those were the only options I had the courage to think about. Using a knife was just too messy.

I entertained these thoughts all summer, before my sophomore year of high school. Then just before school started, God intervened. It appeared that He wanted me to live. He carefully chose three classmates who were able to help me get my mind off suicide. I say that God carefully selected them, because they all happened to be young ladies that I really admired and looked up to. Two of these classmates came to my house to personally invite me to an event with their church youth group and then to church with them the next Sunday. Another classmate was instrumental in encouraging me to come to church as often as I could. She knew that was where I would be fed the Word of God and be encouraged by other believers. They (and others in that youth group) were all from stable Christian homes, and they all lived very wholesome, godly lives. Most of the students in that group were honor students. Two of them were cheerleaders, one of them was a gymnast, and several of them were in the music program. I greatly admired them for their accomplishments. They were all very good friends and made very good role models for me. This really intrigued me and I wanted to know the secret to their success in life. And even though they were successful, they had the normal issues that most teens have. I could relate to them. So after a week of pleading with my parents to let me go to church with them, my parents finally decided to let me go.

This group of Christians at church loved me with a kind of love I never felt at home. In fact, I had never experienced this kind of love anywhere I had ever been before. They also kept saying that they were loving me with *God's love*, and I just wasn't sure that I could accept that. I wasn't sure I could believe God knew anything about love and human emotions. After all, according to my 15-year-old "theology," He, my Father in Heaven, had allowed the incest. During the younger years of my childhood, He had given me a father who seemed to be a good and caring father. Then that father turned into something horrible. My biological father had hurt me with a pain that reached all the way into my soul. He demoralized me with incest and had robbed me of all my hopes and dreams—and that continued into adulthood. With that being the case, how could this God possibly know how to love or protect me? But these friends' love was unique and genuine and began to give me some real hope. The love was powerful and the hope was real enough to cause me to stop thinking about suicide.

Toward the end of my sophomore year and a couple of months before my sixteenth birthday, I was invited to a high school retreat where a representative from Campus Crusade for Christ was our guest speaker. He shared a message based on the "*Four Spiritual Laws,*" the biblical message that teaches that we are all sinners and as such we cannot spend eternity with God, apart from believing the sacrificial death of the Lord Jesus (in which He shed His blood on the cross for us individually), who then, three days later, was miraculously risen from the dead. The sacrifice of God's Son, Jesus, was for my sins, even if I were the only sinner. This means that He saw value in me.

I had heard that message several times before in my life, but this time it penetrated deep into my soul. It sunk all the way down to where the little girl in me who had been violated by incest was hiding with her broken heart. I reasoned to myself that if God loved me that much—enough to sacrifice His one and only Son for me—then, yes, I could believe He *had* to see value in me. So I presented my broken heart to Him. I asked Him to forgive me for making such a mess of my life by hiding my broken heart from Him and thanked Him for dying for my sins on the cross. When I finished praying, for some reason, everyone had already left the room and I was left there alone. There was no rush to leave. The first thing I felt was a heavy weight of anguish fall away. The first of many weights that would go, in the process of healing, was the weight of the wounds of incest. There was a verse that was quoted that night that I have never forgotten:

> *Therefore, if anyone is in Christ, he is a new creature; the old things have passed away; behold, new things have come.* 2 Corinthians 5:17

That verse meant a great deal to me, because I understood it to mean that old things would be wiped away right then and there forever. But my initial understanding of it was not quite right. I thought the old, painful things would be wiped away *immediately*. But, unfortunately, it doesn't work that way. It means that old things *begin* to pass away. It is a metamorphosis, somewhat like the process the butterfly goes through in the cocoon before it emerges into a beautiful creature. There were many things about God and His sacrifice for me and my metamorphosis that I still didn't understand. But I was confident that God would fill in the blanks, as I learned to know Him better.

After I began my relationship with God, through Jesus Christ, my ideas about love and sex and men began to change gradually and radically. I was still in search of love, and, to a great degree, I found it in God Himself and in other Christians. However, I still suffered from many of the fears brought on by the emotional trauma I suffered at the hands of my dad. My dad's problems really affected me in a new way, during that first year after I became a Christian. The nightly visits had stopped, but I still lived with my dad and he continued to have multiple problems. The wounds of the incest still affected me, but my focus had changed from finding a way to escape my current situation to learning to trust God and allowing Him to make me a member of His own family.

After I met the Lord Jesus and accepted Him as my Lord and Savior, everything fell apart at home for me in new ways. My dad didn't like the idea of my going to church. I think he was threatened by the idea that Someone else, more powerful than he, was in control of my life. I had begun to change outwardly, and people began to notice the changes in my life, including my family. I had joy for the first time in my life. I think my dad was intimidated by my joy and the work of the Holy Spirit in me. I also think he just didn't like the idea of my being so happy, going to church, having friends, and seeing the positive changes in my life. He fought it, by trying to keep me from going to church. He ridiculed my joy and new purpose for living. He ridiculed my friends, by insisting that Christian joy was simply another evidence of the use of illegal drugs. When he said this, I couldn't help but break out laughing. If he had known my friends, he would never have said that. I even told him that some of my new friends were honor students, of which two of them, identical twins, eventually graduated from high school as Valedictorians. My father again tried to ridicule my friends, by telling me that most people who get those kinds of good grades consistently all through school need drugs to keep them going. I knew that wasn't true, because I knew my friends well enough to know their character and that they would never come close to the drug world.

My father also tried to destroy my faith by using his limited knowledge of the Bible to confuse me. But it usually backfired on him. I remember one evening very clearly. At the dinner table, my family (led by dad) began firing Bible questions at me, one after the other, so fast that I couldn't answer them. I became so flustered and frustrated that I ran away from the table in tears. The tears had nothing to do with Bible knowledge. They were due to *my hurt from rejection,* because they all seemed to be against me, and they seemed to enjoy seeing me frustrated. My family *didn't want answers,* and, at the time, I didn't have them. They were taunting and ridiculing me intentionally, and *I felt completely rejected–again!! Oh, how the rejection hurt! Yes, I was really being rejected*, but what it was, in reality, was persecution for my new-found faith in the Lord Jesus. This kind of thing has been happening to Christian young people for centuries, but this was new to me. *It felt like my old enemy—painful, hurtful, lonely rejection*. The r*ejection was so painful, that it felt like a knife wound deep in the heart of my soul. It is still something that I cannot handle well to this day.*

There was another time that my father insisted that Jesus was the god of this world. I told him that he was absolutely mistaken about Jesus—that the god of this world is Satan. An argument began shortly after that, with him telling me that I did not know more about the Bible (or anything else for that matter) than he did. I hate competition and I did not feel that I had to be right. But I was tired of his put-downs, and I knew that he was mistaken about God and His Word. Additionally, it was very easy to get sucked into arguing with him. So I got my Bible and let him read 2 Corinthians 4:3-4:

> 3 *And even if our gospel is veiled, it is veiled to those who are perishing,*
>
> 4 *in whose case the god of this world has blinded the minds of the unbelieving, so that they might not see the light of the gospel of the glory of Christ, who is the image of God.*

After that he was hesitant to trample on my understanding of God's Word, as he knew I had been spending many hours in my room reading it. So he couldn't destroy my faith on biblical grounds.

My mom did support me in my new faith. She didn't choose to believe in it or follow it for herself, but she knew that it was what I needed. She knew that if I didn't go to church, I could easily be out on the streets in the arms of the wrong type of person or someone that was way too old for me. Or if I wasn't in church, I could have been out there doing something worse than being involved in a church that differed so much from hers. I could have been involved in a cult. She had taught me moral decency since I was very young, to keep me from dating and marrying too young as she had done. My mom had gotten pregnant at 15 and dropped out of school. She felt that Christianity would be a very good thing for me, and she began standing up to my dad by saying "Yes" to me, when dad was always saying "No!"

Did I say that my dad was always *saying*, "No?" It was more like he was *shouting **"NO!"*** as loud as possible. He delighted in telling me "*NO!*" and restricting and depriving me of my desires. I think he enjoyed using his power and authority as my father to control me. If I wanted something or if it was clear to him that it really meant something to me, he opposed it, scoffed at it, restricted it, *and strongly ridiculed it!!* This made me feel the *utmost rejection*, which cut deep into my broken heart. Even though my father had deeply hurt me and rejected me as his daughter by the incest and other inappropriate behaviors and words, for some reason, I still wanted his approval.

There was also constant yelling. He yelled about everything. He argued and fought about everything. The atmosphere was always explosive, uncertain, and volatile. All this yelling was very intimidating and frightening to me. *I was very much afraid of him and his explosive anger.* I didn't know it was a symptom of his Bipolar Disorder, and I don't think it would have mattered. He ***terrified*** me. All this yelling exacerbated another problem for me: *Post-Traumatic Stress Disorder*, which I still suffer from to this day. I would cringe when anyone yelled or was angry, whether it was for a good cause or not. And I still do.

My dad also began displaying another problem during my high school years. He was a *transvestite*. This was a sexual dysfunction and perversion.

He began wearing my mother's underwear under his clothes. There was one incident when he came to pick me up at church and he was drunk senseless. He could hardly control the car. Besides that, he was wearing one of my mother's brassieres under his shirt, along with a pair of her nylons and a pair of my mother's dress shoes. Although they were under his clothes, they were still quite visible. Since all of this was clearly seen by anyone looking in his direction, I was horrified and embarrassed and ashamed—all at the same time. I wondered which one of my parents he was trying to be.

I was ashamed to be his daughter. His speech was vulgar, and he was constantly making sexual comments. It became so bad that when we came to visit people (family friends and relatives), they would ask us to leave *and to never come back*. When that happened, the whole family suffered. When my father wasn't welcome back into their homes, that meant the whole family could never come back as well. At that time my mother did not have a driver's license, and my father would have opposed us going on a family outing without him. That made this both a personal and group rejection. It hurt me personally, because I was becoming extremely sensitive to that painful, emotional rejection. It was like another knife wound into my heart. I had looked up to some of these friends and extended family members as role models, and now we couldn't see them anymore. Now I had to turn exclusively to the role models at church and school. My options were really narrowing when it came to role models. I have to believe, however, that the Lord was narrowing my path and the direction He wanted me to go in my life, by limiting my access to role models. At the time, this was extremely painful. All these behavioral symptoms that my dad was displaying affected everyone. But I do not recall any family discussions about them. Perhaps there was some discussion, but I was so hurt I couldn't remember. No one knew about the incest yet. I still had told no one. I was still silent regarding that trauma.

When I was sixteen years old, all these problems became too much for my mother to handle—and understandably so. The pressure on her was incredible. My dad had threatened some terrible things, if she ever tried to leave or divorce him. She had pressure from him 24/7. He told her that if she ever tried to leave or divorce him, he would hurt me. In fact, he said he would *murder* me in a very graphic way, most likely, because I was that coveted first daughter. He then threatened to hurt every one of her remaining offspring in a terrible way. To top it off, he threatened to commit suicide. He was extremely intimidating, controlling, and convincing.

In her desperation and being of the Catholic faith, my mother went to her local Catholic Church and spoke to a priest for counseling. When my mother told the priest about all the sexual dysfunction, he asked her if my father had ever touched any of her children inappropriately. My mother immediately denied it. She couldn't believe he would do such a thing. That was either out of the scope of her imagination, or she was in denial that such a thing could have happened. It is possible that she still had a slight amount of respect for him and his former morals. Then the priest assured her that most people who make the kind of extreme threats that my father had made, regarding murder and suicide, rarely follow through on them. He told her they usually commit those kinds of acts spontaneously, without any prior warning, and when they do make those kinds of threats, they are meant to be used as control tactics. He also encouraged her to tactfully do what she could to find out if my father had extended his sexual dysfunction to abusing any of her children.

All the way home from that meeting, my mother had the fear that perhaps he really had extended his sexual abuse to include me. She kept turning it over and over in her mind, because she knew that he was so completely out of control in his dysfunctional behavior toward her and in other ways. When she arrived home, she tried to discuss it with me. She found me in my bedroom as usual, withdrawing into my own world. She asked me if my dad had ever touched me in the wrong way. I gave her such a classic answer that, for someone so naïve, it could never have been contrived. I just turned my back to her and said, "I don't want to talk about it." With that answer, the thing she feared the most came crashing down on her. She knew he had crossed the line of moral decency. She was absolutely crushed and mortified.

When I had counseling years later, my counselor suggested that I may want to consider and accept the option that she was, in fact, in denial. She said that most mothers/wives usually do know when their husband have sexually abused their children. But they bury it deep inside as they just can't deal with it. So she was likely in denial.

The first thing my mother did was to ask my permission to speak to a close family friend. She felt that she might need his support for what she would have to do next. Because of all of my dad's problems, my mother wanted to have him committed to a hospital's mental department. Because I knew my mother had also suffered greatly with my father and I was also sure that she had been through quite enough with him, I gave her my consent. This man and his wife lived out of town, but they were at our house in just a matter of hours. I soon came to regret that consent. I wanted to keep it a secret, in order that no one in our group of friends and extended family would find out and my detestable secret would be protected. This is because you can't control how people are going to respond to news like that. That type of news about people is just the kind of thing that makes the gossip mill turn. In sharing it with one person, my secret was not destined to be kept protected any longer. It was not long before *I felt exposed*—my secret becoming news to everyone in our circle of friends and extended family. This does not mean our friends shared it with each other and everyone they knew. It only means that *I felt* like my secret had been exposed.

I didn't begrudge my mother getting the support she needed. She was suffering with my father in a different way than I had. In some ways it was more intense as his wife. But I did come to regret giving my permission to share my abuse. There were other problems with my dad she could have shared, without sharing the incest, but I didn't realize that at the time. Once my mother gained the support she needed from close family friends, it seemed that almost overnight everyone knew of the terrible thing my father had done, and I felt like I was on display. Or it seemed that way to me. I felt like I was the evil child. To others, I was just an object of interest.

I used to really look forward to the major holidays when the whole extended family would gather to celebrate. I looked forward to seeing my maternal grandmother and my cousins. These holidays were like a big family reunion. But, now, I felt exposed, whenever we had a family gathering. I knew the Lord understood my feelings, and I grew in my faith during those times, as I learned to lean even more on Him; but now it was very painful being around the family when the holidays came around. I felt a huge sense of shame sweep over me, as it seemed like an abundance of eyes were looking at me, up one side and down the other. I always wanted to run and hide and wear twelve layers of clothes, so that I wouldn't be recognized.

After some time, it became so uncomfortable for me with the news being "out there," that the time came for my immediate family to finally confront my father. There had been so much yelling and fighting, that my mother was about ready to crumble. So we confronted my father as a family. Unfortunately, my father responded, first with denial and then with reversal. One day he would break down in tears and say how sorry he was. The next day he would yell and say that he never touched me. As a family, we made conditions for him, if he wanted to continue to live in our home. It was kind of strange, putting conditions on our father, but it had to be that way. Because his response was so double-minded, changing from one day to the next, we wrote up a contract containing a list of things he had to do and things he was not allowed to do, which he was required to sign. For example, he had to promise to stay away from my bedroom and never even touch the bedroom door again. He could never touch me bodily again. Because he had the habit of going outside and watching me through my bedroom window, he had to promise to stay away from that window when he was outside. He could not demand unconditional respect. He could not countermand my mother's permissions for my extra-curricular activities or decisions about us. He had to stay fully clothed when he was outside of his bedroom or the bathroom. Although he willingly signed the contract, *he had broken every promise within a week.*

It was discouraging to have my father renege on the contract so completely, but it was not at all surprising. My mother, as intimidated by my father as she was, became much stronger. I was very proud of her. She followed the advice of the priest and got a restraining order and gave him one week to leave our home. The restraining order restricted him from even stepping onto our property, except during visitation of the younger siblings. She had been previously afraid, because he had threatened to fatally wound me and seriously injure my other siblings, if she ever tried to leave him. What both of my parents didn't realize was that, as a child of God, I was protected by Him, and there was no way my father could have followed up on any of his threats to hurt me. He also threatened to commit suicide, if she ever tried to divorce him. However, after her meeting with the priest, she came to believe that all his words were for the purpose of control and intimidation to retain his power over her and the family. When she presented the restraining order, he soberly gathered his things; and within a few days, he had moved into a rented room not far from our home. This was during my junior year of high school, and he passed away in January of my senior year.

One time he came back to our home, violating the restraining order. He snuck into our home during the middle of the night. We had a dog, which was normally a good watch dog. We had him for several years previous to this incident, so he knew my dad and did not consider him a threat. My dad snuck into my mother's bedroom and just stood there looking at her, until he had startled her enough to wake her up. The dog was just sitting there next to my dad wagging his tail. My mother was furious with him, that he would violate the restraining order. I don't remember why my father pulled that stunt. Perhaps he wanted to show us that he was still in control, and it was still his home. But it didn't work. What it did was to put us all on high alert, until we wised up and changed all of the locks on our doors and secured all our windows.

During that year (my junior year of high school) and until I graduated from high school, I had a part-time job after school. I asked my mom to never let my dad know that I was working or where my job was located. I was so afraid he would come to my workplace and harass me or my employer. One night I missed my ride home and I was very frightened. It was late at night and it was dark. I was concerned that he might somehow find out where I was. He had an uncanny way of showing up where you would least expect him. So I called my mom, and she called a cab for me, just to make sure I made it home safe.

I was surprised when my father passed away. He was not quite 60 years old. He had minor surgery, but it was nothing that should have caused his death. Through the years, beginning with the auto accident and the head injury, because of the incest, the bipolar depression and volatile anger, the lies, the various addictions, the abnormal behavior, and the controlling nature that we suffered under, I would be so terrified of him that I would pray, *"Heavenly Father, please protect us, and deliver us from this prison my father has us in."* I imagined God's way of delivering us from my dad might be having my parents get a divorce (which they did briefly before his death) or having him just leave and move far away. But I <u>never</u> expected God's way of deliverance to be through his death.

I did have a chance to have one last conversation with my father. I wanted to ask him to forgive me for having a disrespectful attitude toward him and for hating him; I wanted to tell him that I had forgiven him. This came after attending a seminar I learned about through my church called "Institute in Basic Youth Conflicts" taught by Rev. Bill Gothard. At the time of that conversation with my father, I was seventeen years old. That forgiveness was the most painful, the most difficult thing I had willingly done in my life, up to that point. When I had this conversation with my dad, I was up close to him again. I had not been that close to him physically since the incest. For me, it was like getting into a cage with a wild animal.

I felt so miserable inside, because I didn't really *feel* like I wanted to forgive him. The emotions were just not there. It was *a step of obedience, a step of faith*, and I believed that if I took that step, *the forgiveness and thus the feelings* would follow. [10] But it didn't work out quite that way. In fact, it didn't work that way *at all*. In my opinion, the jury is still out for me on whether feelings simply follow a step of faith. However, I believe that we are to obey, regardless of our feelings. Either way, it isn't easy. It was extremely difficult to extend forgiveness toward this man, who had brought so much pain, trauma, and turmoil into my life—and not just into my life, but into the lives of everyone I loved and was close to.

He tore up my life and my home. He didn't just make it difficult to grow up, he made it almost impossible. He interrupted my social development, by restricting me so severely, and he added a negative component to my neurological, hormonal, and emotional development. He caused physical complications. It took me a long time to catch up. I ended up with a neurological disorder and Endometriosis, both which can be linked to incest. I didn't know this at the time, nor did I know that my health problems were linked to the physical and emotional stress he brought into my life.

It took a great deal of soul-searching and personal emotional sacrifice to even think of forgiving Him. But I wanted to please the Lord, and I felt that this was an important step in obedience. I went through the mental action of forgiving him, but it took a very long time for the emotional freedom that real forgiveness brings. Just knowing he was coming to visit my younger siblings and then hearing his car drive up, gave me a sick feeling. This told me that the forgiveness was not complete. It made me feel nauseated and guilty. When he came into the house and I heard the sound of his voice, I wanted to vomit. I did not understand. I was sure that my desire to forgive was genuine, even though I knew he did not deserve it. When I forgave him, I was sure that I meant it from my heart.

This went on for months and months. I prayed that I would feel the forgiveness. He would come to the house to visit and I would feel sick at his arrival. I felt like a disobedient, evil child. I finally spoke to my grandmother. She had not been able to come for a visit in a number of years, because all the turmoil in our home upset her so much that it made her blood pressure escalate. But she gave me some very good advice over the phone. She said, "I have been praying for you daily, especially during the time that your family was falling apart." Then very calmly and very gently she said, "Honey, it took a lot of years for the hurt and anger inside you to build and grow, and it will no doubt take a lot of time for the emotional healing process to be completed. *The important thing was that you desired to forgive your father in obedience to God.*" I think she was saying that God is looking at my heart, and the important thing is that my heart desired to obey God.

But I still felt there was more to forgiveness than what my grandmother had told me. Out of respect for her godly wisdom, I believe that the Lord had a standard for me to meet. Yes, the hurt had been festering there for a long time, and it would take a long time for me to be at peace with what I had done in obedience.

I have also come to believe that when the Lord leads us to take a certain action, such as forgiving someone for their acts of sexual perversion, *we should not trust our feelings. We should do what the Lord commands us to do, regardless of our feelings. We should simply obey.*

On the other hand, if the person who molested us is still living and we can have a conversation with them, I would be very careful at this point. *Yes, we must forgive them from our heart*. However, if they do not truly repent, they may take that forgiveness as freedom to simply go about their life as usual, continuing to torment you or others. So *if there is no repentance, I would be very careful about carte blanche extension of forgiveness. When we forgive, it is primarily for our benefit. It releases us from a life of bitterness. We must not keep our emotions in prison.*

Another thing to remember is that *forgiveness is very different than trust*. Just because you have forgiven someone, does not mean you will be able to trust them. That comes with the next step called *reconciliation.* It could take a long time, from weeks to years, before the perpetrator is ready for reconciliation. *There definitely has to be true repentance (which means turning around and walking the opposite direction)* and a real effort on the part of the offending party to change. [11]

My Own Personal Journal . . . Self-Esteem And The Lack Thereof

Early Thirties During Counseling

Not only did my father rob me of my ability to have the freedom to trust others, but there were some other pleasant experiences that I had never been able to enjoy. These were all things that are very important to a growing teenage young woman.

- *It boils down to the freedom to love myself and really enjoy the things that I like. For example, the things that I wanted during adolescence were so ridiculed by my father, that I had to keep them submerged below the surface of my real personality. I wanted to keep them precious, so I had to hide them as much as possible. In a sense, I had to hide my true personality as well.*
- *My physical appearance was especially distressing. My dad made so many comments about my body and so many sexually oriented comments about other women that it created a very negative image to me, of what being beautiful was and what it suggested. I thought that spending time on my appearance would lead to something dirty and bad. I'm not sure what all my thinking was, because it was so submerged; but I was never free to really express*

my femininity fully in the way I looked, carried myself, and felt about myself.

- *When I would fix my hair a new way, my dad always ridiculed it and sometimes restricted it, if it was too contemporary. When I made new clothes, he always ridiculed them in private, and then He would take credit for my talent and creativity in public, making me feel like less than nothing. If my figure was mentioned, it seemed to always have sexual overtones. It was as if my value was basically sexual.*
- *If I wanted to buy clothes, he insisted that they be the style he wanted (always skin tight, etc.), and after I had a job and money of my own, my mother would scold me for spending the money on clothes that I liked. It seemed that what I liked and what I needed wasn't important or worth spending money on.*
- *Another aspect of this was my weight. I could never be free to go on a diet to lose weight, just so that I would look more attractive and feel better about myself. I always felt that the expectation was that there had to be a better reason for losing weight. For example, if it was justified by a medical reason, then it was okay to be on a diet.*
- *One time a friend of mine said that it looked to her like I didn't care about my appearance. But it wasn't true, and it made me angry to hear her or anyone say that. In fact, I had already been to Finishing & Modeling School and had*

learned to dress and wear make-up and fix my hair like a model. But because of my parental conditioning, I didn't really feel free to apply what I had learned. I came to believe that would lead to something bad and dirty. This friend, who later went into a beauty profession, had to re-teach me some of the things that I had already learned in Finishing School, but she couldn't teach me self-respect and dignity.

- *One morning when I was in my early twenties, my mother* and I were in front of the bathroom mirror doing our makeup. She told me that she had always been very jealous of me, because when I was very young (birth to five years old) my father spent so much time with me. She was jealous of the time he spent with me when I was a baby, because he was so happy to finally have a little girl! She said that was the reason she was jealous of me and my appearance now that I was an adult! I couldn't believe that any mother of an infant or young child would be jealous of her own baby and that the jealousy would follow into the child's teen years and adulthood! Then I try to imagine how that jealousy played into her feelings, when she learned about the incest! The incest was immoral and sick, but the original jealousy was also inappropriate and difficult for me to understand, especially because those sinful actions didn't originate with me.*

- *When I think about this stuff, I get very angry. All I can say is "How dare they?" None of this was my doing. It was, in fact, done to me! To think that my parents could rip me off like this angers me. I am who I am, and they had no right to try to make me into something else and tamper with what God had in mind for me.*
- *I intend, to the best of my ability, to be the person I should be— whether they (or anyone) like it or not, whether they wish I were different, whether they believe I am acceptable or not, or whether they (or anyone else) have the opinion that I am beautiful or not. I will be who I am—period!*

**Note: I know that my mother was very insecure. She loved being a mother. So whatever reason she had for feeling jealous of her baby, I have to give her the benefit of the doubt. She was a very good mother.*

I was thinking about all this after one of my counseling sessions. During the same week, I was also reading a very good book titled *The Sensation of Being Somebody ~ Building an Adequate Self-Concept* by Maurice E. Wagner, Th.M., Ph.D.[12] The following quote reminded me so much about this, when I was living with my parents and retreating to my room so I could be my real self. This was a time when I had to be compliant with them, and this quote explains some of the reasons why. Here is what Dr. Wagner has to say:

"Loving relationships instill stable feelings of belongingness, worthiness, and competence in the mind of a growing child.

"Loveless factors disunite people, making them defensive with one another.

"Love is the dynamic of true, positive, liberating fellowship. . . In a loving relationship, there is a minimum of needing to be on guard and a maximum of freedom in self-revelation to the other person. Each social interaction reinforces for the persons involved a sense of being somebody, for the love that is felt validates the elements of self-concept—that they are accepted and wanted, right and good, adequate and competent.

"Unloving relationships . . . make each person involved aware of being a separate individual who must lean entirely upon his own resources for a sense of being somebody. . .

"When a child does not feel loved, he attempts to capture a sense of worthiness from his parents through defiance or compliance. He discovers in his defiance, if he can get away with it, a sense of being autonomous by overpowering the people who attempt to govern them.

"The insecurity factor lies in his needing to remain a rebel in order to hold on to his sense of autonomy; this automatically positions him in an independent, defensive, aggressive attitude of mind. He cannot help being involved occasionally in situations where this attitude does not work, and he is devastated by the consequences of his own willfulness.

"When a child must be compliant, he discovers in his compliance a sense of worthiness in winning parental approval through ascertaining their wishes and complying with them. He must deny and negate his own wishes and feelings to be accepted and feel good about himself. This develops a false security factor, for he is certain to encounter many situations in his lifetime in which he must be clear about his own wishes and feelings and be aggressive in making confrontations; otherwise he will be overpowered by those who are more defiant in their patterns of interaction.

". . . When a child cannot get away with being defiant with his parent and he is too afraid of their wrath to want to try to be pleasing in the compliant modality, he withdraws to himself . . .

"In this frame of reference, he complies with his parents to get his basic needs, then retreats to himself and to his fantasies for a sense of being somebody.

". . . When a child is deprived of loving relationships in the home, the unloving attitudes he must live with teach him that he is undesirable, no good, or inferior.

"His resources for proving to himself that he has value as a person are threefold: He can reflect upon how others regard his appearance and find in their opinion a sense of being somebody. He can reflect upon His own accomplishments as he has met competition and perhaps won trophies for excellence, achieved certain educational degrees, etc."

Health Problems

About a year after my father began his nightly visits to my room, I had a neurological episode. We had gone to the beach as a family, where I had spent the whole day in the hot sun. Being very fair skinned, with blue eyes and very light blonde hair, this was not a good thing for me. This was before the days when sunscreen was strongly recommended for children and for anyone with my skin and hair color. As a result, I came home with a very severe sunburn on my blonde scalp, arms, back, and legs. The next day, on Sunday, I woke up to find my dad fixing breakfast for the family. I came into the kitchen and immediately passed out. When I fell, I hit my head on the corner of the refrigerator. I was unconscious for more than five minutes. This greatly concerned my parents. They wasted no time getting me in to the family doctor, and I was quickly referred to a neurological specialist. This doctor performed an EEG test, and I was diagnosed with abnormal brain waves and a childhood fainting disorder. This was treated with medication, which I had to take three times a day to prevent the fainting episodes. If I missed even one dose, I would faint. This only happened a couple of times between that first episode and my eighteenth birthday, at which time I was to begin weaning myself off the medication under my doctor's care.

A couple of years after the fainting spells started, another physical symptom emerged. It was a pain of unknown pathology. I had all kinds of tests performed, including diagnostic surgery. But no one could ascertain the source of the pain, including specialists at the Oregon Health Science University Hospital (OHSU). After a couple of years, it was finally diagnosed as psychosomatic pain. I didn't know much about this diagnosis, but the sound of it alarmed me. I was 15 years old at the time, and my siblings and mother had been discussing the source of my father's behavior as being from a mental illness. I thought "psychosomatic" sounded like something mental or emotional, and it scared me. I thought maybe mental problems ran in the family and I had inherited some of my dad's problems. But I was mistaken about that. It wasn't a mental disorder at all, but simply a problem that arises from a stressful situation.

The last health problem that I was diagnosed with was Endometriosis. The symptoms of this disorder began (when I was about fourteen years old) with extremely painful PMS and heavy flow with my monthly menstrual cycle. As a disorder, it had only begun to be known as a diagnosis. It was not connected with incest at that time. It was thought to be a "career-woman's disorder," being associated with women who postponed child bearing in favor of a career. I was also told that it is normal to have pain with the menstrual cycle, and so my complaints of severe pain during my menstrual flow were not taken seriously. I am sure that the medical personnel who gave me that information were genuine in their attempt to be accurate. However, they were mistaken. This problem became worse as I grew older, and the hormone imbalance became more pronounced as I aged. In fact, in my late twenties, my "PMS" was accompanied by a severe hormone imbalance that was system-wide, giving me symptoms that made me feel like I had a severe sinus infection, tinnitus, muscle cramps, and water retention. When I was 28, I finally had laparoscopic surgery to diagnose the problem, and it was confirmed that I had Endometriosis. It was not in the form of a tumor but manifested outside the uterine wall and spread all over the pelvic organs. It was also deemed a "minor case." I was also told that the minor cases, that is, the non-tumor cases, are the most painful. Six months later, I had another diagnostic surgery and the same diagnosis was given—only there appeared to be more endometrium outside the walls of the uterus, which had collected all over my bladder.

It took a number of years before I found a doctor who knew the right combination of hormones to give me before the hormone symptoms settled down and a hormone balance was achieved. Even then, it seemed that no one knew there was a connection between this condition and the trauma I experienced with my father. In fact, I have never had a doctor discuss this with me, until recently, when I brought up the subject. I did not learn about this, until I did research for this book.

In doing research for this book, I learned that there are other health conditions that have been linked to experiences of sexual abuse. Some of these include increased levels of cortisol, which can cause increased inflammation and pain. Inflammation contributes to such illnesses as chronic fatigue syndrome, asthma, hypertension, eating disorders, urinary tract infections, alcohol abuse, obesity, chronic stress, headaches and migraines, gastrointestinal disorders, irritable bowel syndrome, fibromyalgia, and chronic pelvic pain. To learn more about illnesses associated with incest, please see the articles in the Appendix. There is much more on the internet, if you choose to do your own research or speak to your gynecologist or counselor. You may have to be persistent and proactive in seeking information on this subject, because many doctors are not knowledgeable on this subject.

My Own Personal Journal . . . Despair and Prayer

Early Thirties During Counseling

I feel overwhelmed and defeated. I feel numb and emotionally paralyzed. I see no future. With so many feelings to express, I need to be able to write. Writing in my journal is so therapeutic for me. I'm not sure how I could cope, if I couldn't write out my feelings.

I think I hate the time it takes to recover. It seems to take so much of it to experience healing. Just when I thought I had hurt, as much and as long as I could possibly endure, God shows me that, before I can experience healing and love, I need to give it time. A LOT MORE TIME. How long will it take? How long can a person wait for love and the feeling of wholeness?

I am so thankful for the gift of prayer. I am so thankful that I can still talk to God. I don't really feel His presence all of the time, and I'm not sure how He'll respond. And that's okay. I have learned that there are many forms of prayer. My Heavenly Father knows my heart and hears my tears and my longings. Above all, even though I don't always feel His presence, I can be assured of the fact that He is always with me, always caring for me, and always working on my behalf. And I can still talk to Him. I know He is great in wisdom, power, mercy, and compassion. And I always know, beyond any doubt, that He is here with me, listening to every word I say, seeing every word I write, and experiencing every tear I shed. The worst thing I could do right now is to stop praying and believing. It is essential. I really need to pray.

I'm also thankful for the many friends that my Lord has given me. I have a whole group of people, who are willing and interested to listen to my tears. Wow! God is so very good!!

WHEN I WAS IN COUNSELING THREE TIMES A WEEK, IN WHAT FELT LIKE THE DEEP TRENCHES OF THE HEALING PROCESS, IT SEEMED LIKE I WAS NOT GETTING ANY BETTER. IT WAS MORE LIKE I WAS WALKING THROUGH FOGGY GLUE, AND I COULDN'T SEE MORE THAN A FOOT AHEAD. I DID HAVE A STRONG DRIVE FOR SURVIVAL, AND I AM SURE THAT IS WHAT KEPT ME GOING. THE DARKNESS OF MY DEPRESSION HAD BECOME JUST ABOUT ALL THAT I COULD TAKE. SO, I TRIED TO IMAGINE, BASED UPON MY SCRIPTURE JOURNAL, WHAT JESUS WOULD SAY TO ME, IF HE WERE TO COME TO ME ON A DAY WHEN I WAS REALLY DOWN AND HAVING TROUBLE RESPONDING. I WONDERED WHAT A PERSON-ALIZED LETTER FROM THE LORD JESUS TO ME WOULD BE LIKE, AS IF THERE COULD BE ANYTHING BETTER THAN WHAT HE HAD ALREADY GIVEN ME IN THE WORD OF GOD AND IN MY SCRIPTURE JOURNAL. BUT THIS IS WHAT I CAME UP WITH, TAILORED JUST FOR MY SITUATION:

My Precious, *Precious* Child,

I know what you have been going through. *I have seen and felt your pain* from the beginning. *I know how you were violated* when you were an innocent child. *I have felt all your agony,* and *I have recorded all your tears and have kept them all* in My bottle with your name on it. *I have been with you* through the whole agonizing process, even until now, and *I will never leave you. I feel your depression* and I know it's difficult for you to imagine, but *I accept you just the way you are this very moment and I always will.*

I understand your feelings and I find them refreshing. I delight in honest human emotions. *I love you so much more than you could ever imagine*, too much to leave you alone in your struggle. You may not always feel My presence or comprehend My love, but don't let that alarm you. *Human emotions are at times very deceiving. Don't ever squelch your real feelings and don't be ashamed of them.* Emotion is a priceless treasure meant to give expression and meaning to your life. As fragile and wounded as your emotions are today, they are a part of you that gives you the ability to know and understand life, to relate to others, and to relate to Me. So, don't try to push them away or turn them off. That is the very part of you that I desire to heal. I designed you to enjoy your emotions and physical sensations, so please don't squelch them. As difficult as it is, *I ask you to bear with the pain and confusion*. It won't last forever. *I promise you that this pain you are experiencing does have a purpose.*

I am always here with you to help you. Remember, I died to heal you from this pain and make you whole. So be patient. It will be over sooner than you think. When you get through this process of healing and recovery, you will realize that the distance through the Valley of Tears was not as far as you thought, and it did not take as much time as you imagined. *And you will know with certainty that you were not alone for even one second of the way. I was there every minute holding your hand, gently guiding you, and at times carrying you.*

When the time comes that you have experienced inner healing, *you will find, for the first time in your life, the joy of being a woman, the crown of all My creation. I will have healed your emotional hurts and restored the treasure that your father took from you. It will be My forever joy to watch you enjoy being yourself~~the woman I created you to be.*

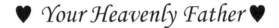

♥ *Your Heavenly Father* ♥

Notes . . .

Chapter 4

Healing Words of Life

So, the Lord commanded us to observe all these statutes, to fear the Lord our God for our good always for our survival, as it is today.

Deuteronomy 6:24

Upon Your Word I Rest

Upon Your Word I rest
Each pilgrim day;
This golden staff is best
For all the way.
What Jesus Christ has spoken
Cannot be broken!

Upon Your Word I rest,
So strong, so sure!
So full of comfort blest,
So sweet, so pure!
The charter of salvation,
Faith's broad foundation.
Upon Your Word I stand,
That cannot die;
Christ seals it in my hand,
He cannot lie!
Your Word that fails me never,
Abides ever.

Frances Ridley Havergal [1]

Healing Words

This book of the Law shall not depart from your mouth,
but you shall meditate on it day and night,
so that you may be careful to do according to all that is
written in it. For then you will make
your way prosperous, and then
you will have success.
~ Joshua 1:8

Introduction

This chapter comes primarily from a journal I kept during the most trying times of my counseling years. When I could not find any good books to read that would teach me how other incest survivors had responded to the wounds that I was struggling with, I turned to the Bible to find "verses of survival." To my surprise, I found them in abundance. For each one that I discovered, I began to write down whatever the Lord brought to my mind as encouragement. At times one verse would keep me going for a whole week or more. When the depression was really bad, these verses would keep me going for even longer than a week, encouraging me to know that I was not scarred for life. It helped me to know that the Lord was in control and that He knew exactly what He was doing with me.

This chapter reads like a devotional. Each page has a verse and what it meant to me, as I was going through my counseling years. You may see references to my story, as I apply how the verse helped me during that time. Many times I would take one verse per day and meditate on it and the encouragement that my Lord gave me.

If you don't have your own copy of the Bible, then I would suggest that you purchase one to read these passages for yourself. There are many easy-to-read modern translations available to choose from. I have used primarily the New American Standard Bible and the New King James Version, which are very similar. The New International Version and the New Living Version are also easy to read and highly recommended. I prefer to have a hard copy of the Bible rather than reading it online, so that I can highlight my "verses of survival" and make marginal notes. But that is simply my preference. You should use whatever format you are most comfortable with.

I would encourage you to begin your own "Scripture Journal", keep a record of it, and date your entries. Keep it with your Bible, where you can write in it every day. You will soon be amazed at the treasures the Lord will show you from His Word that will become personal and precious to you. These could be Scriptures that the Lord gives you (as you walk through this Valley of Tears), along with the thoughts that come to mind (as you meditate on them) and how much they encourage you. I would also suggest comparing the verses that help you the most, in different translations, to see what special insights they give you with regard to your situation. [2] Then read and reread your journal whenever you get discouraged. I would guess that your journal will become even more personally insightful than what I have shared in these pages, as you meditate and pray over God's Word in your time of pain and struggle. It will draw you closer to your Great Physician and the Healer of your soul.

One of the great benefits for you, as a victim-soon-to-be-survivor, is that, as you get to know your Heavenly Father for who He is through the Scriptures, you will find He is not like the sinful, exploitive one who betrayed your trust and stole your innocence. His authority and power are governed by the attributes of His holy and good character. Those attributes will become the focus of your life as a victim/survivor of incest, so that, in your relationship with Him, you will grow to become a person who can confidently pray and trust in your Heavenly Father. As Hebrews 4:15-16 states about our Lord Jesus Christ, He understands our weaknesses and therefore we can be confident to approach Him in prayer:

> [15] *For we do not have a high priest (the Lord Jesus) who cannot sympathize with our weaknesses, but One who has been tempted in all things as we are, yet without sin.*
>
> [16] *Therefore let us draw near with confidence to the throne of grace, so that we may receive mercy and may find grace to help in time of need.*
> (Parentheses added by this author.)

Scripture Applied to the Wounds of Incest

There is none like the God of Jeshurun (Israel),
Who rides the heavens to your help,
And through the skies in His majesty.
The eternal God is a dwelling place,
And underneath are the everlasting arms.

Moses ~ Deuteronomy 33:26-27

There is none to compare with God in meeting my needs. He will move through heaven and earth to support me in my pain and bring healing to my life. This means that He knows exactly what is the best way to dry my tears and stop the bleeding in my soul.

He comes to my aid in His majesty, as my Lord God. At the sight of Him, my enemies will become powerless, insignificant, and completely unable to hurt me.

And who are they, these enemies of mine? They are my weaknesses, fears, anxieties, shame, and self-contempt as well as the scars and memories, my nightmares, insecurities, and post-traumatic stress disorder *(PTSD)*.

But there is an enemy who is furious when God *"rides the heavens to my help"* and when I rest in His *"everlasting arms."* He is the enemy of my eternal soul. Satan—the archenemy of God—the one who delighted in the wounding of incest and who thought it would destroy my life. This terrible enemy had thought I would become so depressed, that I would, indeed, commit suicide and never commit my life to the Lord

Jesus. Satan is the one who is behind all the other forces that have caused me so much pain. When I rest in God's presence as His child, I am covered in His redeeming blood. This causes this enemy, with all his weapons of warfare, to cringe in defeat.

My Father God is my dwelling place. He lives in me and I live in Him. He is my home. His presence is the one place where I can be completely known, understood, loved, accepted, healed, blessed, refreshed, strengthened, and invigorated. It is the one place where I can be held as a child and comforted.

I need Him. Besides being my protection, He is my comfort. When the pain is so overwhelming that I can't think about anything else, I can come to Him to be held in His *everlasting arms.*

Thank You, my Father, that I can always lean and rest in Your everlasting arms. Thank you that You come to me, when I call for help and when You see my need, and that You are my dwelling place. Like none other, I can always count on You to be there for me at a moment's notice. I am so grateful for Your faithful love.

In the name of Your Son and my Savior,
the Lord Jesus Christ,
Amen.

The thief comes only to steal and kill and destroy; I have come that they might have life, and have it more abundantly.
Jesus ~ John 10:10 NKJV

The thief involved in the incest was my biological father, and the thief behind my father's actions was Satan, the devil, who thought he could destroy my life through my biological father's foolish evil actions. The thief stole more from me than I have words to describe. He came close to destroying my life with my thoughts of suicide. He replaced safety and security with fear and deep-seated insecurity.

While he was stealing all these things from me, he was also stealing my child-like faith in my Creator and my Heavenly Father. I could no longer believe that God is good. How could He possibly be good and still allow this unthinkable thing to happen to me? My own father had violated me. He destroyed my ability to trust men. But not just men, I couldn't trust anyone.

Then Jesus entered the picture to give us life. He brought His light and life and focused its pure beam into our miserable home and into my broken heart, in particular. He walked into my life to heal it and to give me newness of life, healing, and joy. He came to apply His redemptive power to my broken soul, in the hope that those around me will see that abundance and crave it for themselves. He came to bring His fresh perfume, the fragrance of His presence, so we could breathe in His wholeness and live in wholeness of life.

But You, O Lord, are a shield
around me,
My glory, and the One Who lifts
my head.
King David ~ Psalm 3:3

Incest makes a person feel defenseless, powerless, and vulnerable. It robs me of my dignity as a human being. It makes me feel like an object of entertainment for another person; it exploits my human value and destroys my self-worth.

God is my protection from whatever I fear and everything I fear, whether it is a conscious fear or not. He is my shield, and He surrounds me with protection. He also lifts up my head. This means that He will restore my worth as a human being, as a unique individual, and as a woman.

My God is my glory. He is the One Who will make my life beautiful, giving me beauty for ashes and a positive self-esteem.

Thank You, my Father, for Your strong hedge of protection around me. Thank You that nothing can change Your sovereign plan. I am so grateful that even when I feel vulnerable, I am safe because of Your gracious protection. Thank You for lifting me up and putting a song in my heart.

In the loving name of my Savior and Lord, Jesus, Amen.

For thus says the high and exalted One
Who lives forever, whose name is
Holy,
"I dwell in a high and holy place,
And also with the contrite and lowly
of spirit
In order to revive the spirit of
the lowly
And to revive the heart of the contrite."
The Lord God to the Prophet Isaiah ~ Isaiah 57:15

I belong to a *holy* God, but His holiness does not make Him unapproachable. This incredible God, Who lives in me, understands every dark corner of my world and every bleeding wound in my life. He is especially close to the contrite, the humble, and the suffering. He is a tender-hearted, compassionate, and loving Father, who is also my Creator and God of the Universe.

That is a lot to comprehend—how my God also lives with broken victims of abuse such as myself. But that is the wonder of my wonderful God. This verse says that His purpose is to revive the spirit of the lowly and to revive the heart of the contrite. Not only is it encouraging to know that He is holy, but, at the same time, He desires to be with the lowly of spirit. This just and merciful God cares about the hurts caused by my father's indiscretion and foolish immorality. It is almost an oxymoron, that in His holiness He would want to get close to the pain caused by something He hates. But that is the wonder of my God! For those who are victims of abuse and suffer from depression for days and months and years, *nothing* could be more encouraging.

In all their affliction He was afflicted,
And the angel of His presence saved them;
In His love and in His mercy He redeemed them; . . .
Isaiah ~ Isaiah 63:9

This verse has always encouraged me. Isaiah tells me that my God is merciful. It tells me that when I am hurting, He feels my pain.

In my affliction, it is God's presence that makes the pain bearable and gives me the power to endure. I need to cultivate a greater sensitivity to God's presence in my life, especially when I am in pain. I need to learn to recognize it, experience it, and feel it, so that I can draw strength from it. God's presence is always there, but many times He is silent. I need to be so familiar with His presence, so that, even when He is silent, I am confident that He is working on my behalf and that He is "accomplishing what concerns me." (Psalm 57:2)

What I need to do is to "practice the presence of God" like Brother Lawrence, [3] the Carmelite monk who lived in Paris in the mid-1600s. Like me, he came to know the Lord early in his life. Then later in his life, he learned to live in God's presence so consistently that, whether amidst the clanging and clattering of the pots and pans or at the Lord's Table, he sensed God just the same. This is a powerful, yet simple form of meditation, and I would like to learn how to do it, as he did.

Since my Lord groans in pain with me when I am in pain, then I need to "practice His Presence" at all times. When my focus is on Him and His strength,

His merciful kindness, or whatever part of His being I need to draw on, I receive that strength to help against that pain when it is the greatest. It also draws me into prayer and meditation. It is so much easier to agonize when the pain is the greatest, but it is not very helpful. By the grace of God, I purpose to meditate on the goodness of Who He is.

My Father, thank you for sharing in my pain. It is difficult for me to comprehend a love so sacrificial that its Giver will experience my deepest emotional and physical pain with me. You are an incredible Person and I never could have known this part of Your character, if not for my own pain seen in light of the Scriptures. I love You for Your wisdom and sovereign plan to bring this all together in my life. You truly do know what is best for me. I praise You, that You will allow me to see victory over all this pain before too much time has passed. I pray that You will use it for Your glory and for the welfare of others.

In the gracious name of my Lord and Savior Jesus Christ,
Amen.

My face is flushed from weeping,
And deep darkness is on my eyelids,
Although there is no
violence in my hands,
And my prayer is pure.
. . . My eye weeps to God.
The Patriarch Job ~ Job 16:16-17, 20

From the time that my memories of the incest began to flood my conscious soul until I began to feel a sense of wholeness, I shed many, many tears (sometimes every day for weeks and weeks and weeks). That is why I chose the title, *Through the Valley of Tears*, for this book. I was so thankful that my Lord understood my deep pain, my loss, and, of course, my response to it all. He truly understood my tears and my inability to hold them back. The depression was so overwhelming. I was sure that I was a marked woman and no one would ever want to be near me or to identify with me.

If you plan to allow the Lord to open the deep recesses of your soul and allow healing to begin to take place, or if you truly want the Great physician to do His work, there will be deep pain. It will be required to allow you to heal. While there may not be pain-numbing anesthesia, there will be many tears that are meant to act as a healing balm. As you shed those tears, you will heal. Those tears are meant to be a spiritual agent designed by your Creator to heal your soul. So then, let them come. Do not hold them back. And do not rush the process. It may take some time.

Does it hurt? *Oh, yes, it hurts!!* I do not know of anything that could hurt more. . . . "But there's hope. St. John of the Cross, the sixteenth-century Spanish monk and mystic, described it as 'the dark night of the soul.' And that dark night has various stages. The first stage is desolation. The last stage is consolation. In between, God holds our hand, purifies our heart, and prepares us for eternity.

"The apostle John, describing Christ in the Revelation, most typically identifies Him as 'the Lamb' or 'the Lamb who was slain.' Perhaps our pain will produce a special affinity and intimacy with Him for eternity, as we cling to Him for eternity, as we cling to Him now while awash in our sorrow. Our deepest spiritual formation occurs not as we flee our distress, but as we face Him and wait on Him. We grow most when we wait.

"Sacred waiting endures and obeys—remains faithful—when everything around us seems tempestuous. Sacred waiting nurtures our deepest strength, hope, and intimacy with Christ." [4]

You have granted me life and lovingkindness;
And Your care has preserved my spirit.
Yet these things You have concealed in Your heart;
I know that this is within You.
Job, the Old Testament Patriarch ~ Job 10:12-13

An incest victim is no stranger to loss. You know from my story that my age was barely into the double-digits when it all began. I was innocent and naïve. I lost a good half of my childhood, and I lost the nurturing of both of my parents. They were both there, but not in the way that I needed them to be. During my counseling years and for many years beyond that, I grieved that loss.

The words of this Scripture verse were spoken by Job, an Old Testament Patriarch, who was a contemporary of Abraham. He was also grieving a terrible loss. He had lost everything in his life that could possibly matter to him. He lost his financial security and income, he lost his children, he lost the respect of his wife and the esteem of his three closest friends, and he lost his health. What else is there in this life, except a righteous person's favor with God? And that is what he is hanging on to. He is hanging on to his integrity. He places his hope in the goodness of God. This chapter in the Book of Job also continues to describe Job's grief and depression. It starts off like this:

I loathe my own life; I will give full vent to my complaint;
I will speak in the bitterness of my soul.
Job 10:1

Then in the middle of the chapter (at about verse eight), he turns his focus toward his Creator. He fears that His life may be over at the hands of God and he cannot understand the severity of his suffering. Who of us who have suffered deep pain have not wondered the same thing? Then he describes in amazing accuracy how God created him in his mother's womb:

Your hands fashioned and made me altogether,
And would You destroy me?
Remember now, that You have made me as clay;
And would You turn me into dust again?
Did You not pour me out like milk,
And curdle me like cheese;
Clothe me with skin and flesh,
And knit me together with bones and sinews?
Job 10:8-11

Then in verses 12-13, in the midst of Job's despair, we see a glimmer of hope. Not only does He see God as the author of life, but he also sees Him as the One who gives him favor and the One who preserves and nurtures his spirit. He sees his Creator, as One who holds him close to His heart. What I see in this is that Job knows that the Lord is close to him in his suffering. He knows that his Creator will not let him down, but will be with him through it all. In all of this, Job has confidence in his hope.

When I was going through my deep depression, I had the same hope. I knew that I was a Child of God and that He would never give up on me or leave me. Even though I was deeply depressed, I knew my Lord had a redemptive purpose in what I was going through, and that purpose was recovery. If you are suffering from abuse and you have suffered at the hands of another, then you can have the same hope. If you are a child of God, He lives within you and will never leave you. As my pastor says, "Whom God chooses, He never loses." He will see you through. If you are not a child of God, please read the Epilogue of this book very carefully, and take the step that is written there.

> *Then he said to them, "Go, eat of the fat, drink of the sweet, and send portions to him who has nothing prepared; for this day is holy to our Lord. Do not be grieved, for the joy of the Lord is your strength." So the Levites calmed all the people, saying, "Be still, for the day is holy; do not be grieved."*
> Spoken by Nehemiah the Governor, Ezra the Priest & Scribe and all the Levites to all the people in Nehemiah 8:10-11

As victims and/or survivors of incest, we know what grief and loss are all about. These people were also grieved, but for a different reason. They were the Jewish survivors of the seventy-year exile in Babylon, who chose to come back to Jerusalem and rebuild the holy city. It was no easy task. They had enemies. They succeeded in building the wall around the city, which was the important first step. Walls were important at that time to keep enemies out. They were like a hedge of protection. In Nehemiah 8, after this task was completed, they all gathered in one place and asked Ezra the Priest to read to them from the Book of Moses (the Word of God in those days). When they heard the words that Ezra read, they were deeply saddened, . . . because, as a nation, they knew that they had been disobedient to God's Word.

Their response was one of remorse, which is a godly, repentant response. The spiritual leaders had compassion on the people. They knew that their hearts were good and that they were grieved over the sins of the nation. So they encouraged them to eat and drink. This is good medicine for the weary and depressed. Then they encouraged them to give portions to those who had none. This is service. It is also therapeutic to focus on the needs of others when your heart is broken.

Why did they give this advice to the people? They said that the day was holy to the Lord. They must not be grieved, because "the joy of the Lord is their strength."

It was a holy day for these people, because, in God's strength, they had completed God's appointed task. They must put their focus and praise toward Him. They must know that "the joy of the Lord is their strength." So how can one have joy, when one naturally feels grief? Well, you first have to understand what joy is. It is not based on circumstances. If it were, none of us would have it for very long. It is not happiness. Happiness is a natural human emotion based on our circumstances. It is unreliable. Joy, however, is a supernatural emotion. It is a fruit of the Holy Spirit. Galatians 5:22-23 reads:

> *But the fruit of the Spirit is love, joy, peace, patience, kindness, goodness, faithfulness, gentleness, self-control; against such things there is no law.*
>
> *The Apostle Paul in Galatians 5:22-23*

Joy is the result of the indwelling Holy Spirit in the life of the Child of God. There are some personality types, who seem to be happy all the time, but that is not the spiritual fruit of joy.

One word of caution about grief. It is natural to grieve a loss, and it is very important to allow yourself to grieve your losses. But it is vital that you do not get stuck in your grief. Do not let your losses define your life. Go through the stages of grief and loss, [5] and then move on with your life. Regardless of what kind of loss you are grieving, always remember that life is for the living. It is for people who are alive. It is also for living people to live life to the fullest extent, especially if they have the Living God empowering them. [6]

And He has said to me,
"My grace is sufficient for you,
for power is perfected in weakness."

Most gladly, therefore, I will rather boast about my weaknesses, so that the power of Christ may dwell in me.

Therefore, I am well content with weaknesses, with insults, with distresses, with persecutions, with difficulties for Christ's sake; for when I am weak, then I am strong.
Apostle Paul ~ 2 Corinthians 12:9-10

His grace is sufficient for me, regardless of how long it takes for my recovery. His love will transform my pain into a thing of beauty. His compassion will give me the strength to handle the pain, confusion, loss, and depression. This is what God delights to do in our lives. He loves to find an impossible situation (or person) and turn them into a miraculous trophy of His grace. He loves to take a dying person and bring them back to life. There have been so many times when I have felt like I was dying inside, because my depression was so severe. But God restored life to me again by His grace. We tend to think that, if a person has experienced certain tragedies, they will be scarred and maimed for life. God loves to prove that idea wrong, when a person is deeply wounded and feels he or she is without hope. Then when they take the risk to entrust their wounded heart to Him,

He does an incredible work of healing in their life. Our God is the One who makes anything possible. He is the God of miracles, and with Him nothing is impossible. So when I am at my weakest, I am really strong, as I trust in Him.

I must rely on the grace of my wonderful God. As I give my pain to Him, He will make me strong! I find great comfort in what it says in Philippians 4:13:

"I can do all things through Christ Who strengthens me."

This is a promise from God.

My Father, thank You for the gift of Your grace. So many times it has given me the strength I need. I could not imagine approaching You in prayer, without the twin gifts of Your mercy and grace. I do not take them lightly. Your goodness is Your glory, and I worship You for being so pure and lovely. Thank you that Your grace covers all the ugliness of the abuse, as does Your blood of redemption. In all of this, I am made strong in You.

In the name of my gracious Savior, Jesus Christ,

Amen.

But now, thus says the Lord, your Creator, . . .
And He who formed you, . . .

"Do not fear, for I have redeemed you;
I have called you by name;
you are Mine!
When you pass through the waters,
I will be with you;
And through the rivers,
they will not overflow you.
When you walk through the fire,
you will not be scorched,
Nor will the flame burn you.
For I am the Lord your God,
the Holy One of Israel, your Savior; . . .
Since you are precious in My sight,
Since you are honored and I love you, . . .
Do not fear, for I am with you; . . ."

The Lord God ~ Isaiah 43:1-5

Regardless of how devastated and overwhelmed I feel, God will lead and carry me through what I'm going through, this time and every single future time. God places unmeasurable value and worth on my life. He is deeply concerned for my well-being. He loves me so much, that He promises to be with me, through the whole ordeal of recovery now and forever.

I was particularly encouraged by the metaphors, of being overwhelmed by rivers (drowning) and being scorched by fire (burned). When I was being violated, I felt like my father was smothering me, and it was hard to breathe. This is very similar to waters overflowing me and suffocating me. I had the feeling of panic.

When the Lord showed me this very encouraging verse and this wonderful promise, that *He will be with me, the waters will not overflow me, and the fire will not scorch me, I hung on to it for weeks. I typed it on a small piece of paper and placed it by my typewriter at work. I read it throughout the days, when I was so discouraged. And the Lord used it to show me He is in control and that He, my Creator, is with me. No matter what.* I could count on this because *I am precious in His sight, and* because *He loves me!*

O Lord, I call upon You; hasten to me!
Give ear to my voice when I call to You!

May my prayer be counted as incense
before You;
The lifting up of my hands as the evening
offering . . .

I cry out with my voice to the Lord;
I make supplication with my voice
to the Lord.
I pour out my complaint before Him;
I declare my trouble before Him.

When my spirit was overwhelmed
within me,
You knew my path. . .

Bring my soul out of prison,
So that I may give thanks
to Your name;

The righteous will surround
me,
For You will deal bountifully
with me.
King David ~ Psalm 141:1-2; 142:1-3 & 7

Incest wounds *make me feel so inhibited, that it's like being in an emotional prison.* During the months and years in counseling, when I was first facing the trauma of incest, my emotions became so inhibited, I couldn't feel anything. Sometimes the depression had me so overwhelmed, that I couldn't feel happy, sad, excited, grateful, or anything. What I did feel was *guilt,* because when I went to church, I was told that I should give thanks and be grateful for any number of things. That was true, but, at that time, I couldn't *feel* those things. I couldn't even manufacture any good feelings. I had trouble concentrating. My health suffered because my emotions were suffering. Sometimes I was so moody, that I didn't want to do the things that I should have been doing. *My soul was in prison. It seemed like depression was in control, but it wasn't. My merciful God was in control of my situation every step of the way.*

> *Oh, Lord, please bring my soul out of prison, so that I may give thanks to Your name. Help me to glorify You, by performing my work and everything I do with excellence. Finally, Lord, let me see Your hand of healing in my mind, will, emotions, and physical health.*
>
> *In Jesus' Most Precious Name,*
>
> *Amen.*

Save me, O God,
For the waters have threatened my life.
I have sunk in deep mire,
And there is no foothold;
I have come into deep waters,
and a flood overflows me.

I am weary with my crying;
My throat is parched.;
My eyes fail while I wait for
my God. . . .
What I did not steal,
I then have to restore.

But as for me, my prayer is to You,
O Lord, at an acceptable time;
O God, in the greatness of
Your loving kindness,
Answer me with Your saving truth.
Deliver me from the mire, [7]
and do not let me sink;

May I be delivered from my foes,
and from the deep waters.
May the flood of water not overflow me,
Nor the deep swallow me
up,
Nor the pit not shut its mouth
on me.

Answer me, O Lord, for Your loving-
kindness is good;
According to the greatness of Your
compassion turn to me,
And do not hide Your face from Your servant,

For I am in distress; answer me quickly.
Oh, draw near to my soul and redeem it;
Ransom me because of my enemies!
You know my reproach and my shame
and my dishonor; . . .
King David ~ Psalm 69:1-4, 13-19

Incest can be characterized by many of the words and thoughts in this Psalm: *deep waters*, *flood of waters, pit, deep mire, overflow, overwhelm, weariness, crying, injustice, helplessness, sinking, paying for the sin of another, reproach, shame, dishonor*, etc. This Psalm has so much that I can identify with. I can read it and think that it must have been written just for me, as an incest victim or survivor, but it wasn't. That's the beauty of God's Word. It's there for me to pray back to my Lord and to meditate on, whenever I am in the pit, or I feel like the flood of depression is overwhelming me.

Because of incest, my innocence, purity, self-respect, ability to trust, and ability to express my real feelings were all stolen from me. The thief is gone, and I am left alone; and now it is my responsibility to put all the pieces back together. This is unjust and unfair!

However, the Lord is fully aware of all of this. He knows my shame and reproach and dishonor. He is listening attentively and is ready to respond with comfort, mercy, and redemption. Although I cannot trust anyone else with the important details of my life at this time, I absolutely can and MUST trust Him.

O merciful Father, thank You so much for this Psalm. It wasn't written for me, but You preserved it for me, to show me that You understand my feelings and situation so completely. Thank You that You will rescue and restore me from any and all prisons of my soul.

In the most precious name of my Lord Jesus Christ,

Amen.

1 I will love You, O Lord, my strength.

2 The Lord is my rock and my fortress and my
deliverer;
My God, my strength, in whom I will trust;
My shield and the horn of my salvation, my
stronghold.

3 I will call upon the Lord, Who is worthy to be
praised;
So shall I be saved from my enemies.

4 The pangs of death surrounded me,
And the floods of ungodliness made me
afraid.

6 In my distress I called upon the Lord,
And cried out to my God;
He heard my voice from His temple,
And my cry came before Him, even
to His ears.

16 He sent from above, He took me;
He drew me out of many waters.

17 He delivered me from my strong
enemy,
From those who hated me,
For they were too strong for me.

18 They confronted me in the day of

my calamity,
But the Lord was my support.

19 He also brought me out into a broad place;
He delivered me because He delighted
in me.
King David ~ Psalm 18:1-4, 6, 16-19 NKJV

This is a very poetic description, of what the Lord did for me and, as a result, how I feel about Him. I do love Him with all my heart, because He has become my Strength and my Deliverer. He is my Fortress, in the sense that He protects me and He is literally a place where I can hide emotionally, when I am afraid. He is also my Shield, which is a way of saying that He will always protect me from harm. To say that He is the Horn of my salvation is loaded with meaning. "Horn" is a symbol which means power or strength. It is also one of the Old Testament names for God, but, in the book of Luke in the New Testament, it is a name given for Jesus.

This Psalm is not just nice Hebrew poetry. It really describes some of what I felt and went through. It says that nothing will stop Him, when it comes to the rescue of His loved ones. It says, *"He delivered me, because He delighted in me" (Psalm 18:19).* This is a Psalm of King David that he wrote after a great deliverance from his enemy. It is easy to see why the Lord delighted in David. But I am at a complete loss to understand why He would favor me. The only reason I can understand this, is that I am His redeemed child, bought with the price of His precious blood and the sacrifice of His only Son. Now He sees me through the blood of Christ. From Ezekiel 22, I see that God hates incest and what it does to innocent lives. He hates what it did to my life. His goodness toward His own is incredible. And, believe me, He truly will rush to the aid of His children, who have been hurt and abused.

My Father, it doesn't seem like You have been in any hurry to bring about recovery and victory in my life. But, then I remember that Your work is never done in haste. It is done in love and mercy and excellence. But I know You have always been at work in my life. You didn't waste any time to protect me, even though I haven't always been aware of it. I am so grateful that You are in charge of this recovery process. I love You, for all you are doing in my life.

In the merciful name of my Lord Jesus,

Amen

The Lord heals the broken-hearted,
And binds up their wounds.
He counts the number of the stars;
He gives names to all of them.
Great is our Lord, and abundant
in strength;
His understanding is infinite.
The Lord supports the afflicted; . . .
Anonymous ~ Psalm 147:3-6

What this says about my God is nothing short of amazing! As I write this, I *am broken-hearted*. There is absolutely no doubt about that. Why would God say that He counts the number of all the stars and gives names to all of them? Because He is their Creator, just as He is mine. He is all powerful. He not only names all of them, He *knows* them *all by name,* just as He knows me by my name. *He is a personal God, and He has a personal relationship with all of His creation. He is abundant in strength and is infinite in understanding.*

All of this means that He is able to support me in my affliction, however severe it might be. He is well able to heal my broken heart and to bind up my deep festering wounds. Since I am an adopted daughter of the Most High God, He takes special notice of me in my need. This means that I can trust Him.

The Lord is near to the
broken-hearted,
And saves those who
are crushed in spirit.
King David ~ Psalm 34:18

The Psalmists agree that the Lord is *near* to the broken-hearted. He is a kindred spirit with the broken-hearted. He *loves* them, and He saves those who are crushed in spirit. *The Lord has a deep understanding for those who are crushed in spirit and for those who have a wounded heart.* Perhaps it's because He knows what it's like to have a broken spirit, due to the betrayal He experienced at Gethsemane, the abuse He suffered on His way to the cross, and the torture He experienced on the cross itself. Or perhaps He understands the crushed in spirit, because it is part of His nature to be compassionate and to know and understand everything about us, especially our pain. The prophecy about the cross states that "*He was a Man of Sorrows and acquainted with grief*" *(Isaiah 53:3 NKJV).* He knows and He understands.

It encourages me to know that He is near to my broken heart and that He does not despise it. He knows how my heart was broken and how my spirit was crushed. Isaiah 53:3-5 says:

3 *He was despised and rejected of men, a Man of sorrows and acquainted with grief. And we hid, as it were, our faces from Him; He was despised, and we did not esteem Him.*

[4] Surely He has borne our griefs and carried our sorrows; Yet we esteemed Him stricken, smitten by God, and afflicted. [5] But He was wounded for our transgressions. He was bruised for our iniquities; the chastisement for our peace was upon Him, and by His stripes we are healed.

A bruised reed He will not
break,
And a dimly burning wick
He will not extinguish;
He will faithfully bring
forth justice.
Isaiah ~ Isaiah 42:3

My Lord will not extinguish me because I am weak. He knows my weakness. He knows that I am crushed in spirit.

This verse tells me volumes about His character. He cares about the afflicted, the disabled, and those who are about ready to give up. He is not One who will walk all over the weak. And He will faithfully bring forth justice. As a victim of abuse, it is important for me to know that justice is very important to Him.

In my case, there was no human justice for me, because my father died before he could pay back what he stole or before justice could be achieved. I don't know if there was any way he *could* pay back what he did or if he could have ever understood the impact it had in my life. When he died, he stood before God, and He exposed my father's wickedness to him. That is something for which he will have to face the consequences forever, wherever he is. My God is the One who will demand ultimate justice. I can trust Him to not only care for me in my weakness but also to execute justice, even though the one who hurt me is gone from my world.

I am comforted to know that "*Christ is building His kingdom with earth's broken things. Men want only the strong, the successful, the victorious, the unbroken in building their kingdoms; but God is the God of the unsuccessful, of those who have failed. Heaven is filled with earth's broken lives, and there is no bruised reed that Christ cannot restore to glorious blessedness and beauty. He can take the life crushed by pain and sorrow and make it into a harp whose music shall be all praise. He can lift earth's saddest failure up to heaven's glory*" (J.R. Miller). [8]

Behold, . . .
I am going to send an angel
before you to guard you along
the way, and to bring you into the
place which I have prepared.
The Lord God to Moses ~ Exodus 23:20

This verse in Exodus refers to the time in Israel's history, when God sent His angel before His people through the desert to the place He had prepared for them. He was protecting them in advance. Psalm 139 says that the Lord knew me when I was being formed in my mother's womb, and the days of my life were written in His book before I was even born. Just as He knew all about me in intimate detail before I was born, He also knew about His people Israel.

In the same way, He also knew what would happen in each of *my* days. He has had His hand on my life. He knew what would happen (good or bad), and He made sure I would be safe.

So, what about the incest? He knew about that as well. It's hard to understand, but He was in control of my father's free will when he hurt me in the worst way possible. The most difficult thing to understand is that God allowed it for my good and for His glory. How can that be? That is one of the secret things that belong to Him and Him alone. It is one of the secret things that I have no choice but to trust Him with. I don't understand it, but I trust my Heavenly Father to always do what is best for me.

I also know and am convinced that my God was there all the time (in each day of my life from the beginning until now), guarding me, suffering with me when I was violated, and now grieving *with* me while I deal with the result of my father's mess. My Heavenly Father is with me now to make sure I make it through the entire recovery process for His glory and for my best welfare. And now He is there for yours.

Hear my cry, O God;
Give heed to my prayer.
From the end of the earth
I call to You, when my heart
is faint;
Lead me to the rock that
is higher than I.

For You have been a
refuge for me,
A tower of strength
against the enemy.

Let me dwell in Your
tent forever;
Let me take refuge in the
shelter of Your wings.
King David ~ Psalm 61:1-4

From that first prayer I prayed, asking God to make my dad stop hurting me, until now, prayer has been a refuge for me. I know that, whatever condition I'm in (whether depressed, feeling weak, or confused), all I have to do is to call on Him. He is indeed a Tower of Strength. He is Someone I can call on, when I feel weary and need to be comforted. His greatest desire is for me to come to Him in prayer, to draw close to Him, and to express my love for Him. This is when I need to remember that God is the One who fights my battles for me. When I let Him fight my battles, "He makes all things beautiful for me in His time" (Ecclesiastes 3:11

NLT). Far too often, I am tempted to take the route of independence and struggle through my problems on my own. The result of this is always disastrous. When this happens, the enemy of my soul believes he has won a great victory. But the Lord Jesus always wins the final victory, because I belong to Him.

> *You are of God, little children, and have overcome them, because He who is in you is greater than he who is in the world.*
> Apostle John ~ 1 John 4:4 NKJV

1 John 4:4 tells me that *we have overcome* <u>*them*</u>. For our walk through the Valley of Tears, seeking recovery for our wounds of abuse, I believe this is referring to depression, fear, distrust, and so on.

> *My Merciful Heavenly Father,*
>
> *"Hear my cry, O God; give heed to my prayer. For You have been a refuge for me, a tower of strength . . . Let me take refuge in the shelter of Your wings."*
>
> *Lord, this is a wonderful prayer that I can pray to You whenever I am in need. Thank You for giving me so many prayers in the Psalms that I can use to express my feelings, when I am at a loss for words to tell You how I feel. Thank You that You also listen to my tears and my silence and know what my heart is saying. Thank You that You understand me like no other.*
>
> *In the blessed Name of Jesus my Lord,*
> *Amen.*

Give ear to my prayer, O God;
And do not hide Yourself
from my supplication.
Give heed to me, and answer me;
I am restless in my complaint
and I am surely distracted,
Because of the voice of the enemy,
Because of the pressure of
the wicked;
Because they bring down trouble upon me,
And in anger they bear a grudge against me.

My heart is in anguish within me, . . .
Fear and trembling come
upon me;
And horror has overwhelmed me.
And I said, "Oh, that I had wings
like a dove!
I would fly away and be at rest.
"Behold, I would wander far away,
I would lodge in the wilderness. . . . "

As for me, I shall call upon God,
And the Lord will save me.
Evening and morning
and at noon, I will
complain and murmur,
And He will hear my voice.
He will redeem my soul
in peace from the battle
which is against me, . . .

God will hear and answer them—
Even the One who sits enthroned
from of old—
With whom there is no change, . . .

Cast your burden upon the Lord, and
He will sustain you;
He will never allow the righteous
to be shaken.
King David ~ Psalm 55:1-8, 16-19, 22

King David says in this Psalm, "*I am restless in my complaint and I am surely distracted.*"

Depression is definitely distracting. It distracts from every meaningful, worthy, and noble pursuit I have ever attempted.

The enemy is multi-faceted. First there is the enemy of my soul, who engineered the wounding of incest and likely thought he had destroyed me. Then there are all the symptoms of incest: depression, withdrawal, suppression, rejection, emotional numbness, loneliness, false guilt, insecurity, inability to trust, and secretiveness—just to name a few.

The one thing I always wanted to do, when I was overwhelmed with the above symptoms, was to escape my circumstances. The writer of this Psalm also speaks about wanting to escape these emotional circumstances:

"Oh, that I had wings like a dove! I would fly away and be at rest. Behold, I would wander far away, I would lodge in the wilderness. I would hasten to my place of refuge from the storms and the tempest."
King David ~ Psalm 55:6-8

My desire to escape led to serious thoughts of suicide—three times. But what I really needed was a relationship with my Heavenly Father. He is the most real personality in the universe. On top of that, He was the only One who really understood my feelings and what I was going through. He is the only One whose merciful kindness will never change, and the only One I can always turn to with the burden of my pain. That is why I responded to Him. He will *always* be just the same today, one hour from now, next week, next year, and always.

Thank You, my Heavenly Father, that I can cast all my burdens on You, and You will not only support me, but meet me right where I am. You are faithful and merciful and kind. I find You always ready to help me the moment I call on You for help. I just need to say, "My Lord, I can't. You can. Please help." Thank You for being there for me, my Lord. You always know what is best for my life.

In the precious name of my Lord and Savior Jesus,

Amen.

Therefore, the Lord longs to be
gracious to you,
And therefore, He waits on high
to have compassion on you.
For the Lord is a God of justice;
How blessed are all those who
long for Him.

. . . you will weep no longer.
He will surely be gracious to you
at the sound of your cry;
when He hears it, He will answer you.
The Lord God to Isaiah ~ Isaiah 30:18-19

I find it amazing that God *longs* to be gracious *and* compassionate to me. I am completely unworthy of this. Everyone is. But that is not the issue. Grace is giving love to those who do not deserve it. It still overwhelms me. It is incredible that in the same breath as He desires to be compassionate and gracious, He also says that He is a God of justice. What an *amazing God!* As one who has suffered great injustice, I can respond to that with great wonder. There is so much injustice in this world, but God will set everything straight in the final outcome. He is already doing a work of healing in me. He is sensitive to me, listens to me, and is ready to respond with gracious compassion and justice.

What is especially amazing is that it says that "*He will surely be gracious to me at the sound of my cry; when He hears it, He will answer.*" Something to remember is that, as God waits on High to have compassion on me, I must wait here in my painful circumstances for His gracious answer. It works both ways. As I am waiting for His answer, He is here to comfort me and protect me. He is here and He is working, albeit in silence, until the right time to reveal His answer. So we must trust and wait.

I have chosen you and not rejected you.
Do not fear, for I am with you;
Do not anxiously look about you,
for I am your God.
I will strengthen you,
surely I will help you,
Surely I will uphold you
with My righteous right hand.

For I am the Lord your God, who upholds
your right hand,
Who says to you, 'Do not fear, I will
help you.'
The Lord God to Isaiah ~ Isaiah 41:9b-10, 13

He has chosen me *and not rejected me*. That is a thought to reflect on. It is music to my ears that there is actually Someone who will not reject me. What is so special about this is that *I am so sensitive to rejection*. But my Lord God will *never* reject me. I will *always* be accepted by Him. Regardless of how I feel about myself or how others treat me, *I am chosen and loved by God!* He knows me intimately and what I feel and agonize over. He knows all I have experienced, and still, *with all that perfect and complete knowledge of me, He still has not rejected me!* Others have rejected me on a lot less knowledge. Instead, my God *longs* to be gracious and compassionate toward me, and He greatly desires to make me a trophy of His healing grace. He will give me all the strength and support I need, until my walk through this *Valley of Tears* is complete.

Do you not know?
Have you not heard?
The Everlasting God, the
Lord, the Creator of the
ends of the earth
Does not become weary or
tired.
His understanding is
inscrutable.
He gives strength to the
weary,
And to him who lacks
might He increases power.
Though youths grow
weary and tired,
And vigorous young men
stumble badly,
Yet those who wait for the Lord
Will gain new strength;
They will mount up with wings
like eagles,
They will run and not get tired,
They will walk and not become
weary.

The Lord God of Israel to Isaiah ~ Isaiah 40:28-31

God knows all about this process of healing and recovery. He knows and understands my depressive weariness. He also has the power to take me through this one day at a time, at my pace, and in His strength.

He will give me new strength as I rely on Him. He will give me the courage and desire to keep going, even when I feel overwhelmed.

I am reminded of what I read in Charles H. Spurgeon's devotional, *Morning and Evening:* [9]

> *Like a shepherd He will tend His flock, In His arm He will gather the lambs, And carry them in His bosom; He will gently lead the nursing ewes.*
> The Lord God of Israel to Isaiah ~ Isaiah 40:11

He first describes the Shepherd, then he describes the way that the Shepherd cares for His precious flock.

> "Who is He of whom such gracious words are spoken? He is THE GOOD SHEPHERD. Why does He carry the lambs so close to His heart? Because *He has a tender heart, and* any weakness at once *melts His heart.* The sighs, the ignorance, the feebleness of the little ones of His flock draws forth His compassion. *It is His office, as a faithful High Priest, to consider the weak.* Besides, *He purchased them with blood, they are His property.* He must and will care for that which cost Him so dear. Then He is responsible for each lamb, bound by covenant engagements not to lose one. *Moreover, they are all a part of His glory and reward.*
>
> "But how may we understand the expression, 'He *carries* them'? Sometimes He carries them by *not permitting them to endure much trial.* Providence deals tenderly with them. Often, they

are 'carried' by *being filled with an unusual degree of love*, so that they bear up and stand fast. *Though their knowledge may not be deep, they have great sweetness in what they do know. Frequently He 'carries' them by giving them a very simple faith*, which takes the promise just as it stands, and believingly runs with every trouble straight to Jesus. *The simplicity of their faith gives them an unusual degree of confidence*, which carries them above the world."

Can a woman forget her nursing child,
And have no compassion on the son
of her womb?
Even these may forget, but I will not
forget you.
Behold, I have inscribed you on the
palms of My hands; . . .
The LORD God of Israel to Isaiah ~ Isaiah 49:15-16

How can you forget *someone* who is inscribed on the palms of your hand? It's so close to your heart. It is the same with our Lord Jesus. Well, *I am inscribed on the palms of His hands!* And I believe the inscription is written in His blood. Each one of us was in His heart and mind as He suffered on the cross. He saw our souls, as He was redeeming us with His precious life blood, written there right on the palms of His hands. Every time those damaged nerves stung with such indescribable pain; He was loving us.

I look forward to the day when I will see Him face to face. I will be able to hold those precious hands in mine and see with my eyes and touch with my own hands the scars of the nail piercing from His sacrifice for my sin—the scars that, like the rest of His body and soul, He suffered with such excruciating pain to make me His child. I was made His daughter by the death that paid for my redemption and adoption into His family. His traumatic suffering, both on the cross and beforehand, provided for my healing from my own trauma, painful memories, depression, and much, *much* more. He will not forget me, and He will never forget what has happened to me.

It's all on the palm of His nail-pierced hands. People may come and go in my life and they may even forget that they ever knew me, but my God will never forget me or the details of my life.

"Because of the devastation of the
afflicted,
because of the groaning
of the needy,
Now I will arise," says the Lord;
"I will set him in the safety for
which he longs."
King David ~ Psalm 12:5

The Lord is aware of my affliction and it is His desire to give me security. His protecting arms are always surrounding me. This shows me the tender heart of my Heavenly Father, *a Father I have learned to truly trust*. Incest is a devastating trauma. It caused me to withdraw into my room or any quiet place I could find for safety. But this verse tells me I can run to my Heavenly Father for safety. I can trust that He will deliver me from my pain and all my fears. When I run to the Lord for my quiet place of prayer and sanctuary, I know He will keep me safe. There is no better place to be.

Thank You, my Father, for being my quiet place of safety. I am so grateful that when I need to run to You, I can pour out my heart to You and tell You everything—all my pain and fears, all my troubles and needs. Because You know what has been going on in my life, nothing takes You by surprise. I can lay it all at Your feet and rest in You, knowing that You will take care of everything. You know the troubles of my soul before I even speak.

I praise You, because I can trust You to take care of the concerns of my life.

In Jesus' precious Name,

Amen.

O LORD, hear my prayer, listen to
my cry for mercy;
in Your faithfulness and righteousness
come to my relief.
Do not bring Your servant into
judgment,
for no one living is righteous before
You.
So my spirit grows faint within me;
my heart within me is dismayed.

I remember the days of long ago;
I meditate on all Your works
and consider what Your hands
have done.
I spread out my hands to You;
my soul thirsts for You like
a parched land.

Interlude

Answer me quickly, O LORD;
my spirit fails.
Do not hide Your face from me
or I will be like those who
go down to the pit.

Let the morning bring me word of
Your unfailing love,
for I have put my trust in You.
Show me the way I should go,

for to You I lift up my soul.
Rescue me from my enemies, O LORD,
for I hide myself in You.
Teach me to do Your will,
for You are my God;
May Your good Spirit lead me
on level ground.

For Your name's sake, O LORD,
preserve my life;
in Your righteousness, bring
me out of trouble.
In Your unfailing love, silence my enemies;
destroy all my foes, for I am
Your servant.
King David ~ Psalm 143:1-2, 4-12 NLT

I have felt and prayed everything expressed in this Psalm. At that time, I didn't know there was a prayer of King David in the Psalms that so clearly communicated what I was pleading before my Heavenly Father. When my father was violating me, I was "*paralyzed with fear,*" not knowing if I should tell his dirty secret or keep it quiet for my own safety. I chose the only route that most victims also choose—*to keep it a secret because of the fear of exposure*. I lost all hope of things getting any better for a long, long time. I would share it with a few trusted friends. Then finally, after many years, I dealt with the secret as openly as I could handle it—in the safety of my counseling session. At times I was back to the paralyzing fear and almost stayed in that state permanently. But as I thought back and remembered all the wonderful things my Heavenly Father had done for me since the time that I was hurt, I reached up and out for help.

I chose to trust in the Lord. It was a hard choice and it was a deliberate choice. It was also a *daily* choice. I knew I needed God's unfailing love every day, for without that assurance I knew I would never recover. Every day I had to make that same choice over and over again to run to the only Father I could trust—my Father in Heaven. I had to depend daily on the gracious Spirit of God to lead me forward, so I would have the emotional stability to face my fears, one fear at a time, one day at a time.

I can remember praying that the Lord would heal me, if for no other reason than "*for the glory of His name and His reputation.*" I felt that, as His child, His reputation was at stake and that might be the only reason He had to make me whole. But I was wrong about that. He desired to make me whole, because He loves me and always desires the best for me like any good Father would. He is incredibly awesome that way. Because of His faithfulness, He brought me out of my deep depression and paralyzing fear. 2 Timothy 2:13 (*NKJV*) says (as part of an ancient New Testament creed) *". . . He remains faithful; He cannot deny Himself."* For my Heavenly Father to be unfaithful to me would be inconsistent with His nature, because He cannot deny Himself. I find that to be incredibly comforting!

As I continued to meditate on verse five of this Psalm, I was doubly blessed. It states:

> *I remember the days of long ago; I meditate on all Your works and consider what Your hands have done.*
> King David ~ Psalm 143:5 NLT

As I was thinking about this recently, I realized that one of my fondest and most cherished memories took place during my years as an employee of Western Conservative Baptist Seminary in Portland, Oregon, and when I was a member at Milwaukie First Baptist Church in Milwaukie, Oregon.

After having my life torn apart at home during my adolescence and teen-age years and having my family "role models" let me down so desperately, the Lord gave me some new role models at these two places. It happened so gradually that I didn't even realize it was happening.

I had been in the worship choir for a few years before working at Western Seminary. At the same time that I was at the seminary, our church hired a new worship pastor who started his tenure at the Seminary in the Master of Church Music degree program. These two ministries dove-tailed so beautifully in my life to give me the mentors that I so desperately needed. The worship choir was truly part of the worship service—in fact, it was central to the worship. It was very special. Our new worship pastor was a master at bringing the music and worship together in such a beautiful way, so that it was truly worshipful.

God was central and He was glorified. That choir grew to at least 60 members, and we were taught to sing as one voice and to sing with excellence to the glory of God. It was such a positive experience and a privilege to be part of such a ministry.

I also had the opportunity to become good friends with the pastoral staff, each of whom had a true pastor's heart. It was heart-breaking to me when, after several years, the Lord led our Senior pastor to another ministry.

In my position at the Seminary, I worked with men and women who became godly mentors to me. One of them was a Church History professor who was about my father's age. When I first began working for him, He approached me and said that he had heard that I was fatherless. I have told about this relationship in another part of this book, so I will not repeat the story here, except to say that he was a good friend and mentor. There were others at the school who had a great influence in my life, and I am good friends with some of them to this day. There are some I remained close to for years, until they passed on. And one of them, a former staff member, is a close life-long friend.

I will always be grateful for those five years, because God used both the church and the school relationships as an emotional and spiritual healing balm for my soul. This is one significant way God had done a great work of mentoring in my life. I remember spending time with the faculty members in the faculty lounge and listening to them discuss different theological issues and serious questions of the faith, along with their theological humor, which I really enjoyed. I knew they had to have a mature relationship with God and extensive training in His Word to be able to have those types of conversations. During that time I purchased a new Bible and began reading through it on my breaks and at lunch. I remember having a thirst for God and knew I would have to grow deep in the faith, in order to be able to join in with them in those discussions. I determined to devote myself to God and His Word, so I would grow in the knowledge of my Lord Jesus Christ. This became my life-long desire and quest.

For He has not despised nor abhorred
the affliction of the afflicted;
Neither has He hidden His face from him;
But when He cried to Him for help,
He heard.
King David ~ Psalm 22:24

The Lord doesn't avoid me because I am in pain. A number of friends that I have had in the past have done that for one reason or another, but my God will never do that. I remember reading in the New Testament about the way Jesus did not hesitate to touch those who were inflicted with leprosy, a condition that was highly contagious in those days. He showed a special compassion for those afflicted with all kinds of contagious conditions that caused pain and suffering. Since He is "*a Man of Sorrows and acquainted with grief*" (*Isaiah 53:3*), He is no stranger to affliction. He has a deep personal knowledge of all my ways and needs, and He will not back off because my pain is ugly and undesirable or because I happen to be a high-maintenance individual.

When I think about the way certain friends and acquaintances have backed away because they didn't want to hear about my pain all the time, and I realized it could have been for a couple of reasons. One reason could have been due to a lack of maturity on both their part and my part. I was so wrapped up in my pain that I couldn't think about or talk about anything else. What I didn't realize was that people got tired of hearing about it. I did not wish to be dishonest or "fake" about what was going on in my life, but I had not learned how to balance my pain with other things in my life and to not "wear my hurts on my sleeve." The few "friends" that shied away from me simply did not choose to be close to the unpleasant aspects of hearing about my pain. One of them actually came to me later and apologized, because she had developed a severe headache that she couldn't get rid of, and so she became much more understanding toward me. She had always been convinced that God could be called upon to pray her pains away until one day when He didn't cooperate with her mistaken theology. He had ceased to be her medical vending machine and she learned to trust Him in a much deeper way. It's amazing how much we learn when we go through similar trials as those we previously judged as weak. However, as time passed I learned to focus more on the interests of others and to not discuss my pain unless a friend actually asked about it.

My Father,

Thank You that You know all about my pain. You do not hide Your face from me because it is unpleasant. You do not avoid me because I am covered with the dirt left on me by abuse. I am so grateful that when I come to You in prayer, You hear me, regardless of what form my prayers take. Like a good Father, You love me no matter what condition I come to You in. You see me clothed in the righteous robes of Your dear Son.

It is in His beautiful Name, the Name of my Lord Jesus that I pray,

Amen

Turn to me and be gracious to me,
For I am lonely and afflicted.
The troubles of my heart
are enlarged;
Bring me out of my distresses,
Look upon my affliction
and my trouble,
And forgive all my sins.
Look upon my enemies, for
they are many;
And they hate me with
violent hatred.
Guard my soul and deliver me;
Do not let me be ashamed, for
I take refuge in You.
King David ~ Psalm 25:16-20

I look to my God for His grace. His grace is His unmerited favor and strength. He gives *that to me freely as His redeemed daughter. He is ready to understand my pain, heal me, vindicate me, forgive me, and comfort me. I just need to lay my loneliness, pain, and broken heart at His feet.* He will hold me in His arms and soothe me in His mercy and love. He will give me the spiritual and emotional rest I need. He is the Great Physician who knows how to heal the wounds of His creation. To me it seems too complicated to ever become completely straightened out. However, for Him, it is not difficult at all. He could do it with a word, but that would happen too quickly and I would not learn anything from the process. Therefore,

He will perform what concerns me over time in the best way for my full recovery.

Then your light will break out like the dawn,
And Your ***recovery*** *will speedily spring forth;*
And your righteousness will go before you;
The glory of the Lord will be your rear guard.

Then you will call, and the Lord will answer;
You will cry, and He will say, 'Here I am.' . . .

<u>Then your light will rise in darkness,</u>
<u>And your gloom will become like midday</u>.
Isaiah ~ Isaiah 58:8-10

This is an incredible promise. Since I have been living in a prison house of dark depression and gloom for such a long time, this reassures me that the light will break out. These are great word pictures. It is a picture of the depression, disappearing like the darkness at dawn, and the recovery, instantly and speedily springing forth! That gives me a huge dose of hope and encouragement.

Until then, God's goodness will protect me. I have to trust Him with that, believe Him for it, and leave the rest to Him. With the state of mind that I am in right now, there is a lot to trust God for.

I know and believe that God's goodness is part of His glory.

Then Moses said, "I pray You, show me Your glory!"

And He said, "I Myself will make all My goodness pass before you, and I will proclaim the name of

the Lord before you; and I will be gracious to whom I will be gracious, and will have compassion on whom I will have compassion."
But He said, "You cannot see My face, for no man can see Me and live!"
The Lord God to Moses ~ Exodus 33:18-20

When Moses wanted to see God's glory, He had a significant conversation with him. In the next chapter of Exodus 34:5-6, *God revealed His glory to Moses*, as much as a mortal man can see of God's glory with the naked eye without dying. Gazing at God's glory would be synonymous to gazing at the sun with the eyes unprotected, only much more intense and devastating. With that being the case, God descended to Moses in a cloud and once again declared His attributes of mercy, grace, longsuffering, goodness, and truth. This is what God revealed to Moses as being His glory.

In Isaiah 58:11, the Scripture states that our needs will be met. My desires will be fulfilled, as in a dry place that has been in a drought. What an amazing promise! God can change the situations that we see as impossible, whatever these difficulties are. He can change them from drought to a lush garden, from gloom and depression to light, from weariness to strength, and from death to life-giving living water.

My gracious Heavenly Father,

Thank You for being a promise-keeping God. Thank You for this assurance that recovery is included in Your promise. Thank You that you will wipe away my depression and allow me to feast on Your rich living water. You are so good and merciful. Help me to focus on these attributes as You bring Your healing to my soul.

In the name of Your Son Jesus,
who shed His blood for me,
Amen.

A father of the fatherless and
a judge for the widows,
Is God in His holy habitation.
God makes a home for the lonely;
King David ~ Psalm 68:5-6a

The role of a good father is to provide for the needs of his children. This means he is to protect, nurture, and lead them. This kind of man would even give his life to care for his children if necessary. My father was a good provider. He didn't make a lot of money at his job as a blue-collar worker, but he worked hard to make a living and brought home a regular pay-check. However, he failed in all the other areas of being a man. He disobeyed Colossians 3:21 in that he "*exasperated his children and made us all lose heart*." He frustrated us and our mother as well. He was over-bearing. He discouraged us as individuals, as we grew out of childhood into adolescence. He was not the father I needed or wanted. He scoffed at my personality, my desires, and my goals, as he did for everyone else.

However, God, *my Father Who is in Heaven*, is my *real Father* in the truest sense of that word. He will never scoff at me or my needs. He is my Provider, my Protector, and the One who nurtures me with His love and guidance. When I was lost, scared, and lonely, He took me into His family, making me His own daughter, as it states in *Romans 8:15*:

> *For you have not received a spirit of slavery leading to fear again, but you have received a spirit of adoption as sons (and daughters) by which we cry out, "Abba! Father!"*
> *(Parentheses added by this author)*

My Father in heaven became my *"Abba Father." "Abba"* is the Aramaic word for father. It is what Jesus called His Father. It is a word a little child would call his father (daddy). Jesus' relationship with His Father was close and tender.[10] God is my Abba, my adopted Father—the One and only Father I could trust.

Just as a father has compassion
on his children,
So the Lord has compassion on
those who fear Him.
For He Himself knows our frame;
He is mindful that we are but dust.
King David ~ Psalm 103:13-14

God is my Father in the truest sense of that word. He truly defines fatherhood. He cares about my feelings and needs. He knows and understands me. Since He is my Creator, He knows how I function as an individual. He knows my limitations and weaknesses as well as my strengths.

He knows how my mind works. He knows how the trauma affected my views on life, on men, and on what I thought I would be when I grew up. He understands my depression and my fear. He is fully aware of my misconceptions about life, myself, and my inaccurate thoughts about Him. He is much more patient with me than I or any other person could ever be. He wants to see me recover from this terrible trauma, even more than I do, but He is waiting for me to reach the place of determination to *want to recover*. He is very patient. This is what the Bible calls *long-suffering*. He will never give up on me, and He will use this experience continually in my life, until I become a special token of His grace and a sparkling jewel in His crown.

Thank You, Lord, that You are my compassionate Father. You know me so completely. You know how I was framed in my mother's womb and that I, like everyone, was made of dust. You know how fragile I am and how much I need You. Thank You for Your gentle compassion that will make me strong.

I pray this in the strong Name of Jesus my Lord,

Amen

"For I know the plans that I have for you," declares the Lord, "'plans for welfare and not for calamity to give you a future and a hope."
The Lord through the Prophet Jeremiah ~ Jeremiah 29:11

It gives me great encouragement to know that God has good plans for me. It is powerfully enabling to know that nothing my dad *did* to me and nothing he *said* to me or about me *can interfere with God's good plan for my life. I have to believe* in God's plan and *decide not to believe* in my dad's lies. God will accomplish all of His good plans for me, and *I must believe this because* my God is faithful. The pain that I am going through right now is temporary, and any future pain, whatever kind it is, will only be as intense as God allows.

I am growing to believe that God has a good future for me, and I am putting my hope *not in the future, but in my God*. I do not have to fear the future, because my God is there and He has prepared the way. At one time, I felt very dirty because of the incest—like it was somehow my fault. I felt guilty—like I needed to be forgiven. I know now that it's not my forgiveness for this act that needs to be sought, but it is my forgiveness that needs to be given. I need the grace to forgive my father. I also need to forgive my Father in Heaven for allowing it to happen in the first place. That keeps me from becoming angry with Him. But as I meditate on His character, I know that He never allows anything into my life that He will not use for good. That is hard to swallow, but it is true. I can confidently embrace His lovingkindness, His tender mercies,

His faithfulness and goodness as well as His righteousness, His grace, and His love for me. I know my God will cleanse me from all the dirty feelings that I once had.

The Lord is good to those who wait
for Him,
To the person who seeks Him . . .

For the Lord will not reject
forever,
For if He causes grief,
Then He will have compassion
According to His abundant loving-
kindness.
For He does not afflict willingly,
Or grieve the sons of men.
Lamentations 3:25, 31-33

This is such an encouraging passage of Scripture! I love it! When God tells me that He loves me, this means so much more than when my biological father said the same words. My father certainly did not mean anything like what is written in these verses. *I must believe in the goodness of God, in order to trust Him. He is good, compassionate, and loving in His attitude and in all His dealings toward me.*

As a person who has been abused, especially one who is a victim of childhood incest, I am very sensitive to rejection and abandonment. They go hand in hand. This verse promises that God will not allow me to experience rejection forever. If God allows me to experience grief, then He will balance it out with His compassion and love. *He does not like to see His loved ones suffer, but He has a genuinely positive purpose in the pain.*

> *For God has not given us a spirit of*
> *timidity (fear), but of power and love*
> *and a sound mind.* (Parentheses added by this author)
>
> *The Apostle Paul to his protégé, in 2 Timothy 1:7 NKJV*

For a victim of abuse, especially those who have been violated in a place of safety like their own homes, there are many things to be very afraid of. But this verse says that even though there are things that we fear, *we should never have a fearful spirit.* God has given us a *spirit of power and love and a sound mind.* Inner personal power is not something that we are born with. The feeling of powerlessness is much more natural. *It takes the power of God to reverse that feeling of weakness, with His Spirit working throughout the healing process. We can't do it on our own.*

See what Jesus says in the Upper Room Discourse about our need for Him to do the work in us to produce the healing process.

> *I am the vine, you are the branches. He who abides*
> *in Me, and I in him, bears much fruit; for without Me*
> *you can do nothing.*
>
> Jesus to His Disciples ~ John 15:5 NKJV

I need Him to produce growth in my life. I need Him to bring about recovery and growth in my life. I need Him to give me air to breathe and food to eat. I need Him for everything.

When Jesus heard that, He said,
"This sickness is not unto death,
but for the glory of God, that
the Son of God may be glorified
through it."

Jesus to His Disciples ~ John 11:4 NKJV

I have been sick with one thing or another most of my life. But after the incest, I seemed to be exceptionally weak and vulnerable. I suffered with an undiagnosed pain in my teen years, which I now believe was brought on by the incest. Having this traumatic experience during early adolescence, when I was developing hormonally and neurologically, it caused my immunity to be compromised. I would define sickness to include anything from a physical ailment to an emotional trauma that contributes to continuing physical pain. All this makes the pain much more complicated and difficult to sort out.

But God is not limited by my childhood illnesses. Nor is His work in my life short-circuited by my dad's indiscretion in violating me. My Heavenly Father has a plan to turn every pain in my life into something beautiful for which to praise Him. He plans to give me beauty for ashes. Pain is not beautiful; neither is sickness. But the work of God is *very* beautiful, and the way He works through it is worthy of our praise.

It is apparent that God has allowed both the incest and the Endometriosis, as well as other physical weaknesses in my life, to bring glory to Him. They did not just appear to give me pain and sorrow. They were there for a purpose. During those times of sorrow and struggle, as He worked in my life and as He intervened, He received the glory. I don't understand how, but He does. It is how He works.

We count those blessed who endured. You have heard of the endurance of Job and have seen the outcome of the Lord's dealings, that the Lord is full of compassion and is merciful.

The Apostle James ~ James 5:11

It is very difficult to endure the process of healing and recovery. Sometimes it seems to take a very long time, and it's easy to get disillusioned with the whole thing. However, it's very necessary to go through this *Valley of Tears*, and it's vital to know and dwell on the character of God. You need to always remember that your Heavenly Father is full of compassion and mercy and that He has enough power and love to change your life completely. Do not quit, and do not give up on the healing process. There were times when I wanted to give up. But I was a survivor and was too far entrenched in the process, so that was never an option. I would advise you to keep in mind the advice of Winston Churchill during England's darkest days of World War II:

"Never, Never, Never give up."
"If you're going through hell, keep going."
"Success is not final; failure is not fatal: it is the courage to continue that counts."

Since the Lord is full of compassion and mercy, we can surely count on Him to strengthen us and give us the endurance to never give up and keep going.

My Father in Heaven,

I ask You to strengthen me with your compassion and mercy to help me to never give up. Please give me the grace to keep going, no matter what, knowing that You're on my side and You will never fail me.

I love You for Your merciful kindness and that You will bring about my recovery before I leave this Valley of Tears.

In the precious name of my Lord and Savior,

Jesus Christ,

Amen.

And in the same way the Spirit also
helps our weakness; for we do not
know how to pray as we should,
but the Spirit Himself intercedes for
us with groanings too deep for words;
The Apostle Paul ~ Romans 8:26

Sometimes it is impossible to express feelings in words. Sometimes the only way to express my feelings to God is by silence in His presence. There are times when words are totally inadequate to express the depth of my emotions. Sometimes the only prayer I can pray is to *cry* in His presence.

Communication with God often transcends the need for words, and His Holy Spirit then takes over and translates any human words I need to speak with His own groanings. It is a very great mystery. I would never try to understand it, but I just need to rest in it. This mystery of the Godhead is utterly amazing.

I am very grateful for this working of His Holy Spirit in prayer. He, God the Holy Spirit, the third member of the Godhead, is interceding for me intensely. His intercession is so deep there are no words to describe His expressions. The Scripture says they are "*groanings too deep for words.*" That is pretty intense. What can be better than that? I am covered. Even when the only prayer I can pray is tears, God sees every tear and hears every groan. And He will answer in the best possible way and time. What an amazing God to entrust my sorrows to!

Depart from me, all you
who do iniquity,
For the Lord has heard
the voice of my
weeping.
The Lord has heard my
supplication,
The Lord receives my
prayer.
All my enemies shall be
ashamed and greatly
dismayed;
They shall turn back, they
shall suddenly be ashamed.
King David ~ Psalm 6:8-10

Tears are a powerful form of prayer. Do not ever discount the times when you are at a loss for words in your times of prayer, and all you can do is shed tears before the Lord. He knows what those tears are saying. They are like a fragrant incense, coming up before Him and going right to the throne of grace and mercy.

During the years following the trauma, when I was deeply depressed while reliving that disturbing experience, I cried oceans of tears. I cried so much at times that my face would hurt, and I looked *terrible!* After some years had passed, I discovered this verse that states that my weeping actually has a voice before the Lord. He *hears* the "*voice of my weeping*"*!* He truly is my awesome God! He knew the *ache of my* *heart,* even when I didn't have the ability to speak it! All I have to do is to shed my spontaneous tears, and He hears my prayer. This is so amazing. Even when I didn't have the words and I wept before Him, He knew everything in my heart—all my loss, all my grief, and all my hurt. *He sees* and *hears right through my tears*.

You have taken account
of my wanderings;
Put my tears in Your
bottle;

Are they not in Your
book?

In God, whose word I praise,
In the Lord, whose word I praise,
In God I have put my trust,
I shall not be afraid . . .
King David ~ Psalm 56:8,10-11

I find this absolutely incredible. Everything God says in His Word is incredible to me. I don't know which verse is my favorite. Since God knows every intimate detail about me, it doesn't surprise me that God keeps track of all my tears. This shows that He is *deeply and personally knowledgeable about everything that concerns me (See Psalm 139:1 NASB).*

First of all, God knows all about my wanderings. This means that God knows about my years of dark depression, when I was convinced that there was no hope for me (before being delivered from my emotional prison). These are not wasted years before the Lord. To me they were wasted years, but to Him they were completely necessary. He knows about them; He takes them into account. He keeps track of them in His book. He knows when they will end. What a library God must have!

Second, He keeps track of my tears. Verse 8 says they are in "His bottle." Well, I don't know how big God's bottle is, but the one for my tears must be the jumbo size! I've heard that little "tear bottles" are sold in gift shops in Jerusalem, and they are shaped in such a way so that the moisture in the bottle will not evaporate. God wants an accurate accounting of my tears. In fact, He also keeps track of them in His book. He cares so much about my suffering that He records my grief in His bottle *and* in His book. In a way, that is like keeping track of my prayers. In his book Growing Strong in the Seasons of Life, [11] Chuck Swindoll has this to say about shedding tears:

> "I wonder how many tear bottles in heaven bear your initials? You'll never have many until you let go and let a little tenderness run loose."

In the case of those of us who have suffered abuse and have been violated, we also need to let "a little tenderness run loose." But we need to go beyond that. We need to let our emotions be completely released. When we begin to shed these tears, we can be sure that we have passed the first of many steps in healing the pain of being violated in such a private and personal way.

What then shall we say to these things?
If God is for us, who is against us?
He who did not spare His own Son,
but delivered Him up for us all, how
will He not also with Him freely give
us all things?

But in all these things (sufferings)
we overwhelmingly conquer through
Him who loved us. For I am convinced
that neither death, nor life, nor angels,
nor principalities, nor things present,
(nor things past)*, nor things to come,*
nor powers, nor height, nor depth,
nor any other created thing, shall be
able to separate us from the love of God,
which is in Christ Jesus our Lord.
The Apostle Paul ~ Romans 8:31-32, 37-39
(Parentheses added by this author)

There is nothing God cannot give me, and there is more that He wants to give me than I can imagine. He will freely give me all things, and this includes release from this terrible pain of incest. This includes the memory of it and the post-traumatic stress disorder. It includes the symptoms of the trauma. He is able and very willing to do this, but He wants to do it in His own way and certainly in His own time. This gives great encouragement to my faith and to my prayer life.

Even more, there is nothing that can separate me from God's love. That includes my *past* and my *biological father* who violated me as well as my *wounds* and the *insecurities* that have continued to the present day. God's love can reach me, in spite of the negatives in my life, and He can do away with any hurt that I am willing to face with Him.

Finally, be strong in the Lord, and in the strength of His might. Put on the full armor of God, that you may be able to stand firm against the schemes of the devil. For our struggle is not against flesh and blood, but against the rulers, against the powers, against the world forces of this darkness, against the spiritual forces of wickedness in the heavenly places.Therefore, take up the full armor of God, that you may be able to resist in the evil day, and having done everything, to stand firm.

The Apostle Paul ~ Ephesians 6:10-13

The battle for emotional healing is instigated by Satan. His desire is to see lives destroyed. That is why incest happens in the first place. He will do anything in his power to prevent recovery. The battle is a spiritual one and you must fight it in God's strength. This is why, when you read through the Psalms, the various writers are constantly asking God to come to their aid and to provide rescue from their enemies.

One of the most common weapons Satan uses against us is a poor concept of God. It is the first weapon he used on mankind, by convincing Eve that God was withholding good from her. For an incest victim, this is a very common struggle. Our concept of God begins with our parents. When a parent violates a sacred trust and exploits the vulnerability of the child, that tends to spill over into the child's concept of God. So the child grows up feeling like no one can be trusted. After all, God was there, and He allowed her to be hurt. In order to resist the attack of Satan in this area, I need to develop a healthy concept of God. I need to get to know Him for who He really is. This begins with the Word of God. He has revealed His personality and character in the Bible. He has told us what He is like, what His attitudes and attributes are, what He is like, and what we can expect from Him. The Scriptures reveal so much about how He feels about us.

For I am confident of this very thing, that He who began a good work in you will perfect it until the day of Christ Jesus.

The Apostle Paul ~ Philippians 1:6

Sanctification is a biblical word that means the work of God through the Holy Spirit, in which he works in our lives day by day, to make us like His Son Jesus. This process begins the moment we become a member of His family through our faith in the Lord Jesus. We have confessed that we believe in the death and resurrection of Jesus Christ for our sins, have asked Him to forgive our sins, and have invited Him to be our Savior and Lord.

Sanctification also includes the good work that God is doing in my life right now, and He *will* complete it. It's important for me to be reminded of that, because it sometimes seems that I'll never change and nothing good will ever happen. God's good work in my life *will be completed.* I can count on it and look forward to it. It is what is called our living hope. I'll be able to look back someday with confidence and thank Him for helping me to keep going. While it includes the recovery from the pain I am experiencing now, the important thing is that it assures me that my faith will persevere. I can also know that He will continue His sanctifying work in my life, until He takes me to heaven to be with Him forever. At that moment, His work in me will be complete. And what God starts, He will finish. As my pastor says, "Whom God chooses, He never loses." I can count on that with great confidence!!

Thank You, Lord, that in You is fullness of joy and the assurance of the Holy Spirit You have given me as a gift, who is always with me and working out my sanctification, until I see You face to face. I know He will keep working until I am complete in You, and this gives me great confidence. Thank you for the assurance that my faith will persevere, because You are living in me. I am so grateful for the gift of Your grace in my life.

In the wonderful name of my Savior, Jesus Christ, Amen.

Ask, and it shall be given to you;
seek, and you shall find;
knock, and it shall be opened
to you.
For everyone who asks receives,
and he who seeks finds,
and to him who knocks
it shall be opened.

Or what man is there among you,
when his son shall ask him for
a loaf,
will give him a stone?
Or if he shall ask for a fish,
he will not give him a snake,
will he?

If you then, being evil, know
how to give good gifts to
your children,
how much more shall your
Heavenly Father give what is good
to those who ask Him!
Jesus ~ Matthew 7:7-11

Prayer is a mystery, and yet it is a very vital part of healing and recovery. God wants us to seek Him in prayer. He has made this very clear. He has said that whatever we need, we should come to Him in prayer, with thanksgiving, and present our requests to Him.

God is a very good Father. He is a better Father than the best of all earthly fathers. He will go beyond all my expectations to bring good to my life.

My soul, wait in silence for God
only,
For my hope is from Him.
He only is my rock and my
salvation,
My stronghold; I shall not be
shaken.
On God my salvation and my glory rest;
The rock of my strength,
my refuge is in God.
Trust in Him at all times, O people;
Pour out your heart before Him;
God is a refuge for us.
King David ~ Psalm 62:5-8

God is my refuge and my strength, and all my expectation is from Him and Him alone. It should always remain that way. I learned to have my expectation come from Him during a dark time in my life. It was when I couldn't trust anyone else, and all my trust had to be in God. So trust Him I did. I poured my heart out to Him. It was the most beautiful and rich time in my relationship with God. It was also when I was involved in a worship choir, and the music was always in my mind and heart. I truly miss that time.

For this reason I bow my knees before

the Father, from whom every family in heaven and on earth derives its name,

that He would grant you, to be strengthened with power through His

Spirit in the inner man, so that Christ may dwell in your hearts by faith;

and that you, being rooted and grounded in love may . . . know the love of Christ which surpasses knowledge, that you may be filled up to all the fullness of God.

Now to Him who is able to do exceedingly abundantly beyond all that we ask or think, according to His power that works within us, to Him be the glory in the church

and in Christ Jesus to all generations forever and ever. Amen.

The Apostle Paul ~ Ephesians 3:14-17, 19-21

What an incredible passage, with such an encouraging message! He is able to fill us with His power to give us His strength. He will dwell in us by faith as we are rooted and grounded in Him. We can know His deep and abiding love that is much more than a cerebral love. And best of all, we can be filled with all the fullness of God! This is an incredible and mysterious relationship. No wonder He is able to bring a victim of child sexual abuse out of deep depression through the Valley of Tears, and all the way to recovery. He is able to do it all! Not only that, but He is willing, based on our faith. Yes it does take time, and that is why we must never give up.

"He is able to do exceedingly abundantly beyond all that we ask or think, according to His power that works within us." That power originates from the Holy Spirit, whose power is limitless. Just think of the power that it took to raise Jesus from the dead—that is the power of the Holy Spirit. That is the same power He has to work in your life and mine. Incredible, huh? No wonder the Apostle Paul said, "to God be the Glory in the church and in Christ Jesus to all generations forever and ever!!"

Thank You, my Father, that You desire to answer our prayers with such greatness and might, beyond all that we can ask or think. You truly are good, benevolent, and wise, far beyond our imaginations. Please do a mighty work in us, and in everyone who reads this book, by Your power working in them.

In the powerful name of Jesus I pray,
Amen.

Come to Me, all who are weary and heavy-laden, and I will give you rest.

Take My yoke upon you, and learn from Me, for I am gentle and humble in heart; and you will find rest for your souls.

For My yoke is easy, and My burden is light.
Jesus ~ Matthew 11:28-30

It is impossible to improve on the words of Jesus. All I can do is to meditate on them and consider what He meant when He said them. During the time of Jesus' pilgrimage on this planet, a yoke used for oxen was custom-made out of a single piece of wood for one particular pair of oxen. It was designed in such a way that the load would be evenly distributed, so that neither load bearer of the two oxen carried a heavier load. This is how it is with our Lord. He desires we each have an even load, so that no one is over-burdened. He offers us His yoke, so that we will learn His ways and will find rest for our souls. His yoke is easy and His burden is light.

It is His desire to meet all our needs. There are times when he "*makes us lie down* in green pastures," so we will get the rest we need to recuperate for the next task. He will then restore our soul for whatever the next challenge is that He has for us. He can *always*, *always* be trusted to take us down the road to recovery. He heals us in whatever way He chooses, no matter how severe the pain may be or how long the walk through the *Valley of Tears* to recovery may take.

As I write this, the pain of the incest is a memory, but there is still pain in my life to deal with. At this time, I am going through a battle with severe chronic pain, due to nerve damage brought on by a very slow-growing tumor called a neurofibroma that was lodged inside my spinal cord a number of years ago. It is estimated that the tumor started growing when I was 24 years old. The result of removing the tumor by high-risk micro-neurosurgery was that neuropathy developed from the L5/S1 level in my back (low back just above my tail bone). This neuropathy extended from my low back all the way down to my feet. This may or may not have had anything to do with the incest back when my neurological and hormonal functions were developing, but I have been suffering with neurological pain for most of my adult life. I have had to learn to trust my Heavenly Father for His strength, understanding, wisdom, love, affection, and His will for every day of my life.

Sometimes when we are in the process of healing from one source of pain, we may encounter another. It is there that the Lord uses what we have learned in one trial to help us cope with another. There are no easy answers as to why we must suffer with pain in this way. It doesn't matter if the pain is physical, emotional, or psychological—only our Lord knows. But we do know these burdens make us stronger, as they force us to look to Him for our strength and wisdom. We can always count on the truth that "*His yoke is easy and His burden is light.*"

The Lord is my Shepherd.
I have all that I need.

He lets me rest in green meadows.
He leads me beside the peaceful streams.

He renews my strength.
He guides me along the right paths,
bringing honor to His name.

Even when I walk through the darkest valley,
I will not be afraid, for You are close beside me.
Your rod and your staff protect and comfort me.

You prepare a feast for me in the presence
of my enemies.
You honor me by anointing my head with oil.

Surely your goodness and unfailing love will
pursue me all the days of my life,
and I will live in the house of the Lord forever.
King David ~ Psalm 23:1-6 NLT

The Lord is my Shepherd. In John 10:11 the Lord *Jesus says, "I am the Good Shepherd. The Good Shepherd lays down His life for the sheep."* It goes on to say that He does this on His own initiative, because He wants to do this of His own free will and in obedience to His Father in Heaven.

The fact that He did lay His own life down and take it up again for us makes everything in Psalm 23 possible. He provides everything I need. That means He gives me what I *need* and not necessarily what I *want* (and not necessarily at the exact moment that *I feel* the need or want).

Psalm 23 states that He *makes* me *lie down* in green pastures. He not only provides a comfortable resting place, but He *makes me rest* at just the time when I need rest the most. We are most like sheep, when we feel helpless and do not know what is best for us. In fact, we are like sheep in so many ways. This is why our Lord Jesus calls Himself our Good Shepherd. He gives us the place and time to rest and allows us to lie down, regardless of what we or other people might think. This could be physical or emotional rest.

My Good Shepherd also leads me beside quiet waters. Running water is very dangerous for sheep. They do not know about undertows. They could easily drown in those fast-moving currents, but they do not realize it. John 10 says that the Good Shepherd knows His own and they know Him. They follow Him because they know His voice, so they will not be in danger of drowning or falling into a number of other dangers.

I remember a specific time when I was working at Western Seminary. I had been working very hard and engaging in other activities in the evening at church. I was taking private voice lessons and singing in a Masterworks Choir, practicing for an upcoming concert. I just didn't know when to say "No" to various activities. I was enjoying my work and activities too much. I began feeling very tired, and my doctor diagnosed my "tired feeling" as mononucleosis, often referred to as "the kissing disease" because it is so contagious. But I did not get this condition from sharing germs with anyone. I got it because I had a compromised immune system and had not listened to the warning signals my body was giving me. I had pushed myself to do too much, both at work and after work.

When I was diagnosed, I compounded the problem by thinking I could short-circuit the rules. I thought I could be the exception to my doctor's advice. I thought I could continue working and just cut down on my extra-curricular activities. When I shared this with my very wise roommate (who was also a nurse), she gave me some very sobering information that my doctor did not share with me. She told me that "mono" is a very serious condition. She said that if I did not treat it as my doctor suggested, by taking bed-rest for a couple weeks, my spleen could rupture. In other words, "mono" could be fatal. So I took a week off work and several weeks off my other activities, slowly recovering from this virus. Our Lord takes our need of rest very seriously.

The prophet Elijah is a very good example. He became very exhausted and depressed to the point of suicide, after an incredible spiritual victory over the evil prophets of Baal on Mt. Carmel. When it was all over, he killed all those evil prophets, thus enraging Queen Jezebel who now wanted to kill Elijah! So he took off and ran to what he thought was a safe place—Mt. Horeb, or Mt. Sinai, as we more commonly refer to it.

He ended up at Sinai, but it was Elijah's Good Shepherd who led him there because He knew that Elijah needed serious down time, along with some emotional and spiritual rest. Elijah also needed some time with the Lord for serious counseling, just like we do when we are depressed and worn out. The Lord took Elijah to this perfect resting place where He fed him, made him rest by still waters, and spoke some needed words of wisdom to the misguided prophet. You can read his story in its entirety in the Book of 1 Kings 18-19.

Yes, the Good Shepherd takes very good care of us. He protects us and provides for us. But the best part is that He restores our soul. *For an incest victim that is everything*. For although incest is a physical assault, what is really damaged is our soul. We can trust Him for protection, when we can trust no one else. *He and He alone is our Protector and our Provider.* To me, this means a greater sense of wholeness.

This Good Shepherd may take us through some very dark times along the way. But it's encouraging to know He is right there with us, as we go through "*The Valley of Tears*", while we are being led through the *Valley of the Shadow of Death*. It is pain that takes us through a temporary dark time. The *Valley of the Shadow of Death* is just a shadow. And a shadow cannot hurt you. It is harmless. You may feel like you want to die, but it's just a feeling that will pass like a long afternoon shadow.

Even though we will go through some emotionally dark times, like the "*Valley of Tears*" and the valley that feels like death in our pain, we need not fear because our Good Shepherd is always with us. For those of us who belong to Him, His goodness and love will accompany us all our lives—every single day of our life on this planet. Then we will, in an instant, go to live in His house forever—free of emotional and physical pain. That is something to live for every day!

Notes . . .

Chapter 5

Special Psalms to Encourage You

My God of mercy shall come to meet me at every corner. (Psalm 59:10 NKJV Lit.)

There are many more Scriptures that became "verses of survival" in my personal journal than what appear in the last chapter, but for lack of space I could not list them all. However, in this chapter I have expanded on a couple of chapters in the Psalms that were and continue to be especially encouraging to me.

During my most trying times when I was in my dark depression, I spent a lot of time reading and meditating on the Psalms. There is nothing like the Book of Psalms that can give me a sense of the nearness of God, an incredible peace, and an understanding of how our Lord responds to His people in their time of need. That is why I have dedicated this chapter to some of my meditations (in their entirety) on some of my favorite Psalms that really helped me during my time of deepest distress.

Meditations on Psalm 139

1 O Lord, You have searched me and
known me.

2 You know when I sit down and when
I rise;
You understand my thought from afar.

3 You scrutinize my path and my lying down,
And are intimately acquainted with all
my ways.

4 Even before there is a word on my tongue,
Behold, O Lord, You know it all.

5 You have enclosed me behind and
before,
And laid Your hand upon me.

6 Such knowledge is too wonderful
for me;
It is too high; I cannot attain to it.

King David ~ Psalm 139:1-6

This is just the first six verses of Psalm 139. Like King David, I find such knowledge too wonderful for *me* to comprehend. When I meditate on these truths about my Father in heaven, I come to know Him a little better and it becomes a little easier to trust Him. As I do this, I am drawn a little closer to Him in the process. Not only do I need to feel secure in myself and in my God, as others observe what I am going through; but I also find that I need a good understanding of the things He has given me to experience.

❖ ***Verse 1*** ***O Lord, You have searched me and known me.***

He knows me to the depth of my soul. For an unbeliever this could be frightening. Before I knew Him, I was very fearful of God's great power and His perfect knowledge of me. The fact that there is nothing about me that is beyond God's scope of knowledge is both encouraging and overwhelming.

This first verse says that God probes my inward being and has perfect personal knowledge of me, because He created me. But God does not probe or search me for something He does not already know. He searches me out, so that He can *reveal to me what I need to know about myself. It is so that I will learn what is inside my soul*. This is interesting:

. . . but just as it is written,
"Things which eye has not seen and
ear has not heard,
And which have not entered the
heart of man,
All that God has prepared for
those who love Him."

For to us God revealed them through the Spirit; for the Spirit searches all things, even the depths of God.

For who among men knows the thoughts of a man except the spirit of the man, which is in him? Even so the thoughts of God no one knows except the Spirit of God.

Now we have received, not the spirit of the world, but the Spirit who is from God, that we might know the things freely given to us by God,
The Apostle Paul ~1 Corinthians 2:9-12

In one sense, the thought of God knowing all my secrets can give me an uncomfortable feeling. It shows that, as much as I value my human independence, I cannot be independent from God's knowledge and His understanding of who I am and what I am like.

The first thought I have about this is rather negative from a human point of view. It means He knows all about my sin and my personal secrets. If I have not confessed my sins to Him, repented of them, become completely open with God, and then made the decision to turn from my evil ways, it will affect my fellowship with Him. The bottom line is that if I choose to be a secretive person, it simply wouldn't work when it comes to my relationship with God. But there is no need to be that way, as He is such a good, loving, and forgiving God. As *1 John 1:9* clearly states:

> *If we confess our sins, He is faithful and righteous to forgive us our sins and to cleanse us from all unrighteousness.*

My second thought on this subject is more positive. When I am afraid and have nightmares, when I can't sleep, when I'm in despair, or when the demons of trauma haunt me—I can always count on my God to be there with me to comfort me and chase the demons of trauma away. Furthermore, He knows and cares deeply with a compassion that comes with indescribable tenderness. This is one thing that makes God so amazing.

The Lord has probed my soul—my heart, my mind, my will, and my emotions. He knows things that I am not even aware of. His knowledge of me is perfect and infinite.

As A. W. Tozer puts it:

> "*God knows instantly and effortlessly all matter and all matters, all mind and every mind, all spirit and all spirits, all being and every being, all creaturehood and all creatures, every plurality and all pluralities, all law and every law, all relations, all causes, all thoughts, all mysteries, all enigmas, all feeling, all desires, every unuttered secret, all thrones and dominions, all personalities, all things visible and invisible in heaven and on earth, motion, space, time, life, death, good, evil, heaven, and hell. Because God knows all things perfectly, He knows nothing better than any other thing, but all things*

equally well. He never discovers anything. He is never surprised, never amazed. He never wonders about anything nor (except when drawing men and women out for their own good) does He seek information or ask questions." [1]

❖ ***Verse 2*** ***You know when I sit down and when I rise;***
You understand my thought from afar.

My Father God knows everything I do: getting up, lying down, going out, and coming in. He knows the reasons for all my strange behavior and He *knows* my past, present, and future. My Heavenly Father could understand me at that time because He was right there with me, grieving the terrible traumatic experience and the loss of my childhood and self-esteem. He had His hand on me and He never left me.

❖ ***Verse 2*** ***He understands my thought from afar.***

He knows every thought that crosses my mind at every moment in time. He knows the thoughts that I dwell on and why I dwell on them. He knows what I stop to meditate on. He knows what I continually wish for. He understands my deepest desires. He knows how difficult it was for me to forgive the man who abused and traumatized me. He knows why he did it and all about his problems. He knows how insecure

I feel because of the trauma. He understands all my thoughts and feelings about what happened to me.

❖ ***Verse 3*** ***You scrutinize my path and my lying down,***
And are intimately acquainted with all my ways.

He (my Heavenly Father) knows everywhere I go and when I sleep. He knows everything about _ALL MY WAYS_. He also knows where I am at every moment. This is especially comforting for those of us who have been abused—when we thought we were in the wrong place at the wrong time, because someone other than an immediate family member abused us, or because we were actually in a place *where we should have been safe in our own homes!* Either way, our Heavenly Father knows right where we are and He knows what will happen to us there. He is the Protector of those who cannot protect themselves, and He protects *all those* who belong to Him.

In the context of God being fully aware of "my path and my lying down," He is aware of every detail of my life on a close and personal level. He always was and He always will be.

This is very difficult to understand. But upon further contemplation, it's comforting to realize that He, knowing the hearts of all of us, did not and would not interfere with my father's free will. He was there, knowing everything there is to know about me and everything about the inner workings of my soul and temperament. He knew what it would take for me to heal, and He set me on that path of healing. As Psalm 139:3 says, "*He is intimately acquainted with all my ways.*" Using that knowledge, He led me to just the right people who would be instrumental in the healing process. *And He will do just the same thing for anyone who seriously desires recovery from trauma.*

❖ ***Verse 4*** ***Even before there is a word on my tongue,***
Behold, O Lord, You know it all.

He knows me so well that He knows what I will say before I speak, and He is aware of what I am thinking about, good or bad.

❖ ***Verse 5*** ***You have enclosed me behind and before,***
And laid Your hand upon me.

God has put a strong hedge of protection around me, and His hand is always on me. This is His way of protecting me from evil. He protects me from evil thoughts and from those who would put those thoughts there (whether they are from people, the media, or something we have read). He protects me from people who would discourage me or cause me emotional pain. He protects me while I am in depressive moods, by helping me to shut out ridicule, fears, and whatever has the power to hurt me. My own thoughts can be destructive, and the enemy can use them against biblical truth.

Another way He protects me is by my intake of the Scriptures. As I read and meditate on Scripture and other good books written by men and women of God, I gain great power and strength against the enemy. The Scriptures are, in fact, a part of His hedge of protection around me.

My past was encompassed by His presence. He was there and His hand of protection was on me, in spite of my being unaware of Him. The same is true of my present and my future. He was there, He is here now, and He always will be.

❖ ***Verse 6*** ***Such knowledge is too wonderful for me;***
It is too high, I cannot attain to it.

The knowledge of these verses is so amazing and wonderful, it is far above human comprehension. I believe that is why King David *says, "It is too high, I cannot attain to it."* It is incredibly powerful. I trust in my Lord that it is true. I choose to believe that my God will use this knowledge to encourage me, comfort me, and give me the confidence I need in every circumstance I face. I know that He knows me better than I know myself, He understands my thoughts and emotions, and He knows all about my environment. He is fully aware of my surroundings and knows intimately all about what happened to me. He is protecting me from all evil, and nothing can harm me apart from His will.

I cannot comprehend this truth in my emotions and find it hard to respond to intellectually, but it is true.

❖ ***Verses 7-8*** ***Where can I go from Your Spirit?***
Or where can I flee from Your presence?
If I ascend to heaven, You are there;
If I make my bed in Sheol, behold, You are there.

God is with me no matter where I am or how I'm responding. He is with me when things are going great and I'm feeling good about everything (ascending to heaven), and He is with me when my spirit is low and I am in the pit of depression (in Sheol – the Old Testament place of the dead). He is *always* with me.

❖ ***Verses 9-10*** ***If I take the wings of the dawn,***
If I dwell in the remotest part of the sea,
Even there Your hand will lead me,

And Your right hand will lay hold of me.

Whether I am literally flying through the visible atmosphere or going to the remotest part of the sea, or whether I am choosing an escape route in my times of deepest depression—God's hand is still holding onto me, regardless of my location or condition. I see this passage as my attempt to escape, hide in my pain, and withdraw, which I found myself doing on many occasions. These were the times in which I reached out to Him for His assurance, and He responded to me with these comforting words, "*You are not alone; you will never be alone.*" This came through spending time in the Scriptures and meditating on Psalms like this one.

- ***Verses 11-12***

If I say, "Surely the darkness will overwhelm me,
And the light around me will be night,"
Even the darkness is not dark to You,
And the night is as bright as the day.
Darkness and light are alike to You.

I was afraid of the prospect of growing up and living as an adult in that dark world. All of this overwhelmed me. But my Heavenly Father sees through my fears in perfect perspective. They are not dark to God and they are not a threat to Him. To Him, all is light, and He knows my future in perfect clarity.

- ***Verses 13-15*** ***For You formed my inward parts;***
You wove me in my mother's womb.
I will give thanks to You,
for I am fearfully and wonderfully made;
Wonderful are Your works,
And my soul knows it very well.
My frame was not hidden from You,
When I was made in secret,
And skillfully wrought in the depths of the earth.

The Lord made me physically, emotionally, and spiritually in every intricate detail. (And He did the same with you and every other human that has ever been created). He gathered all the DNA (that made up the person that I would be) with great expertise and skill in my mother's womb, and He put me together with incredible tenderness. He knows how I tick, and He knows what I can and cannot handle on every level (down to the smallest cell). Since He made me, He knows how to heal me. He is the master craftsman. This means that He can transform the wounded person that I was or am today into a new person of strength and dignity. As it says in 2 Corinthians 5:17, *". . . old things have passed away; behold, the new has come."*

❖ ***Verse 16*** ***Your eyes have seen my unformed substance;***
And in Your book were all written,
The days that were ordained for me,
When as yet there was not one of them.

Since my Lord God saw me and formed me in the womb of my mother, He has known me on a deep personal level since my conception, the first day of my life.

But there is more. This verse says that in His book every day of my life has a journal entry with all the days of my life written down. God knows what each day of my life would bring, whether good, bad, or terrible, and He calls these days "ordained." The events of these days were written in His journal before I was even born! He knew from the beginning what would happen with my father, and He had a plan.

I say with great faith that the same is true of you. He already knows you intimately. He knows all your days and He has a plan for all of them—no matter what tragic event has happened to you, and no matter what trauma you have suffered or are currently suffering from. If that sounds a bit trite, believe me, nothing with our Creator God is trite. His plan is magnificent, loving, powerful, and, as it states in Genesis 1:31, *"it was very good."* If you put your faith in the Lord Jesus, He will not leave you in the condition you are in. He is far from finished with you. If you belong to Him, the outcome will be *very good, indeed!*

Children of the Heavenly Father

Children of the heavenly Father
Safely in His bosom gather;
Nestling bird nor star in heaven
Such a refuge ever was given.

God His own does tend and nourish,
In His holy courts they flourish;
From all evil things He spares them,
In His mighty arms bears them.

Neither life nor death shall ever
from the Lord His children sever;
Unto them His grace He showeth,
and their sorrows all He knoweth.

Praise the Lord in joyful numbers,
your Protector never slumbers;
At the will of your Defender,
Every foeman must surrender.

Though He giveth or He taketh,
God His children never forsaketh;
His the loving purpose solely
To preserve them pure and holy.

— *Karolina Wihelmina Sandell-Berg* [2]
1855

Thoughts from Psalm 25

1 O Lord, I give my life to You.
2 I trust in You, my God!
Do not let me be disgraced,
or let my enemies rejoice in
my defeat.
3 No one who trusts in You will
ever be disgraced, but
disgrace comes to those who
try to deceive others.

4 Show me the right path, O Lord;
point out the road for me to follow.
5 Lead me by Your truth and teach me,
for You are the God who saves me.
All day long I put my hope in You.
6 Remember, O Lord, Your compassion
and Your unfailing love which
You have shown from long ages past.
7 Do not remember the rebellious sins
of my youth.
Remember me in the light of Your
unfailing love,
for You are merciful, O Lord.

8 The Lord is good and does what is right;
He shows the proper path to those
who go astray.
9 He leads the humble in doing right,
teaching them His way.

10 The LORD leads with unfailing love
and faithfulness to all who
keep His covenant and obey
His demands.

11 For the honor of Your name, O LORD,
forgive my many sins.
12 Who are those who fear the LORD?
He will show them the path
they should choose.
13 They will live in prosperity,
and their children will
inherit the land.

14 The LORD is a friend to those who
fear Him.
He teaches them His covenant.
15 My eyes are always on the LORD,
for He rescues me from the
traps of my enemies.

16 Turn to me and have mercy,
for I am alone and in deep distress.
17 My problems go from bad to worse.
Oh, save me from them all!
18 Feel my pain and see my trouble.
Forgive all my sins.

19 See how many enemies I have
and how viciously they hate me!
20 Protect me! Rescue my life from them!

Do not let me be disgraced, for
in You I take refuge.
21 *May integrity and honesty protect me,*
for I put my hope in you.

22 *O God, ransom Israel*
from all its troubles.
King David ~ Psalm 25 **NLT**

If I did not know this was a Psalm of David, Shepherd King in ancient Israel, I would have believed that a victim of abuse must have written it. There is so much in this psalm that a person who has suffered from the trauma of incest can relate to.

The first thing I notice is that there is much that we can learn, about who God is and what He is like, just by reading Psalms like this. There is so much of God's character taught here and throughout the Book of Psalms. I recommend reading this Psalm with a colored pencil and highlighting words that show the character of God. Please note how the Psalmist highlights God's character in verses 5-8, 10, and 16.

Second, I notice the writer of this Psalm knows what it means to be shamed. In verses 2, 3, and 20, he pleads for the Lord to protect him from disgrace and defeat.

Third, this person is very well aware of his need for forgiveness and comes to God in verses 5, 7, 8, and 11. This is so important if a person expects to receive help from The Lord.

Fourth, this person pleads for mercy and compassion. If an incest victim wrote this Psalm, it would make perfect sense:

Turn to me and have mercy,
for I am alone and in deep distress.
My problems go from bad to worse
Oh, save me from them all!
Feel my pain and see my trouble,
Forgive all my sins.
See how many enemies I have
and how viciously they hate me!
Protect me! Rescue my life from them!
Do not let me be disgraced, for in You
I take refuge.
Verses 16-20 NLT

This person is desperate. But this was not written by an incest victim. It was written by an ancient Israeli king seeking deliverance from a person wanting to end his life. This shows me how much God's Word is powerful and relevant to speak to the needs of *anyone who is in deep pain*. He intended it to be that way.

This reminds me of a day when *I was in so much pain* from the wounds I had experienced, I was desperate for God to intervene. In my mind and in my searching, He was my only hope for relief from my pain. In my desperation, I found myself literally begging my Heavenly Father to release me from the prison house of pain I was experiencing. My pain was so deep and intense that the only thing I could think of was the pain I was feeling. God responded to my begging prayers, but He did not respond in quite the way I anticipated.

In my prayer time, I was brought face to face with the Spirit of God who gave me the realization that my focus had been strictly on me. I was concentrating so hard on the outcome that *I* wanted God to produce, that I forgot Who I was praying to for that answer. I was so focused on the gift that I was asking for, that I forgot the gracious Giver of mercy and compassion. The Lord showed me in that moment that I had to put my focus back on to the God of Grace, who loves me with the everlasting love that I craved.

I also had to stop thinking about my comfort and go back to thinking about honoring Him with my life—even if it meant honoring Him with my pain. This meant being thankful for His grace to bring me through each day, for His shed blood on the cross that brought me from darkness to forgiveness, and furthermore, for the blood that redeemed me and made me His child.

Finally, and very importantly, I learned that I had to empty myself and to give my pain to Him. I had to say, "*Lord, this day I give my pain to You. You know what I can handle. In Your sovereignty and blessed control, please help me each day to continue on in Your strength.*"

Besides meditating and memorizing Scripture, it often helps to personalize Scripture. Put yourself into Psalm 25. Make it your own and pray it back to God. This will not only teach you how to pray, but will also aid in the meditation and memorization process.

Where the Psalm uses personal pronouns such as the word "me," substitute your own name. As you journal, in the context of making this verse your own, you may personalize this and other psalms in this way:

O God, ransom ____________________ *(your name here)*
from all her (or his) troubles. *Psalm 25:22*

This prayer is asking God to deliver you from all your troubles. So you may fill in the blank with your name.

My Beloved

by Annie Clarke

"And I will betroth thee unto Me forever; . . ."

Perhaps as the Israelites are called out of Egypt ~ Hosea 2:19

He said: "Will You go with Me
Where shadows eclipse the light?"
And she answered: "My Lord, I will
follow Thee
Far under the stars at night."
But He said, "No starlight pierces the gloom
Of the valley Your feet must tread;
But it leads you on to a cross and tomb—"
"But I go with You," she said.

"*Count* the cost; can you pay the price—
Be a dumb thing led;
Laid on an altar of sacrifice?"
"Bind me there, my Lord—
Or hold me with Your wounded hand;
For I fear the knife and the piercing nail,
And I shrink from the burning brand.
Yet where You go I will go,
Though the way be lonely and dread—"
His voice was tender, and sweet, and low—
"You shall go with Me," He said.

And none knew the anguish sore
Or the night of the way she came;
Alone, alone with the cross she bore,

Alone in her grief and shame.
Brought to the altar of sacrifice,
There as a dumb thing slain:

Was the guerdon* more than the bitter price
Was it worth the loss and pain?
Ask the seed-corn, when the grain
Ripples its ripened gold;
Ask the sower when, after toil and pain,
He garners the hundred-fold.
He said (and His voice was glad and sweet):
"Was it worth the cost, My own?"
And she answered, low at His pierced feet,
"I found at the end of the pathway lone
NOT DEATH, BUT LIFE ON A THRONE!" [3]

*Reward

Meditations on Psalm 86

1 Incline Your ear, O LORD, and answer me;
For I am afflicted and needy.

As a victim of abuse, I feel afflicted and needy. The Lord knows this, and He is ready and willing to answer me when I call upon Him.

2 Preserve my soul, for I am godly;
O You my God, save Your
servant who trusts in You.

For the most part, the wounds of incest are wounds of the soul. He will preserve my soul, and He will save me from this trauma, because I am entrusting myself to His care. He is the One Person who can truly be trusted with my soul.

3 Be gracious to me, O LORD,
For to You I cry all day long

4 Make glad the soul of Your servant,
For to You, O LORD, I lift
up my soul.

The one thing I need when I am in the deep darkness of depression is *God's magnificent grace.* The Psalmist prays for God to be gracious. This is a powerful force of strength from God that I can lean on all day long. *When I know and really believe that His grace is sufficient, I know that I can rest in Him.*

5 For You, LORD, are good, and ready
to forgive,
And abundant in lovingkindness to
all who call upon You.

6 Give ear, O LORD, to my prayer;
And give heed to the voice
of my supplications!

Healing is a matter of faith and trust. It is vitally necessary to *trust in the goodness of God*. I must believe that *He is good and ready to forgive both my perpetrator's sins and my own*. I had to learn that no one is out of the reach of God's forgiveness. As God's child, that means no one in my life should be out of the reach of my forgiveness as well.

7 In the day of my trouble
I shall call upon You,
For You will answer me.

8 There is no one like You
among the gods, O LORD;
Nor are there any works like
Yours.

When I am in pain, I can always call on my Lord Yahweh [4] for help and He will answer me. There is no one like my Lord and no one can match His works!

> 9 *All nations whom You have*
> *made shall come and worship*
> *before You, O Lord;*
> *And they shall glorify Your*
> *name.*
> 10 *For You are great and do wondrous*
> *deeds;*
> *You alone are God.*

When I am overwhelmed, it really helps to get a glimpse of the greatness of God. There will be a time when my God will rule the nations on this earth. They will all come and bow before Him and honor His name. He does great and wonderful things, and all the nations will have to acknowledge Him as King of kings and Lord of lords. When I am blinded by the pain, it really helps to look at my King and realize *He is in control and that He alone is God*. Truly, if He is King of the nations and controls their every move, He can handle the situation of my pain. I know the situation the nations are in, and it seems to me that they are as much out of control as my emotions. But as God is the Blessed Controller of all things, He can easily control both the confusion of the nations and my confused emotions at the same time. My personal Lord and Savior is He Whose name is the King of kings, the Lord of lords, the Alpha and the Omega, and the

Beginning and the End (that is, the One Who sees the Beginning from the End). He is in complete control of every person from the highest ruler to the lowest municipal officer. He has it all in His control.

11 *Teach me Your way, O Lord;*
I will walk in Your truth;
Unite my heart to fear
Your name.
12 *I will give thanks to You,*
O Lord my God, with
all my heart,
And will glorify Your name
forever.

Emotional healing comes when I learn *the ways of my God* and live in His truth. When my heart and mind are no longer so distracted that I cannot concentrate and focus on the task at hand, then my mind and heart will be united to reverence the name of my God. When that happens, I will be able to live in harmony with myself, instead of being controlled by fear.

13 *For Your lovingkindness*
toward me is great,
And You have delivered my
soul from the depths of
Sheol. [5]

When I trust Him and put my focus on His greatness and His wonderful works, *I can't help but see that His lovingkindness on my behalf is very great.* This Psalm says that He delivers King David's soul from the depths of Sheol, the Old Testament place of the dead. It was like saying that God had delivered his soul from death. In the same way, He delivered my soul from deep darkness—the best way I know to describe my most debilitating depression. In order for Him to be able to deliver me from deep darkness, He would have to enter that darkness. This is another way that I am assured that He knows exactly what I have been going through.

> 14 *O God, arrogant men have risen*
> *up against me,*
> *And a band of violent men*
> *have sought my life,*
> *And they have not set You*
> *before them.*

It was only one man who violated me and betrayed my trust. This verse reminds me of him. He seemed to be very arrogant and proud, but over the years I have realized that he wasn't all that proud. I have come to believe that he was very insecure and needed to use others to make himself feel strong. He used his wife and children to build his ego, and he used us in very hurtful ways. This verse describes him very accurately in that it says "*they (or he) have not set You before them.*" In other words, my father was not thinking about what the Lord thought about his actions, when he acted immorally with his alcohol abuse, sexual dysfunctions, and verbal abuse.

> [15] *But You, O LORD, are a God*
> *merciful and gracious,*
> *Slow to anger and abundant*
> *in lovingkindness and truth.*
>
> [16] *Turn to me, and be gracious to me;*
> *O grant Your strength to Your servant, . . .*
> *King David ~ Psalm 86: 15-16*

This is what my Heavenly Father is like. This is what attracted me to Him and what makes me love Him. The positive ending is that *my Heavenly Father, is merciful and gracious, slow to anger, and abundant in lovingkindness and truth*. He is the one I need. I ask Him to turn to me, and I ask for His grace and His strength to encourage me.

The Beauty of Psalm 55

1 Listen to my prayer, O God.
Do not ignore my cry for help!

2 Please listen and answer me,
for I am overwhelmed by my troubles.

3 My enemies shout at me,
making loud and wicked threats.
They bring trouble on me
and angrily hunt me down.

4 My heart pounds in my chest;
the terror of death assaults me.

5 Fear and trembling overwhelm me,
and I can't stop shaking.

6 Oh, that I had wings like a dove;
then I would fly away and rest!

7 I would fly far away to the quiet of
the wilderness.

8 How quickly I would escape—
far from this wild storm of hatred.

Interlude

9 Confuse them, LORD, and frustrate their
plans,
for I see violence and conflict in the city.

10 It's walls are patrolled day and night against
invaders,
but the real danger is wickedness
within the city.

11 Everything is falling apart,
threats and cheating are rampant in the
streets.

16 But I will call on God
And the LORD will rescue me.

17 Morning, noon, and night
I cry out in my distress,
and the LORD hears my voice.

18 He ransoms me and keeps me safe
from the battle waged against me,
Though many still oppose me.

19 God who has ruled forever,
will hear me and humble them.
For my enemies refuse to change their ways;
they do not fear God.

22 Give your burdens to the LORD,
and He will take care of you;
He will not permit the godly to slip and fall.

23 But You, O God, will send the wicked down
to the pit of destruction.
Murderers and liars will die young,
but I am trusting You to save me.
King David ~ Psalm 55:1-11, 16-19, 22-23 NLT

He filled my heart with incredible peace and he gave me Christian friends who supported me. What a gracious God I trust! What a loving and faithfully true Father I have, who has redeemed me from my overwhelming fears! He showed me I can always come to Him with my troubles, regardless of my circumstances. He will always take care of me.

Who is God to an Incest Victim?

Because incest generally happens during childhood when our concept of life is just being formed, it greatly affects our view of God. It usually gives us a distorted, damaged idea of what God is really like and how He feels about us. Yet, if we are to experience deep inner healing, we *must* know God for who He is.

A child's concept of God is wrapped up in his (or her) parents or in whoever is responsible for him. If my parents were kind and generous, then I would naturally believe that God is kind and generous. [6] However, if my parents were strict and demanding, what I believe about God would take on that characteristic as well. In the case of incest, if my parents (or even one of my parents) violated my trust, took advantage of my vulnerability and weakness as a child, stole my personhood, and deprived me of the emotional raw material needed to cope with life, how could I possibly trust a God who is infinitely more powerful and who has absolute authority over my life?

As I ponder these thoughts, I realize the only way to trust God is to find another way to get to know Him more accurately. This is exactly what He wants us to do. He doesn't want us to be afraid of Him or to think of Him in an inaccurate way, because of the false example set by our parental role model.

The only way to develop this kind of relationship with God is to spend a lot of time with Him. It is just like developing a relationship with any other person. The more time you spend with someone, the more you get to know them. God has revealed Himself in the Bible, and that's where we get to know Him.

Divine healing requires a type of radical spiritual heart surgery. If one is to undergo this type of heart surgery, this person must be able to trust the Surgeon. Read books on the attributes of God. *I can't emphasize enough how important it is to spend time with God every day. Pray for understanding and clarity of mind.* He is faithful to true seekers and *He will reveal Himself to those who search for Him with all their heart.*

The following is an article by A.W. Tozer, which is titled "God is Easy to Live With" and reprinted with permission.

God is Easy to Live With

A.W. Tozer

Satan's first attack upon the human race was his sly effort to destroy Eve's confidence in the kindness of God. Unfortunately for her and for us he succeeded too well. From that day, men have had a false conception of God, and it is exactly this that has cut out from under them the ground of righteousness and driven them to reckless and destructive living.

Nothing twists and deforms the soul more than a low or unworthy conception of God. Certain sects, such as the Pharisees, while they held that God was stern and austere, yet managed to maintain a fairly high level of external morality; but their righteousness was only outward. Inwardly they were "whited sepulchers," as our Lord Himself told them. Their wrong conception of God resulted in a wrong idea of worship. To a Pharisee, the service of God was a bondage which he did not love but from which he could not escape without a loss too great to bear. The God of the Pharisee was not a God easy to live with, so his religion became grim and hard and loveless. It had to be so, for *our notion of God must always determine the quality of our religion* (or our faith).

Much of Christianity since the days of Christ's flesh (the time He spent on earth) has also been grim and severe. And the cause has been the same—an unworthy or an inadequate view of God. Instinctively we try to be like our God, and if He is conceived to be stern and exacting, so we ourselves will be.

From a failure to properly understand God comes a world of unhappiness among good Christian people even today. The Christian life is thought to be a glum, unrelieved cross-carrying life under the eye of a stern Father who expects much and excuses nothing. He is austere, peevish, highly temperamental, and extremely hard to please. The kind of life which springs out of such notions must of necessity be but a parody on the true life in Christ.

It is most important to our spiritual welfare that we hold in our minds always a right conception of God. If we think of Him as cold and exacting we shall find it impossible to love Him, and our lives will be ridden with servile fear. If, again, we hold Him to be kind and understanding, our whole inner life will mirror that idea.

The truth is that God is the most winsome of all beings and His service one of unspeakable pleasure. He is all love, and those who trust Him need never know anything but that love. He is just, indeed, and He will not condone sin; but through the blood of the everlasting covenant He is able to act toward us exactly as if we had never sinned. Toward the trusting sons of men His mercy will always triumph over justice.

The fellowship of God is delightful beyond all telling. He communes with His redeemed ones in an easy, uninhibited fellowship that is restful and healing to the soul. He is not sensitive nor selfish nor temperamental. What He is today we shall find Him tomorrow and the next day and the next year. He is not hard to please, though He may be hard to satisfy. He expects of us only what He has Himself first supplied. He is quick to mark every simple effort to please Him, and just as quick to overlook imperfections when He knows we meant to do His will. He loves us for ourselves and values our love more than galaxies of new created worlds.

Unfortunately, many Christians cannot get free from their perverted notions of God, and these notions poison their hearts and destroy their inward freedom. These friends serve God grimly, as the elder brother did, doing what is right without enthusiasm and without joy, and seem altogether unable to understand the buoyant, spirited celebration when the prodigal comes home. Their idea of God rules out the possibility of His being happy in His people and they attribute the singing and shouting to sheer fanaticism. Unhappy souls, these, doomed to go heavily on their melancholy way, grimly determined to do right if the heavens fail and to be on the winning side in the day of judgment.

How good it would be if we could learn that God is easy to live with. He remembers our frame and knows that we are dust. He may sometimes chasten us, it is true, but even this He does with a smile, the proud, tender smile of a Father who is bursting with pleasure over an imperfect but promising son who is coming every day to look more and more like the one whose child he is.

Some of us are religiously jumpy and self-conscious because we know that God sees our every thought and is acquainted with all our ways. We need not be. God is the sum of all patience and the essence of kindly good will. We please Him most, not by frantically trying to make ourselves good, but by throwing ourselves into His arms with all our imperfections and believing that He understands everything and loves us still.[7]

God of the Impossible

Oh God of the impossible!
Since all things are to Thee
But soil in which Omnipotence
Can work almightily,

Each trial may to us become
The means that will display
How over what seems impossible
Our God has perfect sway!

The very storms that beat upon
Our little barque so frail*
But manifest Your power to quell
All forces that assail.

The things that are to us too hard,
The foes that are too young,
Are just the very ones that may
Awake a triumph song.

O God of the impossible,
When we no hope can see,
Grant us the faith that still believes
ALL possible to Thee! [7]

—J.H.S.

**a sailing ship, typically with three masts, in which the foremast and mainmast are square-rigged and the mizzenmast is rigged fore-and-aft.*

Notes . . .

Chapter 6

Getting Through the Recovery Process

God always hears, and He never forgets. His silence does not mean that He is not listening and is not planning . . . He is patiently waiting for the moment to arrive when He may prove His love and His power . . . God is always on time; never behind and never ahead.

–Men Who Prayed

The Recovery Process

Before I get into the recovery Process part of this chapter, I would like to clarify what I believe recovery from the trauma of incest *is* and what it *is not.* When I was going through the most painful part of the counseling process, I desired and craved what I thought of as "complete recovery." Part of my problem was impatience and unrealistic expectations. I wanted to get through the painful process quickly so I could get on with my life. I wanted to get past the first step I was on, so I could move to the next step and the next. But then I came to the realization that perhaps a victim of father-daughter or adult-child incest *never completely recovers in the "normal" sense* and that some the deepest scars may stay with him (or her) for life.

Now don't get me wrong. If you are a victim or a survivor, don't let that discourage or demoralize you. You *can* get to a place, where you can become free from a great deal of the pain and trauma. I also believe that the scars will always be there to some extent, and they can be opened at any time. You need to be prepared for that possibility. When a person goes through counseling or any kind of therapy for these wounds, sometimes all the issues are not addressed before the circumstances of life interfere, and the counseling relationship has to be terminated.

When I say that I believe a victim of incest never fully recovers, you may think that sounds like a lack of faith on my part. Well, it's not a lack of faith. It is reality. Life happens, and sometimes it interferes with your best-laid plans for recovery. But God's plans for our recovery *always* continue. This is why you must always be pro-active in your pursuit of growth and healing. My hope is to encourage you to get started on your journey toward recovery and to help you develop a *recovery mindset,* as you walk through *The Valley of Tears*.

There were times during the recovery process when I was so depressed that I could not function. During these times, the greatest effort I could perform was to get out of bed in the morning or produce a smile, since it was necessary for my job. Most of the time, all I could do was to survive. If I didn't need my job for financial survival, I wouldn't have even moved all day. That is what I will call *ground zero*. Ground zero is a place where I was so numb I couldn't describe what I felt or why. I couldn't concentrate on anything vital. Because I was suicidal twice in three years during my counseling years, it was risky to live alone or carry any responsibility, and yet, I did what I had to do—just to survive.

There will always be some residual scars and wounds that are never dealt with for one reason or another. What we are talking about is the *progress* of surviving on an emotional and relational level. It is growing in our faith through a very close and personal relationship with the Lord Jesus, trusting Him every day, one step at a time, to take us up from ground zero to a place of joy and trust.

Do not let this thought become a discouragement to you. And do not entertain the thought that all you have to look forward to is partial recovery. Spanning the distance between ground zero and thriving emotionally, *even with scars from past wounds,* is a very long distance that I never could have traveled without the work of God in my life. It is definitely something that I give praise to God for, rejoice over, and thank Him for every day.

Some of the steps in the recovery process may include facing our pain personally or include confronting the person responsible for causing this pain (especially if he or she is living, if we have access to him, or he has some involvement in our lives). In my case, my father died before I graduated from high school, and my mother was not able to help with my emotional pain. She did help briefly when she learned about the incest, and as a family we did confront my father. But then she realized that my father would not cooperate with the restrictions the family placed on him. She didn't understand my need for emotional support and healing. It was a process of time, and it would require outside help. It required *counseling.* My mother further didn't realize that giving me emotional support would require a process of time and that *it would* involve outside help. But I believe she feared the exposure that acquiring outside help might mean *for her.* It might mean that she would be considered "an enabler." But for me, at that time being a victim, it meant that I would receive much needed counseling, and someone I could talk to who would truly understand my feelings.

The first time I asked her if I could see a counselor, I was still in high school. My father had just slapped me into a corner, because I had failed to perform an after school chore. Physical abuse of this nature was not his usual behavior. This type of abuse, coupled with the strain of the sexual, verbal, and emotional abuse I had been under for the previous five years, was too much for me emotionally, and I just couldn't take it anymore. But the slapping itself wasn't treated with concern by my mother, because she didn't connect the dots. However, it did greatly concern and upset me.

When my father left the room, I was physically shaking. I felt like I had enough of my dad's abuse, so I approached my mother to ask her if she would send me to a counselor. This was not a spontaneous thought on my part. I had been thinking about it for some time. I had even thought about going to my school counselor, but I knew I could not put any more pressure on my mother by going behind her back. In this case, my mother was distracted by dad's yelling and told me that she didn't believe that I had a problem that required counseling. She thought that my father was the only one who had *problems* in our family that warranted that kind of help, and he wasn't likely to cooperate. It seemed apparent to me that my dad's problems loomed so large in her mind, that what anyone else was going through was inconsequential. Or perhaps she was afraid the incest would get her into some kind of trouble as an enabler. I later realized that perhaps she tried to discourage me from seeking counseling because of what it might reveal about her. Yes it would likely help me, but it would certainly make her feel very uncomfortable about what had happened.

When I finally did seek counseling on my own, I was in my late twenties. After my mother realized I was actively seeking counseling—a good fourteen years after the incest came out in the open—*she was very upset*. She couldn't understand why I would need to see a counselor about something that happened "*so long ago.*" She assumed that my pastors, youth pastors, and mentors at the seminary would simply "take care" of my emotional and spiritual needs. I wasn't able to discuss with my mother the deep wounds I had been struggling with at the time the incest was happening or at any time afterwards. I had never felt comfortable enough explaining the emotional impact of what my father had done. I didn't even understand it fully myself.

My father obviously *did* have problems. He left his family in a state of emotional turmoil. I was nineteen years old when I left home, and my father had already passed away. Even though he was already gone, I still had to leave home just for my own emotional survival. My mother had remarried and planned to move to Eastern Oregon to a lifeless canyon far from any of the friends or churches that I knew.

However, long before I left home physically, when I was only 14 years old I left home emotionally. This was when I realized that with all the dysfunction and turmoil with my parents, I would need some stable role models to pattern my life and goals after. I knew I didn't want to grow up to be like my parents. I didn't want my life to be like what I was beginning to see what they had become. I really do not know where I got that idea. I wasn't a Christian yet and had dropped out of the Sunday School my parents had been sending us to. But I knew I would not find any good role models or advice at home from my immediate family. When I was fourteen, I began to look for role models in adults at school and in some extended family members. I primarily turned my focus outside of my immediate family and looked for mentors in school teachers, music leaders, and classmates that I respected. These were people who had a very positive outlook on life. I also found them in honor roll classmates, for whom I had great admiration. I desperately wanted someone I could look up to and respect.

After I became a Christian at the age of sixteen, I also began looking for role models at church, which led to some sense of independence away from the family. It was at this time that I asked my mother for advice about college and she refused to give it to me. I was very hurt and felt rejected. I wanted advice from *my mother* because she had known me my entire life. I later realized that she gave me the most loving answer she could give me. She was feeling very insecure and very fearful that she would give me bad advice and suggested I speak to my Youth Pastor.

After I moved away from home, there were times when my mother would call me in the evenings while being intoxicated. She was driving me crazy! I believe she was calling out of guilt, because of the terrible thing that my father had repeatedly done to me. I guess she hadn't realized the impact of what he had done when I asked for counseling when I was in high school; now she felt powerless to protect me from the consequences of it. I believe that she was worried that it might have residual effects that would keep me from growing to be an emotionally and physically healthy woman. Well, she was right about that in some respects. She desperately wanted to see me marry and have a family of my own. So did I. When she called while being intoxicated, I believe she thought the alcohol would give her the "courage" to tell me how disappointed she was in me, in that I had not yet married (at the age of 26) or had given her any grandchildren. At first these calls came only once a month, sometimes twice. When they began coming more often, I knew that I had to begin standing up to her, which I eventually did.

I prayed about making a clean break from some of the attitudes and painful memories I had grown up with. But this was a very difficult thing to do. Whenever I spoke to different members of my family about seeking counseling, I received a variety of responses. After praying about this for a couple of years, I realized I could not make a complete break from the toxic thinking of my past, until I moved away from my home town in Portland, Oregon. This was where I was raised and where so many reminders of the past were all around me, constantly invoking so many negative memories. I had read that women who were abused often had to move away from the town or area where the abuse took place in order to heal. So after more than a year of prayer and planning, I moved to Southern California where many of my good friends had formerly lived. While in Southern California and with godly counsel from former California and Portland mentors, I made the decision to see a Christian counselor.

When I told my mother about the counseling, she appeared to be disappointed and hurt. She gave me the impression that she was really opposed to the idea and personally offended. It was as if my seeking counseling had a reflection on her as a mother. In a way it did, because as mentioned before, I had never been able to trust her with my wounded emotions. I believe it played into her guilt over the incest. I had formerly believed that it played into her guilt over the incest. But as time has gone by and after years of counseling and research, I have concluded that it also played into her feelings as an enabler. So she could not have been supportive of my needs. Some members of my family backed her up in opposing my decision, since she shared it with them from her point of view. But there were one or two who seemed to support me. The unspoken attitudes toward me were, "Why, *after so many years* did I need to leave home and get involved in counseling over something that happened so long ago? After all, wasn't this something *we all just wanted to forget?*" The unspoken suggestion was that maybe I should forget about it as well. Maybe I should just move on with my life, find a nice man, and get married. [1]

Oh! I would have loved to have forgotten about the incest, to have found a nice man to settle down with, and to get married! But I couldn't just forget about it, and I couldn't just get married, until I had dealt with the issues of my past, because I knew the problem of incest would likely destroy my marriage no matter how well it started off at the beginning. Everyone wants to forget about the toxic part of incest, but, unfortunately, it is something that refuses to be forgotten.

I think that was the point. It is the most unforgettable, shameful memory in any family. And no one ever wants to talk about it in a positive way that is actually helpful to the victim. There's too much shame, blame, and secrecy. They pretend to be "experts," who have the least accurate information on the topic. When it happens, everyone is shocked, saddened, and grieved; once they have voiced their opinions, they just want to forget about it. They walk on egg shells around the whole subject. [2]

You rarely hear about a family who will stand behind one of their own who is a victim struggling through the long process of healing—no matter how long it takes. At least I never had heard of such a family. I have known a number of women who had to bear the truth of their ugly secret alone. Families will talk about the victim and treat him (or her) as if she is strange or different, instead of standing behind her in an understanding way, knowing that her "peculiarity" is not something to be rejected, but is something that needs to be understood as a symptom of being violated.

It is almost unheard of to hear about a family who gives any kind of positive helpful support to one of their own who has been victimized by another member of their own family. There may be some initial support, such as, "Wow, that's *terrible!* I can't believe he did that!" Tragically on the other hand, I have a friend (and have read about others) whose mother had a reaction something like this: "I can't believe he would do such a thing like that to you. *You must have imagined it.*" (Yeah *right!* Like a young girl is really going to imagine something like that.) or "*You probably had a bad dream.*" or "*Oh, not my Johnny. How could you say such a thing? You should be ashamed of yourself for even suggesting such a thing.*" More often, the reaction is shock and the reluctance to talk to the victim about it or anything else. This is "walking on egg shells" and denial behavior, which only causes deeper trauma, shame, and rejection for the victim.

In my case, the family did confront my father together as a group, because he had so many other sexually dysfunctional behaviors. I was so thankful for that united front. Confrontation is a very important step to take *as a family*. But after the initial confrontation and death of my father, as I remember it, everyone seemed to stop talking about it. We spoke of other problems my dad had, but the topic of incest came up only a few times. Perhaps my siblings went quiet about it to respect my privacy or because they didn't know what to say about it. I think everyone had their own wounds left by my father and didn't have the strength to worry about mine. But whatever the reason, I was left holding on to my wounds and clutching my broken heart, which I unfortunately chose to bury. I didn't bring it up, because I feared rejection. Once my father was out of our home and after he died, life seemed to go on for everyone. It *seemed that way*, but I knew that he had spread his damaging hurt around. Everyone got a taste of pain, which they carried in different directions. But that is their story to tell, not mine.

I believe that for the rest of the family, it was somewhat of a relief to have him gone. With him deceased, we knew he couldn't come back. The wounds he left behind were not discussed as a family any more. It was easier to deal with that way, but not very healthy. That's very different from saying there were no wounds to discuss. No, there were plenty of wounds. They were definitely *there, buried by denial and shame; however, they were not forgotten.*

The point in all this is that we need to confront the individual(s) involved in causing our pain. Other family members who know about it may or may not be of any help. This may be either by choice or because they don't know how to help. Depending on the age of the victim, however, the abuser must be confronted. Facing our pain may include going to one-on-one counseling. After I spent fourteen years in the company of Christian mentors and friends, while living mostly away from my family, *I chose one-on-one counseling. This was the primary step #1 for me*. I say it was the primary step #1, although confronting my father was the initial step #1 for me. I doubt that I would ever have confronted him without my family's support. I was too much afraid of him.

My own personal bold step #1, going to <u>one-on-one counseling</u>. It was a very difficult step to take, especially at first. *But I had to do it alone*. I did take this step on the advice of friends and mentors, but the actual step of making the phone call and making personal contact was mine and mine alone to take. I had to take all my personal blinders off to realize that I needed help in dealing with my problems. I had tried but concluded that I couldn't handle it very well on my own. I had to keep telling myself that it took a lot of courage to see a counselor, and I would be respected for it in the end. The most important aspect of that would be self-respect. I had to talk myself into going to the first appointment. I had to encourage myself that *I was really okay* and that I needed as much help as anyone who had been through the nightmare that I had experienced. I needed this "self-talk" to give myself the strength to actually follow through with the first contact.

The primary way that I tried to deal with facing my pain on my own was by journaling. I had to realize that my feelings were more overwhelming than my ability to cope with by using a pen and paper or computer, and I needed more knowledgeable help and accountability. Ironically, I later learned that I also had two friends who had decided to have professional counseling (for reasons different than mine) at the same time that I did. They had never met each other and they lived in two different states, which were hundreds of miles apart. I had respect for these friends, because I knew it took a lot of courage to seek professional help when it is needed. I thought if they could do it, I certainly could do the same. I also convinced myself that there was no shame in seeking help.

I knew I was going down this road by myself, because I did not have much family support and I had moved to an area 1200 miles away from most of my family, close friends and mentors. Counseling is a difficult process, and it became even more difficult without a strong support system. I was pretty much alone. It was just the Lord and myself and the few acquaintances I had acquired in my new home in Southern California. I would have to remember and relive that terrible experience all over again. I would have to talk about the feelings I was afraid to describe and the feelings I could not express at the time that it happened.

During this process, I would have to get in touch with the feelings I buried when the abuse happened. *I knew this process would be very difficult and very painful!* Now I would be going through the Valley of Tears alone and head on. The second time you go through something difficult always seems to be more painful.

The following section "Steps to Recovery" lists some steps to healing that I recommend.

Steps to Recovery

Now that I've faced the pain of my trauma, what are the steps *I should take* for *the Lord to do a work of recovery?* I worded that very carefully because it is God who does the work of recovery, but we must be willing participants. There are things we can do that will help the process along, and other things that will be a hindrance. For example, I can stubbornly deny I was ever abused and refuse to deal with my emotional pain. Or I can stuff my painful emotions deep inside and not share them with anyone, toughing it out. Either way it's my choice.

But there is one other option: I can draw close to the Lord in prayer, open my heart to Him about my wounded soul, and allow Him to do His work of healing and recovery. The Word of God makes it clear that we should involve others with our troubles in order to be healed:

13 Is any one of you in trouble?
He should pray.
Is anyone happy?
Let him sing songs of praise.

14 Is any one of you sick?
He should call the elders of the
church to pray over him and anoint
him with oil in the name of the Lord.

15 And the prayer offered in faith
will make the sick person well;
the Lord will raise him up. If
he has sinned, he will be forgiven.

16 Therefore, confess your sins to each
other and pray for each other
so that you may be healed.
The prayer of a righteous man
is powerful and effective.
The Apostle James ~ James 5:13-16 NIV

Where there is no guidance,
the people fall,
But in abundance of
counselors there is victory.
King Solomon ~ Proverbs 11:14

Without consultation, plans are
frustrated,
But with many counselors they
succeed.
King Solomon ~ Proverbs 15:22

Listen to counsel and accept
discipline,
That you may be wise the rest
of your days.
King Solomon ~ Proverbs 19:20

Let's say that I can clearly remember what happened to me, what do I do now? Here are some ideas I wrote down as I was concluding my counseling process.

1. Get in touch with your experience and your feelings. This is not fun or easy, but it is very necessary. As discussed previously, the first step in overcoming any difficulty in life is to face it. Emotional trauma and the symptoms that accompany it are no different. So, learn to express your feelings in every way possible:

a. Writing: Learn to write about all your thoughts and feelings. This should be done in a very private journal. Initially I filled many store-bought journals, and then I kept my thoughts and feelings on typewritten pages in a notebook. Gradually I began keeping it on a computer. If you're worried about privacy, you can always password-protect your journal document. The important thing is to write down your feelings. Chuck Swindoll is one of my favorite authors and a former employer of mine at Insight for Living along with his wife Cynthia. He has this to say about journaling:

   Thoughts disentangle themselves over the lips . . . and through the fingertips. How true! The old gray matter increases its creases when you put it down on paper. Start a journal. A journal isn't a diary. It's more. A journal doesn't record what you do—it records what you think. It spells out your ideas, your feelings, your struggles, your discoveries, your dreams. In short, it helps you articulate who you are. [3]

b. Drawing: If you have the talent, go for it. I had a former roommate who was going to write a story about herself in a store-bought journal book. One night she came home to an unexpected event. A man had broken into her apartment where she lived alone. When she came home from work he was there waiting for her. She was subsequently raped at knife-point. She might have been murdered in the process, except that she was able to convince the perpetrator that she had a friend coming to meet her for dinner. The journal that was intended to be a story about herself became the book where she vented her feelings about the rape. She wrote about it and drew many pictures expressing her anger, depression, and plans to prevent it from ever happening to her again. Although it was an integral part of her healing process (along with weekly counseling sessions), it remained a very private story.

c. *Crying*: *Don't keep it inside!!* Let it *all* come out. Find a safe place and just cry! My friend who had been raped scheduled her counseling on her day off. This was the day she walked through her *Valley of Tears*. I don't know how she did it (saving her tears to cry all on that one day). She seemed to be very strong in handling her emotions. I seemed to cry every night when I was going through my counseling, reading books, journaling, or whenever I was thinking about my pain (which seemed to be all the time).

d. *Yelling*: Make sure you're in a safe environment, such as with your counselor or in your car or at home (if it won't alarm your neighbors, family, friends, or roommates). This sounds a little crazy, but one idea I heard about is to go out of town into the woods or a remote area. Make sure there's no one around. Then just yell at God or yell at the trees (role-playing and picturing them as the perpetrator).

e. Remembering: If at all possible, relive the event. Find a person you can trust and talk through the incident. Either your counselor, your best friend, or perhaps your support group can help you with this. If you choose to relive the event with a friend, make sure it is a friend you can *really trust*. This is a highly sensitive part of your life*, and you must be able to know that this person will not repeat what you share in the strictest of confidence.*

f. Grieving: *This is vital!* The perpetrator has stolen something precious from you and it's something you will never get back. He has stolen a first-time physical experience that you should have been able to save for your husband or wife. Worse than that, he stole the innocence of your young soul. You need to go through a grieving process, just the same as if you had lost your best friend or a family member. So, grieve your lost childhood and innocence—grieve *everything* you lost. In many circumstances, you must make up for what has been stolen from you and for which the thief has gotten away with. Usually it seems like the thief will never be punished. Now you must allow yourself to feel the injustice and pain of that loss and embrace it.

If you have difficulty remembering all the details, you have probably suppressed your feelings and memories. These need to come to the surface so that you can deal with them and hopefully resolve them. If this suppression becomes a roadblock to you, ask the Lord to bring everything to the surface and help you to remember the details. He's very interested in seeing you healed, and if there are things you still need to remember, He will bring them to the surface.

2. It is very important to maintain relationships with people who know you and with people you can trust who will support you. The one big mistake I made was that I moved 1200 miles away to another state (away from all my close friends), before I started counseling. I had good reasons for doing this; but in some ways, it boomeranged against me. *I do not recommend doing that if you can help it.* You need your close friends, people with whom you have a history, who know you well enough to give you support. Another option is that you can join a support group. This is a safe place where you can vent your feelings and make supportive friends at the same time.

   I took the more difficult route. I did not have much of a history with anyone in the local area I lived in, *and* I did not join a support group. It was unfortunate that besides being chronically ill, working full time, and going to counseling up to three times a week, I felt that I didn't have the time for a support group. I didn't realize it would turn out that way when I decided to move, but it eventually worked out for my benefit in the end. This, however, made my counseling years a very lonely time. Most of my local peers didn't have a clue as to what I was going through. As a result, I was very lonely and depressed. However, I did keep in touch with my best friend in Portland, who was also going through counseling. We supported one another and shared our grief through the mail and on the phone.

3. Spend time with God and in His Word, the Bible. This is *VERY IMPORTANT!* This was where I drew my strength. I recommend that you become familiar with the Psalms and the Gospels. The Psalms are extremely helpful because they contain expressions of every kind of emotion, and they teach us how to deal with our emotions in a spiritual context. They also have much to teach us about the character of God, how to trust Him, and how to pray. Incest victims often have problems with their concept of God and in trusting Him, relating Him too much with their perpetrator (especially if the perpetrator was their father, step-father, uncle, or another male authority figure). The more you can build a proper idea of who God is and what He is like in relationship to you through Scripture, the better. This is a profound

problem for victims of childhood sexual abuse. According to Dr. Dan B. Allender,

"*The abuse victim's fundamental enemy, then, is sin: the fearful refusal to trust a God about whom she is deceived. The Spirit of God is hard at work in her to reveal God's true nature and confront her fear and mistrust, but His work is a battle that requires her cooperation.*" [4]

This is why time spent getting to know God's character is so important. Look for His character in Scripture and work on developing a trustful relationship with Him. One helpful way that I have found to do this is to read Psalms every day. If you read five Psalms each day, you will read the entire book in a month. This way you can read all the Psalms every month. Look in the Psalms every time an attribute of God is mentioned and notice how trust in God is expressed.

In the Gospels (Matthew, Mark, Luke, and John), the Lord Jesus is ministering first and foremost to the people of Israel. His character, as our Lord and Great Physician, is the same then as it is now. Notice carefully how Jesus responded to the afflicted people He encountered while He walked this earth. Since He has not changed at all in the way He responds to those He loves, He will have the same compassion toward you in your pain, as He had for those who hurt and for those whom He healed while He was on earth.

Remember that God is the most "Wonderful Counselor" *(Isaiah 9:6).* He understands all your feelings. Don't get discouraged if you lose interest in "spiritual things." God is not looking for a spiritual or religious performance from you. He wants a personal relationship with you.

Spend time with God learning how to know Him in a close relationship. Reveal yourself to God on a personal level and get to know Him and feel comfortable with your real self in His presence. This takes time in His Word, in prayer, and in learning how to listen to His voice.

4. Get counseling. This has already been discussed and it cannot be emphasized enough. Find a counselor of your same gender, who is trained and experienced in the area of incest. I have found that there are different types of counseling techniques. Some counselors will sit and say nothing while they let you have control of the topic, ask the questions, and even allow you to come to your own conclusions. Some counselors don't want you to come prepared, but to just come and learn to be comfortable with them and learn to open up about the issues that trouble you. Others will be more interactive by asking and answering questions, making suggestions, recommending books, giving you homework, and recommending

support groups. If you are not comfortable with one type of counseling, try another. You need to feel comfortable with your counselor to receive the greatest benefit. Remember, this is about you and your emotional health, not about your counselor and his or her chosen technique.

5. Understand that counseling and healing is a process of time that requires your cooperation and takes real effort on your part. It also requires God's work within you. God is always working in your life, so don't get discouraged if it feels like nothing is happening or happening too slowly. Don't quit and don't give up. You have to hang in there. Change must be relatively slow to be permanent. Change also requires adjustment time. The process of healing will change you radically, in ways you can't even imagine. If you change too fast, you might find yourself in a state of mental and emotional upheaval, and you will feel very awkward about yourself. Be patient. God loves you and He is actively involved in your recovery process.

   I can honestly say that I would not be where I am today, if not for my years of counseling or "talk therapy." If I had to do it over, I may have done things a little differently, but I am so grateful that I went through those painful years. I always felt that our sessions ended too soon, because verbalizing my feelings was so therapeutic. I highly recommend this process.

Do as much reading as you can. Try to find as many books as you can about what other victims of incest and rape have experienced. What kinds of emotions did they have? How did they feel about their counseling and their recovery process? The value in this is knowing that what you are feeling and going through is normal for the trauma you experienced. Many who have experienced it have recovered from it. As I was going through my counseling, I made a list of all the emotions I was feeling. It made me feel somewhat depressed, but I did write them down. Eventually, it helped me understand myself better. Perhaps doing so will help you understand yourself a little more. I made a list of some of those emotions, included it in this chapter, and titled the list "Feelings Caused by Incest." Maybe you will come up with a different list. The important thing is that you come up with your own list and write about these things in your journal. It will be very therapeutic for you.

My Own Personal Journal . . . Fulfillment, Loss, and My Concept of God

Early Thirties During Counseling

I had a friend who frequently pointed out that I had a negative attitude toward life and a very poor concept of God. He also said I had a very negative view of myself. Well, considering what I'd been through, is it any wonder?

When I worked at Western Seminary, I had a more positive view of life. Things were not always perfect, but I had a great roommate and great friends. I absolutely loved my job and co-workers. I was completely committed to my church and loved my music activities. I derived great fulfillment from all of it. During that time I was really growing and blossoming emotionally in all my relationships. I can remember telling people that I enjoyed my job and church activities so much that none of it seemed like work to me.

Then after about five years of enjoying my work and church relationships and activities, in the space of one year, I lost it all. My roommate became engaged and moved on. My health deteriorated. Because of my health issues, I had to leave my job, and my boyfriend was gone. Because I couldn't work anymore, I lost the ability to support myself. I also had to have surgery. It seemed like everything that gave me self-confidence, identity, and fulfillment was ripped out of my life. *What in the world was God doing?! He certainly had something in mind. But what was it? It was certainly painful.*

Much of what made up my self-identity has been replaced since that time, but I have never really been able to feel the level of satisfaction and enjoyment that I felt before. No job has been able to compare with what I had at Western. No roommate or living situation (except when I lived alone) has proven to be as beneficial—until I got married. The only thing that had really given me a significant challenge was the move to California.

Why is it so difficult for me to have a positive frame of mind and to experience fulfillment? I've learned that there is a very fine line between finding fulfillment in my work and relationships and putting my security in those things. I'm *deeply afraid* that, if I were to really enjoy something or someone and find a lot of fulfillment, they will be taken away from me. I'm afraid to enjoy life because the moment I do, I will lose what means the most to me.

This says a lot about my concept of God. The problem started with my biological father who would not allow me to enjoy *anything* after the incest began. Everything I enjoyed was sharply criticized, ridiculed, and taken away. In fact, there was one day I told my father that I wanted to attend Bible College. He told me that, if I did that, he would disown me. Talk about the ultimate ridicule and rejection! To me, God became a killjoy, and the experiences of the past couple of years only accentuated that.

On the contrary, I *know* that God is good. There is no question about that. He is the Author and Giver of Joy. And He gives blessings *for our benefit*. He is a *good* Father. But for some reason, those characteristics of my Lord God seem to be miles away from my current experiences. It has become very clear to me that my understanding of my Heavenly Father's character must be improved. If I don't strive to know Him better, I wouldn't be able to have a more meaningful relationship with Him. The only way to improve my understanding is to spend more time with Him in His Word. That is something I need now and will need to do for the rest of my life.

Cycles

As I continued in my counseling, I experienced a cycle that I went through each week. I developed a habit of trying not to focus on my emotions during the week. I thought I had to ignore them in order to cope with my life at work. But I couldn't escape from them. I will write more about coping later.

Every week I went through an emotional cycle. Since my counseling session was on Wednesday evenings, I began a sort of recovery on Thursday from the overwhelming feelings that had been discussed. Then emotional heaviness and physical fatigue would linger over the weekend until Monday and Tuesday, when those dark feelings would gradually subside. By Wednesday morning I felt pretty good, until I contemplated going to my counseling session again. By that evening, I would struggle with getting back in touch with the hurtful emotions again. It was a painful cycle that I would rather have not gone through. I had mixed feelings about it, because I actually looked forward to my counseling sessions because they were so good for me. It was sort of like a massage. It hurt, but it was good pain. It was *pain with a purpose*.

During Those Sessions My Issues For Counseling Tended To Be:

1. Feeling like I was sitting all by myself in a dark dusty dungeon where no one wanted to visit.
2. Feelings of aloneness, abandonment, fear, anger, and depression.
3. For a long time, I felt a seething rage and the need to express it without being ridiculed, condemned or punished for it. This was anger I had always identified as a deep hurt—a hurt that didn't feel wrong or sinful. It took me over two years to recognize the difference between my *anger (rage)* toward my father and what I was identifying as a *deep rage* that he had caused me. *I didn't know that what I was feeling as a deep hurt was really a seething rage I had harbored toward him.* I didn't know how enraged I was. It was a very strong anger that over time I came to recognize as an explosive bomb inside of me that was going to go off if I allowed it to, and I was terrified of it. Until I went through counseling, I didn't know that it was okay for that rage to come out in emotional words and tears—all good expressions in the correct context; *and then, finally, relief!* Since

it had to come out, my counseling session was the safest place for that to happen.

4. But let me caution you! While it is understandable for a victim of childhood abuse to have this type of rage, *it is not a good thing!* Anger that has turned to seething rage can turn very dangerous if not dealt with very carefully. Anything can set off the emotions of a person who has rage like that. This is why, regardless what age you are at the time, it is very important to seek out a counselor who is trained to deal with the wounds of childhood trauma and the anger and rage that comes with it.

Another important point to remember is that it *must be recognized and released.* Anger, like bitterness, can make a person ill. When Dr. Englizian (my friend at Western Seminary) learned about the incest, as grieved as he was for my sake, he stressed *very strongly* that my depression was most likely caused by a lack of forgiveness in my heart. He further told me that as much as my father did not deserve the forgiveness, *I needed it!!* By releasing my father from the prison of guilt and anger I had him in, my forgiveness would gradually release that rage that had me so depressed. Otherwise, I would spend my life with bitterness and resentment. As it states in the Book of Hebrews:

> *See to it that no one comes short of the grace of God; that no root of bitterness springing up causes trouble, and by it many be defiled; . . . .*
> *Hebrews 12:15*

This means that I had to forgive my father so that no root of bitterness would spring up in me, cause a lot of trouble, and defile many—beginning with me. I did not want to become bitter, so I knew I would need to continue in the process of forgiveness toward my father until it became final. Dr. Englizian also cautioned me that bitterness taking root in my heart *could cause a lifetime of illness*. He said it is always better for the offended to forgive. Until I had fully forgiven him, I never wanted to see him again. I was glad I was separated from that possibility by death forever.

Joyce Landorf, in her book *Irregular People,* wrote about the letters that people had written to her about their "Irregular Persons"— people in their life who had been anything from an irritant to an abuser toward them—and how they had dealt with them based on Joyce's teaching seminars. In the last chapter she described the nightmare she suffered with her own "Irregular Person" for most of her life. It was her father who had been a very abusive, alcoholic man. His form of abuse was verbal. She states in her book *Irregular People*:

> "This daily pain has immeasurably warped my attitudes, responses, and behavior towards others.

> And it has vastly changed ("destroyed" is a better word) my abilities to think and write.
>
> "C.S. Lewis expressed a theory that 'God whispers to us in our pleasures, He speaks to us in our consciousness, and He shouts to us in our pain.'
>
> "I think God *has* to shout to us in pain because the agony of suffering is so deafening. But, in this past year, I've alternated between hearing the shouting of God and understanding the silence of God. . ."

After coping with this severe pain for some time, she was referred to a cranial specialist. After extensive testing, this very wise doctor told her the following (in her own words):

> "The doctor explained it was as if my whole body and soul had gone on overload. My physical and emotional resistance had been down, so consequently all the darts shot from my Irregular Person had found the targets within me. *It's effect, the doctor pointed out, had been like a massive coronary, a stroke, or a grand mal epileptic seizure; the inside of me resembled a massive battle ground—terribly wounded and probably scarred forever.*
>
> "Everything within me had broken down, and the emotional pain had been joined by penetrating physical pain. The doctor was right. I knew he spoke the truth, because God instantly confirmed it in my soul.

> "The doctor had been quietly talking to me for some time, and I really thought he was about to bring me his conclusions, when abruptly he said, 'Now Joyce, I've got to talk to you about another matter . . . your Irregular Person.' And before I could react, he added, '*Because there is a definite connection between him and your pain' . . . I was stunned as the doctor accurately described my earlier feelings of anger, bitterness, and abandonment."* [5]

This quote illustrates how innocently-received emotional pain can turn into bitterness and resentment without the purity that forgiveness can bring. Forgiveness is a process in which we need the help of the Lord and, at times, other professional counsel to achieve.

Feelings Caused By Incest

GUILT *I felt guilty,* as if it were somehow my fault. I felt unloved. The initial attention was nice, but it made me feel dirty. As it continued, I no longer enjoyed the attention because it wasn't the right kind of attention. It was dirty sex. *The guilt continued because I could never discuss it with my mother or, for that matter, with anyone else. I was afraid she wouldn't understand or believe me. It had to remain a dirty secret—one that I was defenseless to escape from.*

FEAR I was *afraid of punishment*. If I resisted dad (in other words, if I disobeyed), I was afraid that I would be punished. *Not pleasing dad always brought punishment.*

FEAR I was *afraid that the incest would be discovered*, and I would be blamed. *I would either be blamed for submitting to dad's wishes, or I would be blamed for keeping it a secret.*

FEAR I was *afraid of men*, which led to my hatred of men. *I wanted their attention, but I did not want their control—the kind of control my dad wielded over me.*

FEAR I was *afraid of feeling smothered* physically. I felt emotionally raped and beaten, vulnerable to the power of twenty. I was afraid of being attacked. I felt like an animal had attacked and smothered me.

FEAR I was *afraid of sex*. To me, it was gross, and it really hurt.

FEAR I was *afraid of my dad's body*. It was too much to handle emotionally at age 11-12 (while he was in his fifties).

The incest created a deep desire and need for pure love (not the dirty kind) as well as pure and gentle affection. It was an exaggerated need at my age. I desired:

1. Attention
2. Cuddling and Physical Affection
3. Praise
4. Approval
5. Affirmation
6. Respect

But I never seemed to get it. It created *insecurity*. I began looking to physical things and things outside of myself to make me feel loved. Things like:

1. Physical Appearance — (which became ALL IMPORTANT)
2. Clothes – (*I became a seamstress and made all my clothes in high school. I found myself wanting to make more and more as our finances would allow.)*

3. Friends and/or (the desire to have) Boyfriends
4. Other People's Approval — *(If I didn't get it, I felt like a failure and withdrew into depression.)*
5. Physical Surroundings
6. Fads *(especially during high school)*
7. Out-of-Proportion Priorities for my age (*like materialism)*
8. Abilities
9. Jobs *(Before I was married, my work was my whole identity.)*

The incest also created a *fear of rejection* and *a dirty feeling* inside of me, which led to *withdrawal* and *emotional isolation*. This created a tendency to day-dream and to come up with fantasies of who I wanted to be. It also led to manipulating people by compliance, so I would at least feel loved.

None of this was good or satisfying. These were all behaviors that had to be corrected. Over time they disappeared, as I progressed in the healing process. The more time I spent with God in His Word and the more I went through the counseling process, the less I experienced these detrimental feelings and symptoms.

Letter to My Dad

THIS LETTER WAS WRITTEN MANY YEARS AGO WHILE I WAS STILL IN THE HEALING PROCESS. MY FATHER WAS NO LONGER LIVING, SO I COULD NOT RECONCILE WITH HIM. AS THINGS ARE TODAY, I MAY HAVE WRITTEN A VERY DIFFERENT LETTER BECAUSE MY RECOVERY IS MUCH FURTHER ALONG. BUT IT WAS VERY THERAPEUTIC FOR ME TO VERBALIZE THESE FEELINGS AT THE TIME I WROTE THEM. IT MAY BE SOMETHING YOU MIGHT CONSIDER AS YOU ARE WORKING THROUGH YOUR FEELINGS TOWARD THE PERSON WHO VIOLATED YOU.

Dear dad,

I want you to know that I have a number of happy childhood memories that I am very grateful to you and mom for. These are memories of family vacations and holidays. During our summer vacation I would go to sleep with my brothers and sister in our sleeping bags in the back of our family vehicle, while you and Mom drove to our vacation destination. Then we would wake up in the morning at the beach or the mountains, where we would set up our camp site to go fishing, beach combing, or hiking. I always loved to go hiking.

I also remember our drive to California to see your family and to visit Disneyland and Marineland of the Pacific. But as I look back on the trip to California when I was 10 years old, and my two elder brothers were twelve and fourteen, I later realized that the trip was really—at least in part--an opportunity to introduce my two elder brothers to their biological father. But there's more. I later realized that you had committed incest with my mother when she was some 23 years your junior. Then you married her when her husband—your own son in the military—was overseas. I was born some ten months after you married my mother. Did you think we wouldn't figure it out? It's not much of a legacy for me and not much of a family heritage. But I will tell you that from May 8, 1972 I am henceforth a child of the Living God, saved by His grace and adopted into His forever family. Because of my second birth on that date—my spiritual birthday—I claim a heavenly birthright. I am a citizen of heaven and I no longer (and have not for many years) bear the shame of being your biological daughter.

Now back to my childhood memories. We had so much fun on our many visits to Grandma & Grandpa Smith's farm in Woodland, Washington. But you weren't really there. You drove us there and then you made yourself scarce by going down to the Lewis River to fish.

We had many very special holidays because of mom's endless planning, sewing, shopping, and baking. I know that you would stay up all night on Christmas Eve putting toys together (and drinking) so that there were always toys under the tree and you were always drunk as well. You also did carpentry work to make furniture toys for us, but it was mostly mom who made our Christmas mornings special. She created the atmosphere.

Every Easter I received a beautiful corsage from you to wear with the special dress mom had made for me. Every Valentine's Day I received a small box of chocolates shaped like a heart, similar to the larger one that you gave to mom. When I was very young you showed your love for us, when we were young children, in doing many wonderful things for us and with us. During these vacation times and holidays, you seemed to be a family man and a good father.

But when we became adolescents, things changed. You wanted us to stay young. You didn't want us to become teenagers or to grow up. What was that all about?

And now, these memories are a blur. In fact, it's difficult to remember you with any kind of fond memories ***BECAUSE YOU DESTROYED ALL OF THEM.*** You literally tore our family apart. Once my eleventh year rolled around there were no more nice family vacations or Holiday memories. Oh, mom really tried to keep our family traditions going, but it wasn't quite the same because of your attitudes and drinking.

But worst of all, it wasn't the same because of the incest. You really crossed the line of immorality by committing incest with me just like you did with my mother. With my mother it was a little different because she was a consenting adult. But it was still incest, terribly immoral, and deeply wrong. What did you think you were doing? Did you think you could just help yourself to whatever female that happened to be living under your roof with no consequences? Well, I'm sorry, but it doesn't work that way.

Because of your abnormal behavior, I don't even want to remember you. Every thought of you and our relationship is seared with pain. You gave me so much frustration and pain during the last 7-1/2 years of your life, my memories of you are filled with pain and nausea. You made me fear men and sex; you made me fear people and hate myself. You made me feel that as an individual, I was worth less than nothing. You inflicted deep wounds on me that I didn't deserve, and then left me to bleed out emotionally and deal with all of that on my own. Then you had the nerve to say that you loved me.

You put me to shame. You caused family and friends to reject and avoid all of us. During our teenage years you wouldn't allow me or anyone in the family to have any friends or close peer relationships.

You were gross. I was ashamed of you—too ashamed to have anyone come to the house. You were drunk all of the time. You were either angry or indifferent toward everyone. You had no sense of decency. When you were inebriated, you would frequently lie around naked in your drunken stupor. You didn't care what part of the house you were in or if you were in the yard or who saw you. How do you think that made your wife and children feel?

You were vulgar and abusive and *very negative*. All of this hurt me very deeply. If I liked something, you showed contempt for it. And you didn't stop there. If I was partial to something or wanted it, you restricted it. If I had a dream or a goal, you scorned it or restricted me from taking steps to achieve it. You denied me the rights of self-respect and personhood, and it made me very angry. I was too naïve to know what you were doing; but now I know, and it really infuriates me!

You intimidated me and destroyed my self-confidence. You frightened me into a weak, timid, and defenseless person, before I was mature enough to fight back. You forced me to be inhibited, by not giving me the opportunity to vocalize my real feelings, good or bad. You led me to believe that being passive and inhibited was more desirable than being real and open and honest. What it all boils down to is that you were too insecure and threatened by me and the others when we wanted to be ourselves. You were afraid that we would get more positive attention than you would. That must have really bothered you. But it backfired. There were less than 25 people at your funeral. Yes, there was sadness when you died. There was sadness because there was no one at your memorial service who would be considered a friend of yours and very few relatives. We had to search for people who would be willing to be pall bearers for you. Since we no longer had to be afraid of you showing up unannounced at our house or coming in at night without notice to hurt us, we were relieved.

As I write this, I am in my late twenties, very passive, inhibited, and still single. All I ever wanted was to be loved and valued. But by the wounds you inflicted, you have so far prevented that. All I ever wanted was to be married and have children. Your night-time visits may have prevented that as well. I always wanted you and mom to be proud of me, but you never had a good thing to say to me or about me (either in my presence or in front of other people). What I did, what I looked like, and what I accomplished was never good enough for you. That seemed to be exactly what you wanted. It is exactly what you predicted. You never thought I could be loved. It would have really been a blow to you to find out that there might be a man somewhere who would love me with a far better quality of love than you had for me. You used to brag about how "I would never find a man as good as you, so I might as well not even try." Those were your very words. I wonder how disappointed you would be when I do marry someday, or if you will have any feelings of regret at all?

What really makes me angry, dad, is that I didn't realize you were sick. You had Bipolar Disorder and you weren't even man enough to face it, to stop drinking, and to accept treatment—if not for your own self-respect, then for the welfare of your family. You used my innocence and the vulnerability of those under your care to try to build your ego and it literally destroyed me. Because I thought you were so unchangeable and so powerful, I felt responsible and guilty for all of the pain that resulted from the wounds you inflicted. Consequently, I learned to be ashamed of myself and to despise myself.

However, I have learned that it wasn't the diagnosis of alcoholism that caused all your abnormal behavior. It also wasn't the diagnosis of Bipolar Disorder that caused your erratic behavior. It was the willful evil in your heart. Those conditions have treatments that had you sought them; our family life would have been far different. But you chose to be willfully evil and took it out on your children and grandchildren.

But I want to let you know I will recover from all of this horrible trauma. You will find that many of your predictions about my adult life will never come true. I don't know if I will ever have children, but I believe that one day I will marry. I will marry a godly Christian man, a man who will love me for who I am and who will respect me. Unlike your prediction, this man will be better than you, simply because he will respect me and love me with tenderness.

I meant it when I said that I forgave you. Not because you deserve it, but because I do. I will not hold you in the prison house of bitterness for my entire life. And the truth is, it is not for me to judge you. That is God's responsibility, and He will do a very good job at it. But I will never be able to trust you again. That would take years of healing in our relationship, which your death has prevented. It's really a shame that you never lived to see your daughter and other children live and grow and overcome the wounds you inflicted. Maybe you could have come to realize how wrong you were. We may never know. How sad for you, and how sad for us. We could have had a real biological father and, for some, a real biological grandfather. But you chose by your actions that we would never have that kind of father. What a shame!

Tammy

P.S. ~ dad, I am adding this addendum to my letter to you several decades after the original writing of the preceding letter. I just want you to know that in spite of all the anger expressed in this letter to you, I want to assure you that I truly did forgive you. It took a very long time. As Grandma explained to me, there was a lot of hurt and rage that had built up inside me, and so, of course the recovery from that took a long time. And had I not taken that one vital step of faith to forgive you those many years ago when I was 17 years old, that seed of forgiveness never would have begun to grow and bloom. Sometimes forgiveness is a very long process. But with the damage you inflicted, I really do not know how I could have survived without forgiving you. You see, forgiving you was step #1 in my recovery process. I am sure that you have no idea of the damage you inflicted in my life. That includes all the emotional damage you caused and all the physical agony you brought into my life, with one illness after another. All I can say is that my true Father, my Father in Heaven knew about all this from the beginning of time, and you couldn't have superseded or even have had the least idea of your part in His divine plan. He knew and always does know what He is doing in the lives of His children. I therefore give Him the glory for my recovery and for giving me the grace to forgive you. And if He can forgive me for the evil in my heart, then I can certainly forgive you for the evil in yours. Sin is sin in the eyes of God, no matter what we do, whether it is an action or a thought. That does not lighten the burden of what you did to me. But that is between you and the Lord. It is no longer between you and me.

"Trauma reshapes a person's life. People are thoroughly different afterward. Survivors are more cautious, often less trusting, and at the least more aware of their immediate environment. Recovering victims of trauma, especially where loved ones were involved, will tell you that values such as security, safety, attachment, and predictability become all-important to them."

Dave Carder, M.A.
Secrets of Your Family Tree [6]

Survival

After the unthinkable abuse had occurred, the first thing I (or any victim) need to understand is how to learn to survive in my current circumstances, to figure out a way to change those circumstances, and to avoid future abuse. Since I was so young, there wasn't much I could do to change my circumstances and avoid future abuse. This will mean different things to different people, depending on the circumstances of the abuse. But for all, the first and only thing at the beginning is survival.

It's like being dropped into the ocean. The first order of business is survival. I must keep my head out of the water and keep breathing. This will take all my thought processes and all my energy. So, I build my existence around treading water. I learn to pray, and I pray with all the faith I can muster that God will give me the strength I need to save me. He is the only hope I have. I don't know if I can count on human help, but I pray for it anyway. Until my prayers are answered, I must do what I can to survive, or I will die. It's as simple as that.

As time goes by, I eventually find my way out of the deep (getting past the initial shock of abuse). It's become natural to use all of my energies to survive, even when I don't need to. Now my main focus must be to get out of the survival mode, see the need to take some risks, be spontaneous, and to allow life to be more meaningful.

In all the years I have been learning to heal and cope with the consequences of abuse, I have learned three things about survival:

1. You won't make it unless you learn to survive initially. Knowing how to survive is essential to life and health, and sometimes, life and death.
2. Survival mode is meant to be a *temporary* mode of functioning, a coping mechanism to get through the rough spots. It's not meant to be a lifetime habit.
3. Learning to overcome the negative aspects of survival is a *lifetime process* of spiritual and emotional growth.

What Is Survival Mode?

I believe the Lord wants us all to know how to survive in this world, but He wants us to *make **Him** the focus of our survival.* In other words, *our survival must depend upon Him.*

> *So the Lord commanded us to observe all these statutes, to honor and respect the Lord our God for our good always and **for our survival,** as it is today.*
>
> *Moses ~ Deuteronomy 6:24*
>
> *Now faith is the substance of*
> *things hoped for, the evidence of*
> *things not seen.*

By faith we understand that the worlds were framed by the word of God, so that the things which are seen were not made of things which are visible.
Hebrews 11:1, 3 NKJV

Therefore, since we have so great a cloud of witnesses surrounding us, ***let us also lay aside every encumbrance,*** *and the sin which so easily entangles us, and let us run with endurance the race that is set before us,*

fixing our eyes on Jesus*, the author and perfecter of faith, Who for the joy set before Him endured the cross, despising the shame, and has sat down at the right hand of the throne of God.*

For consider Him *who has endured such hostility by sinners against Himself, so that you may not grow weary and lose heart.*
Hebrews 12:1-3

When your life focus becomes geared around nothing else except survival, then the dependence is shifted from the Lord to us. That's when it becomes something fleshly, carnal, and ineffective.

In my experience, survival mode has meant many things. The Lord had taught me what it would mean to survive, without dependence upon any other than Himself. He did use people along the way to help me, but only after I pleaded with Him for help. He taught me how to do the responsible thing to make sure my obligations were met, even if I were sick, upset, tired, or not in the mood. This relates to my job, my finances, my involvement at church, and my friendships. In the beginning, learning what it meant for me to survive without anyone except the Lord to fall back on was a good thing. However, after some time, survival mode turned into something else.

Survival Mode Overload

How can I live in "Survival Mode"? When I was growing up as a teenager, my father used to make authoritative predictions about my future. He would say that, in the world in which I would be an adult, only the strong would survive. He would tell me the weak would be swept away to make room for the strong. His intention in telling me this upsetting news was probably to help me snap out of adolescent immaturity and insecurity. Or perhaps it was to pull me out of the adolescent dream world he seemed to think I saw myself through. I will give him this. His intentions may have been good, in spite of their tragic results in my life.

His words to me at that time in my life resulted in an overwhelming fear of the future, of growing up and of facing my life in the world as it was. I was very insecure about myself as a result of the abuse, and these comments made by my father only made it worse. I didn't totally live in a dream world, but I found that my dreams and desires were a comfort, an emotional coping mechanism, and a temporary escape hatch. But they were not something that would last and hold me together.

What is ironic about my father's predictions is that he did not survive to see if they would come true. He didn't live to see my eighteenth birthday. Looking back, I sometimes think he was expressing his own insecurity about the world we were living in and his own inability to be a survivor. As an impressionable teenager, his words were authoritative as they had always been my whole life. It didn't matter if they contained any truth. If he said them, they had the power of truth. I couldn't get away from them—at least not back then.

But he was wrong! *So very wrong*! And this is what you need to understand. The lies you hear, whether they are from the person who abuses you, those who believe your abuse was inconsequential, or even the lies of the enemy, Satan himself—they're still lies. It will be up to you, victim soon to be survivor, to confront those lies in your own life. *God's truth is more powerful than any lie that has been used against you*. You need to realize that you can claim the truth of God's Word as He reveals it to you. *You <u>must</u> claim that truth!*

I needed to learn balanced life skills in order to survive, and I did not learn them from my father. My father certainly wasn't speaking God's truth. He was merely stating his own mistaken conceptions, conceived out of his own set of fears, insecurities, and things from immoral science fiction books that he read.

I'm very grateful for my mother, who taught me some valuable life skills. When I was about 15 years old she began taking me to work with her on Saturdays. She worked at an office in downtown Portland where she was a bookkeeper. She gave me basic jobs to do to help her—things like alphabetizing items for filing. This was my first experience working in an office. Certain skills my mother taught me helped me throughout those years. I had to learn how to get up on my own by an alarm clock. If I wanted to go with her, I had to be ready to go with her by a certain time. If I wasn't ready, I couldn't go. We took the bus downtown. That was how I got to work for the first seven years that I worked. And that was just the beginning.

I never learned any survival skills from my father, because I had come to learn that he had nothing to teach me. And he didn't even really try. Except there was one thing I remember him saying. He said "It's better to be a half hour early than one minute late. That's it. He had a very strong work ethic and he expected us to work all the time. It was almost demoralizing.

When I became a young adult in my twenties, I had to learn how to take care of myself, because there would be no one to bail me out if I failed. Even the skills I had learned from my mother were for the purpose of survival. After I passed into "adulthood" at the age of eighteen, I was considered "on my own" by my mother.

During the first year of self-survival, I had two surgeries, which my mother helped me with financially. She also took care of me during my recovery time. But when I moved into my own apartment, I still had to work in spite of constant illness. I had to put my needs and feelings aside to do the "responsible thing." I learned to live on my own, depending on no one else. It was just me and the Lord. I did move back "home" with my mother and step-father twice during my early twenties. Both times resulted in relational disaster. This only reinforced the concept of the need to be on my own. No one else was likely to step forward to take care of me physically, emotionally, or financially. It was not likely that a knight in shining armor would rescue me.

Unfortunately, I didn't really know how to trust the Lord, but He was right there taking care of me the whole time. If I had been more aware of that, my life would have been a whole lot less stressful and recovery might have come more easily. But, like most people, the best lessons the Lord taught me came through repetition, difficulty, and time—His best teachers.

In the years that followed, I made new friends, and I realized what I had to do to keep those friendships alive and well. Many times, it meant completely sacrificing what I wanted for what they wanted. I kept remembering two things my mother used to say to me, "*Tammy, you can't always have what you want*," and what she wrote in my childhood diary, *"True friends are like precious gems, choose each one wisely."* Over the years, the Lord gave me some very precious gems. But with regard to the first thing she told me, sometimes I wondered if I could *ever* have what I *really* wanted. I was very impatient, and I finally concluded that maybe it would happen later on in life. But for now, I thought I would have to keep the friendship boat from rocking at all cost. My friends were so precious to me and I was blessed to have some very godly Christian friends, who were trying to serve the Lord, just as I was.

One of the greatest blessings was my church in Milwaukie, Oregon. They had a very active youth group with a number of spiritually mature young people my age and with the same kind of life goals that I had. I believe this was part of God's hedge of protection. I was very blessed during those early years to have great role models in my church, who helped me to grow in my relationship with the Lord and who also taught me valuable life skills.

By my mid-twenties, I saw myself as having a strong "instinct for survival," and I thought it was a good thing, a gift from God. During this time, He taught me many lessons in personal survival. I believe they were primarily meant to take me through the difficult transition from being the fearful, weak, dependent daughter, sister, and friend to being able to live on my own. I don't believe the Lord ever meant for these lessons to be a permanent lifestyle.

I believe from my own experiences that learning through the changes and challenges of life are very necessary. But if that's all you learn, it can become bondage.

On the other hand, if you only know how to survive, you won't be able to live the abundant life Jesus promises in John Chapter 10. When I think of the Abundant Life, I am reminded of Jesus' high priestly prayer found in John 17:3 where He states these words:

This is eternal life, that they may know
You, the only true God, and Jesus Christ,
Whom You have sent.

This Abundant Life of knowing God the Father and Jesus His Son, and living the Eternal Abundant Life they give is a life of faith and trust in Him.

Moving on with Survival mode, when you operate in it alone, living spontaneously is far too risky and sometimes impossible. You have to carefully plan for each event in your life, because doing something of value on the whim of the moment is extremely hazardous. In fact, taking a risk of any kind is very difficult for a person existing only to survive. Spontaneous risk and survival don't usually go together. I found myself living just to make sure my basic needs of work, food, and shelter were met. And that took every resource I had. There was no room for creative exploration or growth. I had entered the dark tunnel of survival mode overload.

Survival Mode Overload is the misuse of something God intended to be used as a temporary gift, a way to help us through difficult times in life. It's a lot like another gift He gave us: food. You see, you have to eat to live. But if all you do is think about food and build your life around eating; you will develop what is called an eating disorder. It can make you sick. If left untreated, an eating disorder can take your life. In the same way, building your life around survival will put your soul and spirit in a deep freeze. If left unchecked, it can suck the emotional and spiritual life right out of you. As with an eating disorder, you can't see that what you're doing is unhealthy, until you are so deeply entrenched in it that you won't be able to get out of it without professional help.

Like food, if you rely on survival as your means of coping all the time, it will become second nature to you and soon you won't even know you're doing it. You will think that it is standard operating procedure. Going from survival mode to abundant living was a long process for me, and I have to continually make sure I haven't slipped back into the comfortable, safe, and unproductive mode of survival. To even see that what I was doing was unhealthy required the peeling back of many layers of denial. I genuinely believed survival was the only way to live or *at least the only way that I could live.* After a while, I got tired of it. It is a lonely existence when your life is so consumed with self-preservation.

Living for self can get pretty boring. There's not much room in my life for anyone or anything else.

What is ironic about this self-centered way of living is that my personal needs never get met, I can never get nurtured, and I can't nurture anyone else. I'm too busy keeping the survival engine going, so there is no energy left for anything else.

There are two things I credit the Lord for doing that helped get me from survival to abundant living. The first was my counseling process. It helped me to see what I was doing, why I did it, and how it made me feel. Becoming aware of how making choices to merely survive looked increasingly like bondage. When I recognized the bondage I was in, I knew I had to learn some different ways of functioning.

The second thing the Lord did to help me out of the rut of survival mode was the most effective. He gave me an incredible husband who is very spontaneous, loves life, and is not afraid to take wisely calculated risks. He loves the Lord and puts his trust in Him completely. With his encouragement and example, I'm still learning how to relax the survival techniques and to allow myself to have fun, enjoy life, take a few calculated risks, and not worry so much about rocking the boat.

Now just because I have written this does not mean I never go back to the old ways. It is a lifetime process and a constant learning experience. There are times when my husband has to tell me to relax and stop being so independent. Today I need to just enjoy God's peace and presence in my life. I have to go through the process of looking at my behavior and asking the Lord to help me live by faith, to help me live for Him, and to live not for myself and not in my own comfort zone.

Symptoms of Survival Mode Overload

While being in Survival Mode Overload, you may not be at a point in your life where you have someone you can trust to help you see what you're entrenched in. I haven't always had someone helping me in that way. But I have learned to recognize some of my own symptoms of Survival Mode Overload. Here are some things I have seen in my behavior that may help you to spot these symptoms in your life. By themselves, some may not be unhealthy behaviors; but as seen in the context of Survival Mode Overload, they may be something to consider. You should seek the Lord for wisdom to help you see, in perspective, what you're doing with your life. You need to be careful to watch out for these things:

1. Becoming a slave to my "to do" list.
2. Being too busy or too tired to have fun.
3. Realizing I haven't done anything creative in so long, I can't remember what it would be like.
4. Taking myself so seriously I have forgotten how to smile.
5. Realizing it has been too long since I've had a good laugh.
6. Feeling seriously guilty if I "waste" time relaxing or reflecting.

7. Being disappointed that I can't perform up to my own expectations or the expectations I believe others have of me.
8. Being defensive about my lifestyle.
9. Being so consumed with survival it seems like all I do is work and sleep.
10. Feeling frustrated because I've been too busy doing it all by myself and making sure it gets done, that I think I'm the only one who can do it.
11. Being so consumed with my own independence, I forget important events such as birthdays, anniversaries, special plans, special people, vacations, etc.
12. Thinking that time off work is time to get things done. Thinking vacation time is catch-up time, instead of a time to relax, enjoy myself, and take a vacation from all the "have tos."
13. Approaching life with what I like to call a martyr complex. I saw this in my mother for years, and never realized I was doing the same thing. The martyr complex is choosing the hard way to handle life because that's what I have become accustomed to. It is in making choices that force me to live with less, because the extras in life aren't consistent with survival. It is the feeling of "I'm not worth it anyway, so what's the use?"
14. Finding I am so busy taking care of my personal needs and keeping people in my life "happy." I began to realize no one else will

make (or take) the effort to help me to become happier and more self-confident.

15. Recognizing I'm in a lopsided existence, where I am doing all the work and getting none of the benefits.
16. Being so busy I don't want or need anybody else's help with my plans.

I'm sure you can come up with other symptoms you have experienced in your own life. These are the little alarms that go off to alert you, in order for you to evaluate whether or not surviving on your own efforts is really necessary for what you are doing today.

Things I Have Learned in Review

My negative concept of God was a _symptom_ of a deeper wound. Wounds have to be healed at the source before symptoms will go away. Therefore, the hurtful experiences have to be dealt with first.

The *facts* are that God is always with me. He was there when I was hurt, and He is present with me now and always will be. It did not give Him joy or satisfaction to see me hurt. Instead it brought Him deep grief and, in our terms, it brought tears to His eyes and, quite frankly, made Him want to vomit. He was not powerless to stop the pain, but out of respect for the free will that He gave to each one of us, He did not nor could not interfere with my parent's actions (except to let them reap what they had sown). God was never offended by my negative feelings toward

Him, but instead He understood them. He was and is willing and is very interested in healing my broken heart. He understands my limitations, as He created me out of dust. God is infinitely intelligent and wise. He understands why things happen as they do in my life, which is far above my ability to comprehend. It absolutely amazes me.

There is no magic formula for experiencing the love and benevolence of God at the heart of my emotions. Regardless of how I feel, God must be given the freedom to be exactly Who He is in the recovery process. I must allow Him to be in charge as the Lord of my life. In fact, He refuses to be any other.

Another very important thing to remember is *why* I feel the way I do. When I was being hurt, I was not a Christian. I was afraid of God and I saw Him as my enemy--just like my dad was. Even though I called on Him in desperation for help, I knew I couldn't trust Him any more than I could trust my dad. Therefore, it makes perfect sense that while I was overwhelmed with the hurts and emotions of those past experiences, my misconception about God was a part of that.

During my counseling years, I needed to express my anger and seething rage. This was something I had a very difficult time recognizing and doing. *Anger really scared me*. The primary reason was that, as I was growing up, I was taught that expressing my anger (childhood tantrums) was bad and ugly and usually followed with punishment. This developed into my becoming afraid of expressing my anger and afraid of the anger expressed toward me. My father had hurt me deeply. He had robbed me of my childhood. He destroyed my innocence. It's as if he had rubbed mud on my uniqueness and self-worth—and then ignored me. It seemed like he was jealous of me to the point of hatred and slander. He denied me the privilege of becoming a person in my own right. His actions caused wounds that prevented my deepest desires from being fulfilled. Why would I willingly submit to that kind of treatment and think of it as okay and normal? It was *not* normal—it was sick and hurtful and damaging. His behavior toward me was unacceptable. In spite of the fact that he was my parent, I had the right (and responsibility toward myself) *to be angry!!* I *needed* to be angry with him and not feel guilty about it.

I learned that my anger should not have been focused toward *God*, but toward my *father's behavior*. There was a big difference. Additionally, my anger should *not* have been focused at my *father as a person*, but toward *his actions. It is okay to hate abuse. It is never okay to hate the abuser.*

Here is an important point: It is vitally important to forgive those who hurt us, even though they may not realize the extent to which they have hurt us and whether or not they come to us in repentance—especially if the one(s) who hurt us is one or both of our parents. The reason for this is a command. In fact, it is one of the Ten Commandments:

> *You shall honor your father and your mother, that your days may be prolonged in the land which the Lord your God gives you.*
> *God through Moses ~ Exodus 20:12*

In spite of the fact that we are also commanded to forgive those who have offended us, this doesn't mean that we have to trust them. We can forgive them *from our hearts*, but that does not mean we should put them in a position of trust where we will allow them to hurt us again. For example, when my mother removed my father from our home with a restraining order, she did not take the role of fatherhood away from him for my younger siblings. She allowed him to have supervised visitation with them. She couldn't trust him to be a member of our household any longer. That's the difference between forgiveness and trust.

As far as my mother was concerned, because of all my father's problems, she was unable to give much nurturing to me after I reached the age of thirteen. Actually, she wasn't available to me even when I was younger. By "younger" I mean that when I was in elementary school, she took in day care to supplement the family income. This created a situation of neglect and she expected me to be the "mature elder daughter" and to help out whenever I could. That was very difficult for me, because I still had some growing up needs and really needed her to be my mother. This "*neglect*" was not intentional, but there just wasn't enough of her to go around. In our home my mother was raising five of us, watching three or four more daycare children, and also trying to run a household. When I was eleven she went to work outside the home and was completely unavailable. Again, the purpose was to provide added income for the family.

Then as my father's unhealthy behaviors escalated, my mother became increasingly distant and even more distant to my growing emotional needs as an adolescent. However, to give her credit, everything she did was for her children. She loved being a mother and wanted to do what was best for each one of us, as difficult as that was. Her emotional resources were stretched as far as they could go, and as a damaged adolescent I didn't see the entire picture. I loved her and I wanted to be like her. When I wanted to be around her, she simply did not have the time or the energy to give to one individual child. When she couldn't give me the nurturing I desired, I felt rejected. This caused me to withdraw, which led to depression and a new lack of trust. This was also perhaps one reason I could not confide in her, when my father molested me night after night.

Coping

How is it possible to live day in and day out with deep emotional pain? How do I go about my life and fulfill my responsibilities of school and work with such a distraction of emotional pain and inner turmoil?

I'll tell you from my experience with both physical and emotional pain, there's never an easy way. When it all started I lived with my family, and that was not easy. Then I lived with roommates I met at church. These were Christians I knew and felt I could trust. This was during the time that most of my pain was buried, and I was doing quite well. But when my emotional pain was at its worst, I was single and was in my late twenties and early thirties. When I moved to Southern California, I was 1200 miles away from my hometown. I lived in rented rooms with families I didn't know, in an area of the country I wasn't familiar with. My emotional pain was so profound that I was desperate. It was at that time that I felt the need for one-on-one counseling sessions.

Most of the families I lived with did not have a clue as to the emotional process I was going through. I rented rooms with different families as they became available, because I lived in a high rent area in Southern California. It was a different culture than my hometown, and some of these strangers were not very understanding. However, part of that time I was able to live alone. During those times when I was blessed to live in my own rented apartment, it became a place of peace, a place of rest, a refuge, and a place to heal. It became my haven.

This was a very lonely time for me. All I could really count on for comfort was God's Word, His presence, and the encouragement of Christian music. Within myself, I had the determination God had given me to help me get through the recovery process.

This recovery process, which I call my journey through *The Valley of Tears*, is very, very difficult. It is the most difficult thing you will ever have to go through.

You have to be totally committed to it *and never, never give up*. Your focus has to be on God, your Healer and your Great Physician. A focus on God and His Word is the only real strength you can count on, and there are a number of things you can do to keep God's Word stronger in your heart than the painful shouts of the enemy.

1. Spend time with Christian friends or join a support group. Many of the larger churches offer these support groups and you can find groups in your area on the Internet.
2. Find a Counselor who is trained in the area of incest. I always felt that my counselor and God worked as a team to heal my broken soul and bring me to a place of recovery. God was my healer, and my counselor facilitated my time to help me understand what was going on in my broken soul.
3. Do something creative, such as gardening, sewing, athletics, or whatever your area of interest is. It's very tempting to think only of the pain and get lost in it. *You must not let this happen!* I found that growing flowers really helped. Even in most rented apartments and rented rooms, your landlords will allow you to have a window box of some sort to grow some flowers. They're there to greet you in the morning and when you return from work at the end of the day. I really encourage it.

4. Another coping mechanism I used was a journal. As I mentioned in an earlier chapter, I would write everything in my journal. I expressed all my emotions. I could be honest about how I felt, even about landlords, roommates, and co-workers who couldn't understand what I was going through. I applied God's Word to my emotions. I searched for promises that I could hang on to for each thought I encountered.
5. *I would even tell myself that God's Word was truer and more real than my pain, regardless of my feelings. I would focus on it during my free moments throughout the day. I would tell myself that the truth found in the Word of God is more real than anything else in my life. And it truly is. Additionally, God's Word, His truth, lasts forever, and my pain won't last any longer than this lifetime.*

Since the journal was for my eyes only, I could be brutally honest. I thought that when I got to the other side of this part of the process, I knew I could either destroy it or save it as a reminder of God's faithfulness.

You will keep him in perfect peace,
Whose mind is stayed on You,
Because he trusts in You.
Trust in the Lord forever,
For in YAH, the Lord, is everlasting strength.
Yahweh God to Isaiah 26:3-4 NKJV

Watch over your heart with all diligence,
For from it flow the springs of life.
King Solomon ~ Proverbs 4:23

For I consider that the sufferings of this
present time are not worthy to be
compared with the glory that is to be
revealed to us.
The Apostle Paul ~ Romans 8:18

Do I Really Need God to Heal?

Some people have asked me why I need to bring God into a book that is about recovery from the trauma of incest. Some of them have even suggested that the reason I have such a strong commitment to the Lord Jesus is because I needed a "crutch", when I didn't have anywhere else to turn. But this is not true. I have met many types of people since I became a Christian. When I worked at Western Seminary, I met people from all over the world who were committed to the Lord Jesus and who came from different cultures. I have known individuals who were raised in strong Christian homes with parents who were committed to Jesus and the Bible. These people were just as strong in their commitment as their parents and sometimes stronger. I have also known some who, for whatever reason, were embittered against their parents because of their strong commitment to their faith. And there are many who had such a strong faith in the God of the Bible (against the wishes of their families), without a traumatic event like mine that led them to what is known as a "crisis of faith" (like thoughts about suicide). Their parents thought they were wasting their lives, throwing away their undergraduate degrees and natural talents by seeking a graduate degree at a biblical seminary. There were also some scholars who have studied the Bible in depth (whom I have had the privilege of knowing and working with) and who, as a result of their study, are committed to Him and love Him to the point that they would even die for their faith in Him. God has His reasons for bringing those He chooses to be members of His family (for reasons only He knows).

Even knowing all of these things, I am confident that my despair was not the only reason I was called into the Family of God. I had a number of opportunities to respond to His call before I actually became His child. This was in spite of the fact that I was absolutely desperate for Him to make something meaningful out of my life. It was truly my last resort, before I had taken seriously the options of suicide or running away from my broken, dysfunctional home.

I have spoken at length about how it took a personal relationship with God through His Son, the Lord Jesus Christ, for me to go through the recovery process and find peace for my broken and bruised soul. I *couldn't* go through it on my own. It's not only true for the incest victim, but for victims of childhood abuse and other violent crimes.

Besides my research into this terrible trauma, I know this to be factual because I have personally known people and have read testimonies of individuals whom God spared from making the decision to end their life. As I was contemplating taking my own life, it was the hand of the Lord who pulled me away from the doorway leading to a suicidal death. It was an intensely emotional experience, as He lifted me out of that deep pit of dark despair. At one point, I knew I was looking right into the pit of hell, and I was more frightened than I could begin to describe. I turned to Him immediately and was received into His arms with the warmth of heaven's fellowship. It was a profoundly spiritual and deeply emotional experience that I shall never forget.

It wasn't until I searched in the Scriptures about God's character and read what scholarly men had written regarding Him, that I began to think deeply about who this Holy Being is. I had to spend some serious time thinking and meditating on all this information to gain some kind of understanding about the One who had created me and carried me through the Valley of Tears. Even so, my understanding was still very limited. But I didn't give up. As I spent time meditating on Who He is as a Person, He spoke to me and drew me into His embrace. You see, it wasn't simply an academic search, but it was also a spiritual quest which brought me into the arms of Jesus.

There have been some who continue to believe that I responded to Jesus because of the pain I was in and because I needed that so-called "crutch" to make me feel stronger. But to those who still believe I needed a crutch to help me get through the pain, I would ask, "How would that explain the devotion of the many friends and acquaintances I have, who never had the same type of trauma I've had, for whom the Lord became their "Tower of Strength?" There have been *so many* who have taken the claims of Christ seriously, as they have read books like *More than a Carpenter* by Josh and Sean McDowell or *The Case for Christ* by Lee Strobel. Both of these authors were avowed atheists who set out to disprove the claims of the Bible and became believers in their attempt.

The scholar who taught me the most about the remarkable nature of the Person of God was a man named A. W. Tozer. He wrote a classic book titled *The Knowledge of the Holy*. This book *really* made me think. When I first read it, I would read a line or two, and then I'd have to think about it for a while before I could continue. Sometimes it would take a week or so and sometimes even longer before I could finish the sentence or paragraph I had been reading, because the thoughts in this book are so unfathomable. I would meditate on them and go over in my mind what I had read, trying to wrap my mind around the truth of the statements made by this very intelligent and deep thinker. The thoughts that he pulled from the Scriptures are nothing less than profound. I learned from Him that the nature of God is deep and unfathomable, far beyond what the human mind can understand. And so God says:

> 8 *"For My thoughts are not your thoughts,*
> *Nor are your ways My ways," declares the* LORD.

9 "For as the heavens are higher than the earth,
So are My ways higher than your ways
And My thoughts than your thoughts.
Isaiah 55:8-9

God is a mystery, and yet He wants us to know Him. If we desire to know Him, He will communicate with us and show us who He is in His Word.

Notes . . .

Chapter 7

A Song of Healing and Praise

While I live I will praise the LORD; I will sing praises to my God while I have my being.

Psalm 146:2

Do you believe that a soul that has been torn by abuse and neglect before it has had a chance to grow up can actually heal and mature? My opinion is that on its own, I doubt it. But with God, all things are possible. Jesus believed this and said this very thing in Mark's Gospel just as he was about to heal a young boy no one else could heal.

And Jesus said to him, "'All things are possible to him who believes." Mark 9:23

I fell in love with the following Psalm when I was memorizing and meditating on Scripture. It might help illustrate a path of healing for you.

Psalm 40

This is a wonderful Psalm that presents the process of healing. I have chosen some select verses that apply to the victory over my wounds of incest and perhaps your wounds of abuse, as well.

- ***Psalm 40:1***

  I waited patiently for the Lord; and He
  Inclined to me and heard my cry.

Healing always requires work. The three most important ingredients of that work are *patient waiting, faith, and prayer.* Sometimes God doesn't answer our prayer for the deliverance from our pain right away. We must be careful to always listen to Him, as He is ever listening to us, waiting to hear our prayers. During that waiting time, He is doing the work of healing in our hearts. This is why we must *wait patiently* and *continue to pray*. He even counts our tears and groans as prayers. Remember this:

Depart from me, all you who do iniquity, For the
Lord ***has heard the voice*** *of my weeping.*
King David ~ Psalm 6:8

O Lord My God, I cried to You for help,
and You healed me.
King David ~ Psalm 30:2

Ask, and it will be given to you; seek, and you will find; knock, and it will be opened to you. For everyone who asks receives, and he who seeks finds, and to him who knocks, it will be opened.
Jesus ~ Matthew 7:7-8

"The task of healing is one of great faith. Sometimes it is hard to take that step of faith, trusting that the Holy Spirit will lead you as you actively search for the help you need. But in the end, it will be worth it."

Earl Henslin, Psy.D.
Secrets of Your Family Tree[1]

❖ *Psalm 40:2*

He brought me up out of the pit of destruction,
out of the miry clay, [2]
And He set my feet upon a rock,
making my footsteps firm.

When I was in the deep darkness of depression, it felt like I was walking through fog laced with glue. I couldn't move forward emotionally any more than a person whose feet were stuck in Wadi mire [3] could move forward physically. It's incredible how our emotions are tied to our physical beings. It's more than we would like to think, and they can stop us dead in our tracks. When I described this sticky fog-like feeling to my counselor, she thought perhaps some medication might help.

In some cases, a chemical imbalance occurs in which certain neurotransmitters become depleted in the brain and spinal fluid. These brain chemicals cannot be replenished on their own, just like we cannot cope with our emotional and spiritual battles on our own. We need help from an outside source. When my counselor realized this was the case, she sent me to a Psychiatrist for a consultation. I was put on a very low dose of anti-depressant medication. There was no immediate change. But after about six weeks, *very gradually* I began to notice a change. It was not like a drug high; it was gentler, like the first sign of spring after a very long winter. I can tell you in my experience the Lord used that doctor's expertise with the medication to fill my heart with life and joy again!

I had been so severely depressed for such a long time (at least ten years), that my system—that is, my brain and spinal cord chemistry—couldn't withstand the pressure and it became severely imbalanced. This was very similar to the chemical imbalance that occurs when a person becomes depressed as a result of hypoglycemia (low blood sugar). In fact, I once knew a pastor who had that very problem. He became so depressed that he was put in a mental hospital. When his diagnosis was finally complete, it was hypoglycemia! As a result of his treatment, the sun came out and there was joy once again.

God used the medical treatment to set my feet upon a rock, a solid place, making my footsteps firm. Feeling a sense of security is the most wonderful feeling in the world after you have lived for years in the pit of despair, as this and many other Psalms describe. It gives you a sense of joy that cannot be contained.

❖ *Psalm 40:3*

He put a new song in my mouth,
a song of praise to our God;
Many will see and fear
And will trust in the Lord.

The new song is the result of healing. It's like being born again, which will result in a wonderful testimony to the glory of God. If you're like I was in the pit of destruction, you don't care much about the testimony at the time. You will later, and you will want to tell everyone you see. But at first you'll just want to get past the pain and get on with your life. What you must understand is that God cares about both your pain *and* your testimony. He *never* wastes our pain. I don't know how He does it, but it is simultaneously for our good *and* for His glory. He's amazing that way. It's very difficult to imagine how it can be for our good when we're in this pit, but that's when we must understand the goodness of God. *I concluded that the reality of God and His character was more real to me than what I was feeling at that moment.*

The enemy of my soul is a master of deception, and he would have me believe that my pain was all there was, and that God was off somewhere taking a nap.

Jesus tells us in John 8:44,

> *. . . He (Satan) was a murderer from the beginning, and does not stand in the truth, because there is no truth in him. When he speaks a lie, he speaks from his own resources, because he is a liar and the father of lies.*
>
> *(Parentheses by author)*

I repeat, "The goodness of God and God's personal care of me is more real than my pain." I wanted to ponder on this thought and believe it more strongly than anything else until I was out of the pit, looking down from where my footsteps were firm. As a result, I found my God to be continually faithful. *As I meditated on the reality of God and His character, He lifted me from the pit of despair and He raised me up to where my footsteps were firm and secure.*

After that initial experience, whenever I became overwhelmed with past or present feelings of insecurity in my heart, He would continue to be just as faithful and compassionate. I realized that God is much more aware than I am, and that healing i*s a pro*cess. None of my growth happens immediately or quickly.

Of course, once you are on that plateau where your footsteps are firm, then you'll be able to sing like never before. <u>*You'll want to rejoice*</u>, and you will want to share with others the wonderful things the Lord has done for you. You won't be able to contain it or to stop smiling!! Additionally, there are times when you will be able to sing even before your footsteps are firm.

In Acts 16:25, there is the story of the Apostle Paul and his companion Silas in the Philippian jail. They had just been beaten and should have been discouraged and feeling sorry for themselves. But instead, they sang and rejoiced with songs of praise because their concept of the reality of God and His deliverance was so much greater than their present circumstance.

❖ ***Psalm 40:5***

> *Many, O Lord my God, are the wonders*
> *which You have done,*
> *And Your thoughts toward us;*
> *There is none to compare with You.*

If I would declare and speak
of them,
They would be too numerous
to count.

It is impossible to imagine all that God has done for us and all His thoughts about us every day and every moment. The very idea is overwhelming. He is truly incomprehensible. There is no way to wrap my mind around God. He's thinking about me constantly. No, there is absolutely none who can compare with Him! God, who can lift me from the dark depression I was in, is surely amazing and worthy of all my commitment and praise!

Shortly after the anti-depressant medications began to work their wonders in my system, I met the man who would be my husband. God's timing is always perfect. I had prayed for the man I would marry for fourteen years, and this was the time that God chose for us to meet. I prayed that he would be a godly man, a man of character, and a man of integrity. And he truly is. I prayed for him all those years that God would protect him and bring him to me. As it turned out, the Lord brought me to him. He brought me all the way from Portland, Oregon, to Southern California to meet him. If I had met him any sooner, he would have met a woman who was very depressed and insecure. As it was, my husband could see me gradually coming out of my shell of insecurity. I could confidently share with him what my biological father had done, in the context of God's work of healing in my life during the years that I suffered with post-traumatic stress disorder. I could enjoy giving glory to God for His work in my life—all because of God's perfect timing. And he could accept it all with great joy and gladness. He could see that God had done a great work of healing in my life, instead of looking at a defeated, depressed woman.

❖ ***Psalm 40:6***

Sacrifice and meal offering You
have not desired;
My ears You have opened;
Burnt offering and sin offering
You have not required.

I believe the Lord isn't looking for any kind of performance from me, as a result of His work of healing in my life. He simply wants me to continue to put my trust in Him, to meditate on Him through the Scriptures, and to keep it in my mind and in my heart.

❖ ***Psalm 40:11***

You, O Lord, will not withhold Your
compassion from me;
Your loving kindness and Your truth will
continually preserve me.

I must always keep my focus on the character of Yahweh, my God. It's His compassion that will keep me safe, and I'll be preserved by His lovingkindness and truth for all eternity. My flashbacks or nightmares will come back from time to time and I need to keep my focus on the Lord and His Word.

❖ ***Psalm 40:13-14***

Be pleased, O Lord, to deliver me;
Make haste, O Lord, to help me.
Let those be ashamed and
humiliated together
Who seek my life to destroy it;
Let those be turned back and
dishonored
Who delight in my hurt.

Even as the Lord lifts us up out of the grime of depression and sets our feet upon a rock of stability, we can still fall back into it. Someone can say something, we begin to feel embarrassed or exposed by something from our past, and BAM!! Down we go into that same old pit of despair. It's in these times that we need a refresher course. The first thing we need to do is seek the Lord in prayer. My pastor tells us "Much prayer, much blessing; little prayer, little blessing; no prayer, no blessing." You cannot pray about this part of your life too much. Then we should make a call to our counselor, our pastor, close friends, or a support group.

Those who have had to suffer with secret wounds know exactly what I have been writing about. It is the secret wounds, the ones that won't heal, that cry out for comfort and healing. Nothing will happen until we pull it out of hiding and present it to the Lord. There will be no healing of the festering wound, until we hold it up to our Lord and say, "Here it is, Lord, here's my broken heart. I can't fix it. I can't even live with it. But You can transform it. Please heal my wounded, broken soul." When we do that, all those wonderful promises you have read on the previous pages of this book can be put into action. But you have to keep praying, making that first step of faith, and trusting our Lord to heal you.

Letter to My Heavenly Father

As I was going through my counseling years before I was married, it was suggested to me by a caring friend that I write a letter to God. This friend suggested that I tell the Lord just how I felt about my situation, about Him, and His sovereignty (that I should honestly express everything I was thinking and feeling at the time). What follows is my letter to the Lord of my Life as I had grown to know Him:

My Father in Heaven, Holy, Holy, Holy is Your wonderful name!

What a difference it is when I address You as my Father, as opposed to how I would address my biological father. It is because You are so very different than he was. I am so grateful for the opportunity to know You as my Lord and Savior and Best Friend. Thank you for your unchangeable, unconditional love!

Thank You, my Father, in that You know me so completely. You know my ups and my downs. You understand why I struggle with trust. This is my biggest problem of all. I wish it wasn't always that way, but You know all about my deep emotional wounds. You know why my moods change, and the fact that they won't affect Your love for me really baffles me. You understand why I am so inhibited, even in Your presence. When I was going through my dark times of despair, I hated myself. Even now that I am Your child and have the advantage of Your Spirit speaking to my heart, I still get depressed at times, but I'm reassured to know that You love me even in the midst of that darkness. When I'm in the dark, I am tempted to ask You "Why?" and "How long will this last?" During those times I feel abandoned, even by You.

I can't comprehend it, but I accept it. This is why I'm so grateful for Your Word. I'm so thankful for the promises that guarantee You're always with me, that You have a purpose for my pain, and that You will work all of this agony out for a good and holy purpose. Thank you for all the godly friends You have given me, who have encouraged me to not give up.

Even when I am in the dark, You are my light. You "understand my thoughts from afar" and You see me with perfect clarity. You not only have the advantage of intimate and perfect knowledge of me from within, but You also can see from a distance what is happening in me. You see the big picture. I'm so caught up in the small details, that all I can see are my own problems. I feel surrounded and smothered by my emotional pain.

Lord, You know what my days are like. You know the defeat I feel every night, when I go to bed all alone and then wake up in the morning . . . all alone. You know why my life is like this, and You know how I feel about it.

You understand my confusion and questions, my anger, restlessness, and impatience. You know my emotions, and yet You accept me and love me unconditionally.

You alone can make sense out of the futile attempts I make to verbally express my emotions. There aren't enough words, phrases, and illustrations to adequately express the pain and loneliness I feel. My pain is beyond verbal description. There aren't enough tears in me to express and ventilate all my hurt emotions. I love what You say in Psalm 56:8 that *"You have taken account of my wanderings, You have put all my tears in Your bottle, and You have recorded them in Your book."* I love how You keep track of all the expressions of my pain. You also say in Psalm 6:8 that You even consider my weeping as prayer to You. You are truly an amazing God.

You need neither tears nor words to understand how I feel. You know me in detail to the depths of my being.

Lord, You are the most Wonderful Counselor. All I have to do is to position myself in Your arms and embrace the fact that You understand me, intimately know me, and accept me the way You created me to be. I'm far from perfect, but You still accept me just the way I am. You also understand the fact that spiritual comfort is not enough. I also need physical arms around me and human understanding. It takes a lot of faith to believe in You for this. But my lack of faith does not affect Your ability to understand me, empathize with me, or support me in all that I think, say, or do.

You know my pain is so deep that I'm unable to lift myself up right now. I'm unable to be encouraged into feeling good again. I believe You can and *will* heal me by Your love, through Your Spirit within me, and with the encouragement of friends and my counselor. I'm depending on You for my life and to make me whole again.

I know in my heart that there will come a day, when I will be free of all these limitations. I pray that You will allow me to be married someday to a man who will understand how the trauma of incest has altered my life. My loving Father, I humbly ask that You will use my changed life for the glory of Your Name and to encourage others who have gone through this same pain and deep darkness.

All this I pray in the grand and holy Name of Jesus, my Good Shepherd and the Healer of My Soul,

Tammy ♥
Your hurting Child

My Own Personal Journal ~ Growth and the Acceptance of Self

Early Thirties, Before Marriage

I am growing . . . in many ways. Memories of my wounds still hurt. Some fears of relating with other people still hurt. Rejection still hurts. But I like myself, and I won't sell myself short to anyone. I believe I'm worth loving, and that's all there is to it. But I'm still lonely. I need close relationships and I don't have very many. The intimate friends I do have are great. There is no question that God has given me some quality friends. They're the best I could ever ask for, but I still need more.

There are still people who can't accept me for the way I am. There are some personalities who can't accept anyone who's different than they are. Let me explain. I'm an introvert. Some extroverted people have a hard time talking with me, because I prefer to be reserved in my conversations. I guess that's a loss for both of us.

There is a family I was acquainted some years ago, who were all extroverted, every single one of them. I really liked all of them, but they had difficulty relating to me because I tended to be very quiet around them. The truth is, together as a group, they could be rather overwhelming. But the fact that they couldn't relate to me as a quiet person made me sad. I would have loved to fit in with them and to get to know them better.

But I think they felt safer in their extroverted, center-of-attention mode.

A member of this particular family made a statement to me one weekend. It was about my personality and it stung like rejection. It really hurt and made it very difficult for me to respond to her. She expressed disapproval for my quiet personality, and it hit me much harder than mere disapproval. I felt completely discredited, devalued, and misunderstood. It made me feel defenseless and weak. It also made me wonder how secure she really was around people who are different from her own extroverted personality.

After that weekend, I discussed the rejection episode with my counselor. She said that having a quiet personality is, on the contrary, not a bad thing. To my surprise she told me it doesn't equal being insecure. Insecurity can be expressed through any personality, whether you are an introvert or an extrovert. My quiet spirit and personality has brought relaxation and refreshment to a lot of people, or so I've been told. It's sad that some people cannot appreciate it. I guess that is a fact of life for everyone. She was right.

Notes . . .

Epilogue

As I traveled through the *Valley of Tears* to obtain healing for my wounds, I experienced much time in deep, dark depression. This led to three separate times of suicidal depression, which were dangerous times for me. The first time was when I was 15 years old and living with my parents. I was serious enough to think about suicide and how I would accomplish it.

The second time, I was 27 years old. I was even more depressed than the first time and living alone. I knew this was dangerous, but, fortunately, I had been working at the seminary with professors who were also pastors with experience counseling individuals who were suicidal. Besides that, I had read the right books. So I knew I needed to talk with someone and express how I was feeling. With that knowledge, I told my supervisor at the Christian University where I worked. The third time was the same scenario as the second. However, my counselor referred me to a psychiatrist, a medical doctor, who evaluated my condition and prescribed anti-depressant medication.

The medication worked beautifully. Within six weeks, the depression had subsided and I felt joy again. I was on this medication for about eighteen months, and then slowly weaned off of it because I didn't need it anymore.

Now I want to exhort you, if you are in the same state that I was in and *if you feel the need to escape, that is your first warning sign*. If you're not in counseling, you need to be. I personally recommend a Christian counselor, because what has been wounded is your soul—your soul being your mind, will, and emotions—primarily your emotions. I wouldn't entrust the healing of my soul with anyone who does not personally know my Creator. However, that's up to you.

I cannot stress enough that the first thing you need to do is to *tell someone how you are feeling and why you are feeling it. Do not wait! Talk to someone! Pray about this decision!* Your Heavenly Father loves you more than anyone on this planet, and the last thing He wants is to see you take your life. Tell Him *everything you feel*. Your Father in Heaven *is the Best Friend* you will ever find, and He truly understands your feelings.

If you are not a Christian, I would like to encourage you to consider what He has done for you. He loves you so much that He, being the eternal God of the Universe, humbled Himself to become one of us. He came to this earth as Jesus of Nazareth. But He was different from any other man that ever lived. He lived a perfect and sinless life, and He willingly offered His life as an offering for our sins on the cross. This was the cruelest form of death in His earthly lifetime or really any other time. He died on that wooden cross and was buried for three days. Then He was resurrected by the power of God to show that His love and sacrifice for our sins was acceptable to God the Father. Have you ever known anyone who would die for you, because they loved you that much? Well, that's what Jesus did. In fact, He said, "*Greater love has no one than this, that He lay down His life for His friends*" (John 15:13). To become His child, all you have to do is confess your sin to the Lord and by faith believe in your heart that He died for you and that God raised Him from the dead, and you will be saved. In prayer, say to Him that you believe and accept what Jesus did for you on the cross and that you also want Jesus to be your Savior and the Lord of your life. In 1 John 1:9 we are reminded that:

> *If we confess our sins, He is faithful and just to forgive us our sins and to cleanse us from all unrighteousness.*

If you prayed this prayer and you really meant it, God came into your life, and you will be filled with His precious Holy Spirit. Congratulations! Welcome to the family of God! You are now one of His adopted children.

Keep in mind that when you prayed the prayer of faith, you may or may not have experienced euphoric feelings. Don't let this determine whether you think the Lord has or has not come into your life. Once you pray that prayer, you will be born-again for all eternity and nothing will ever change this truth, no matter what you feel or what anyone else tells you.

The next thing is, according to Romans 10:9-10, it says the following:

. . . that if you confess with your mouth Jesus as Lord, and believe in your heart that God raised Him from the dead, you will be saved; for with the heart a person believes, resulting in righteousness, and with the mouth he confesses, resulting in salvation.

This means after you pray and confess your sins asking Jesus to be your Savior and the Lord of your Life, believing that He died for you and God raised Him from the dead, you must verbally confess that this is true. You must tell someone such as a close friend or a neighbor.

Then it would be very helpful for you to obtain a Bible and to find a Bible-believing church. Try to find out if it's a church where the pastor teaches straight from the Bible. If you can, get involved in a weekly Bible study. Additionally, get to know fellow believers who attend your church and Bible study. Make some new friends, people whom you can learn to trust. It may take time, but it will be life-changing.

You will find that, as you continue through *The Valley of Tears,* there will be a divine Companion who will be your Great Physician and Comforter.

Appendix I

Bibliography

Allender, Dan B. *Wounded Heart: Hope for Adult Victims of Childhood Sexual Abuse*. Colorado Springs: NavPress, 1990.

Banner, Lois. *Marilyn: The Passion and the Paradox*. New York: Bloomsbury Press, 2012.

Brother Lawrence. *The Practice of the Presence of God*. Edited by Donald E. Demaray. Grand Rapids: Baker Book House, 1975.

Carder, Dave, Earl Henslin, John Townsend, Henry Cloud, and Alice Brawand. *Secrets of Your Family Tree: Healing for Adult Children of Dysfunctional Families*. Chicago: Moody Press, 1991.

Carmichael, Amy. "Nothing in the House." In *A Braver Song to Sing: A Biography of Patricia Ann "Pann"*

Baltz, authored by Marilee Dunker, 6. Grand Rapids: Zondervan Books, 1987.

Clark, Annie. "My Beloved." In *Springs in the Valley*, edited by Mrs. Charles E. Cowman, 242-43. Los Angeles: The Oriental Missionary Society, 1945.

Cowman, Charles E. (Mrs.). *Streams in the Desert*. Grand Rapids: Zondervan Publishing House, 1965.

Ferguson, M. P. "The Consoler." In *Springs in the Valley*, edited by Mrs. Charles E. Cowman, 53. Los Angeles: The Oriental Missionary Society, 1945.

Havergal, Frances Ridley. "Upon Thy Word I Rest." In *Springs in the Valley*, edited by Mrs. Charles E. Cowman, 122. Los Angeles: The Oriental Missionary Society, 1945.

J.H.S. "God of the Impossible." In *Springs in the Valley*, edited by Mrs. Charles E. Cowman, 132. Los Angeles: The Oriental Missionary Society, 1945.

Kruse, Kevin. "The Joy of the Lord." Sermon, Laurelwood Baptist Church, Vancouver, WA, June 23, 2019.

Landorf, Joyce. *Irregular People*. Waco: Word Books, 1982.

Matheson, George. "O Love that Will Not Let Me Go." 1882.

Missildine, W. H. *Your Inner Child of the Past*. New York: Pocket Books,1963.

Moore, Beth. *Get Out of That Pit: Straight Talk About God's Deliverance*. Nashville: Integrity Publishers, 2007.

National Center for Victims of Crime. "Child Sexual Abuse Statistics." Last accessed April 2018. https://victimsofcrime.org/media/reporting-on-child-sexual-abuse/child-sexual-abuse-statistics.

Quote by J.R. Miller: "Christ Is Building His Kingdom With Earth's Broken Things." Goodreads. Last accessed July 13, 2019. https://www.goodreads.com/quotes/333341-christ-is-building-his-kingdom-with-earth-s-broken-things-men.

Radmacher, Earl D., Ronald B. Allen, and H. Wayne House, eds. "Abba, Father"; "14:36 Abba"; "8:15 Abba." In *New King James Study Bible*, 2nd ed., 1581, 1778. Nashville: Thomas Nelson, Inc., 2007.

Razzi, Emily. "Finding Beauty in Tragedy." *Our Daily Bread*. Published September 28, 2017. https://ymi.today/2017/09/finding-beauty-in-my-tragedy/.

Roberts, Deborah. *Raped*. Grand Rapids: Zondervan Publishing House, 1981.

Sandell-Berg, Karolina Wihelmina. "Children of the Heavenly Father." 1855. Translated by Ernst W. Olson. 1925. Tom Fettke, ed. *The Hymnal for Worship & Celebration*. Waco: Word Music, 1986.

Smith, J. Danson. "The Gift of the Thorn." In *Springs in the Valley*, edited by Mrs. Charles E. Cowman,

273. Los Angeles: The Oriental Missionary Society, 1945.

Spurgeon, Charles H. *Morning & Evening*. Peabody: Hendrickson Publishers, 1995.

Swindoll, Charles R. *Growing Strong in the Seasons of Life*. Grand Rapids: Zondervan Publishing House, 1983.

Ten Boom, Corrie, John Sherrill, and Elizabeth Sherrill. *The Hiding Place*. Minneapolis: World Wide Publications, 1971.

Timms, David. *Sacred Waiting: Waiting on God in a World That Waits for Nothing*. Minneapolis: Bethany House Publishers, 2009.

Tozer, A. W. *The Knowledge of the Holy*. San Francisco: Harper Collins Publishers, 1961.

Tozer, A.W. *The Root of the Righteous*. Harrisburg: Christian Publications, Inc., 1955.

Wagner, Maurice E. *The Sensation of Being Somebody: Building an Adequate Self-Concept*. Grand Rapids: Zondervan Publishing House, 1975.

Appendix II

About the Author

Tammy Lansaw grew up in Portland, Oregon, in a large family. As a child she always wanted to grow up to be like her mother, get married, become a homemaker, and have children.

As she was growing up, the backwash of the incest and her father's emotional problems caused many negative issues in her home, leading Tammy to deep suicidal depression. Fortunately, God had his hand on her life. Classmates from her high school invited her to church, and within a year she accepted Jesus Christ as her Savior and Lord of her life. This was the beginning of her healing process and her walk through *The Valley of Tears.*

Tammy's dream of marriage and children never died, and she began praying for God's best for her life. She prayed continually, as one of her mentors had taught her, that she would never take anything less than God's best. Fourteen years after beginning that prayer for God's choice for a husband, she met her life-partner, Victor Lansaw. He is a veteran of the Coast Guard, who has a deep love for the Lord, evangelism, and group Bible study.

Upon graduating from high school, one of Tammy's goals was to attend a Bible College. She was not able to achieve that goal, because of the emotional pain and insecurity caused by the incest. However, after being married for 25 years, she attended North Portland Bible College, completing four terms of Old Testament Studies. This is something she loves and hopes to continue in the future.

Tammy has always loved to write but hesitated to write on the topic of her abuse and family dysfunction, because she did not wish to dishonor or embarrass her mother or siblings in any way. With the passing of her mother and after discussing writing this book with her siblings, she learned that they were in full support. Most of all, with the support of friends and her pastor, she felt the Lord was definitely leading her in this direction.

In addition to writing, Tammy loves singing. She loves Christian music and had spent many years singing in church choirs. Tammy also loves gardening and sewing her own clothes and quilts. She currently lives in Battle Ground, Washington, with her husband, Victor, to whom she has been married for 32 years.

Appendix III

Recommended Reading

Allender, Dan B. *Wounded Heart: Hope for Adult Victims of Childhood Sexual Abuse*. Colorado Springs: NavPress, 1990.

Allender, Dan B. *Wounded Heart: Hope for Adult Victims of Childhood Sexual Abuse – A Companion Workbook*. Colorado Springs: NavPress, 1992.

Brother Lawrence. *The Practice of the Presence of God*. Edited by Donald E. Demaray. Grand Rapids: Baker Book House, 1975.

Carder, Dave, Earl Henslin, John Townsend, Henry Cloud, and Alice Brawand. *Secrets of Your Family Tree: Healing for Adult Children of Dysfunctional Families*. Chicago: Moody Press, 1991. Republished as Carder, Dave, Earl Henslin, John Townsend, Henry Cloud, and Alice Brawand. *Unlocking Your Family Patterns*. Chicago: Moody Press, 2011.

Cowman, Charles E. (Mrs.), ed. *Springs in the Valley*. Los Angeles: The Oriental Missionary Society, 1945.

Cowman, Charles E. (Mrs.). *Streams in the Desert*. Grand Rapids: Zondervan Publishing House, 1965.

Finch, Thomas. *Unmapped Darkness: Finding God's Path Through Suffering*. Chicago: Moody Publishers, 2006.

Frank, Jan. *Door of Hope: Recognizing and Resolving the Pains of Your Past*. Nashville: Thomas Nelson, 1995.

Hansel, Tim. *When I Relax I Feel Guilty ~ Discover the Wonder and Joy of Really Living*. Elgin: David C. Cook Publishing Co., 1979.

Jeffress, Robert. *When Forgiveness Doesn't Make Sense*. Colorado Springs: Waterbrook Press, 2000.

Kerr, William F. (Compiled by). *God, What Is He Like?* Wheaton: Tyndale House Publishers, Inc. 1977. 111-127

Landorf, Joyce. *Irregular People*. Waco: Word Books, 1982.

Lockyer, Herbert. *How to Find Comfort in the Bible*. Waco: Word Books, 1977.

McDowell, Josh, and Sean McDowell. *More Than A Carpenter*. Carol Stream: Tyndale House Publishers, 2009.

Missildine, W. H. *Your Inner Child of the Past*. New York: Pocket Books,1963.

Moore, Beth. *Get Out of That Pit: Straight Talk About God's Deliverance*. Nashville: Integrity Publishers, 2007.

Seamands, David A. *Healing for Damaged Emotions.* Wheaton: Victor Books,1981.

Strobel, Lee. *The Case for Christ: A Journalist's Personal Investigation of the Evidence for Jesus.* Grand Rapids: Zondervan Publishing House,1998.

Swindoll, Charles R. *Growing Strong in the Seasons of Life.* Grand Rapids: Zondervan Publishing House, 1983.

Swindoll, Charles. *For Those Who Hurt.* Grand Rapids: Zondervan Publishing House, 1977.

Tozer, A. W. *The Knowledge of the Holy.* San Francisco: Harper Collins Publishers, 1961.

Wise, Robert L. *When There Is No Miracle.* Ventura: Regal Books, 1977.

Wright, H. Norman. *The Rights and Wrongs of Anger.* Eugene: Harvest House Publishers, 1985.

Appendix IV

End Notes

Chapter 1

1. Megalomania is obsession with the exercise of power, especially in the domination of others.
2. Lois Banner, *Marilyn: The Passion and the Paradox*, (New York: Bloomsbury Press, 2012), 54-55.
3. W. Hugh Missildine, *Your Inner Child of the Past*, (New York: Pocket Books, 1963), 29-30, 43-44.
4. National Sexual Violence Resource Center, "Child Sexual Abuse Statistics," accessed April 2018, https://victimsofcrime.org/media/reporting-on-child-sexual-abuse/child-sexual-abuse-statistics.
5. Note on grieving at the grave of Lazarus, friend of Jesus: Commentators say this was quiet

weeping, in contrast with the usual Jewish wailing at a Jewish funeral.

6. Emily Razzi, "Finding Beauty in Tragedy," *Our Daily Bread*, published September 28, 2017, https://ymi.today/2017/09/finding-beauty-in-my-tragedy/.
7. Corrie ten Boom, John Sherrill, and Elizabeth Sherrill, *The Hiding Place*, (Minneapolis: World Wide Publications, 1971), 215. Corrie quotes her sister Betsie just prior to her death.
8. Mrs. Charles E. Cowman, *Streams in the Desert*, (Grand Rapids: Zondervan Publishing House, 1965), 15-16.

Chapter 2

1. George Matheson, "O Love that Will Not Let Me Go," 1882.
   As I was researching this beautiful hymn, every source I looked into told me that George Matheson wrote this hymn in the midst of suffering. He was going blind; and because he was going blind, his fiancé broke off their engagement. And with a broken heart, he wrote the words of this hymn. It tells of God's faithful love toward us in any and all of our circumstances. Although Matheson lost his eyesight and his fiancé, he allowed God to use these losses for His glory. He wrote these words reminding us of God's constant and consistent love for us. It was Oswald Chambers'* favorite hymn; it is also one of mine.

*Oswald Chambers was an early twentieth-century Scottish Baptist and Holiness Movement evangelist and teacher, best known for the devotional *My Utmost for His Highest*.

2. My experience with forgiveness is described in more detail in Chapters Five and Six. See also Recommended Reading List for books on forgiveness.
3. At that time, Bipolar Disorder was known as Manic Depressive Disorder.
4. Deborah Roberts, *Raped*, (Grand Rapids: Zondervan Publishing House, 1981), 133.
5. J. Danson Smith, "The Gift of The Thorn," in *Springs in the Valley*, ed. Mrs. Charles E. Cowman (Los Angeles: The Oriental Missionary Society, 1945), 273.

Chapter 3

1. This chapter contains graphic, intimate sexual information and is intended for mature readers who are ready to face their pain with the enabling of the Spirit of God.
2. Missildine, *Your Inner Child of the Past*, 29-30, 43-44.
3. Dave Carder, et al., *Secrets of Your Family Tree: Healing for Adult Children of Dysfunctional Families*, (Chicago: Moody Press, 1991), 15. See Recommended Reading List. If you are interested in purchasing this book, please note that this book was republished in 2011 as a revised

edition titled *Unlocking Your Family Patterns*. (Carder, Dave, Earl Henslin, John Townsend, Henry Cloud, and Alice Brawand. *Unlocking Your Family Patterns*. Chicago: Moody Press, 2011.)

4. Joyce Landorf, *Irregular People*, (Waco: Word Books, 1982), 145-46.
5. TMJ, short for *Temporomandibular Joint*, is a painful condition that develops in the jaw muscles. This pain may be due to a combination of factors, such as genetics, arthritis or jaw injury, clenching or grinding the teeth, or stress.
6. I suffered from Endometriosis from the age of 14 until after I was married at the age of 32. It wasn't diagnosed until I was 26 years old. Some doctors link Endometriosis to incest. See the article in Appendix VI.
7. M. P. Ferguson, "The Consoler," in *Springs in the Valley*, ed. Mrs. Charles E. Cowman, (Los Angeles: The Oriental Missionary Society, 1945), 53.
8. Amy Carmichael, "Nothing in the House," in *A Braver Song to Sing: A Biography of Patricia Ann "Pann" Baltz*, auth. Marilee Dunker, (Grand Rapids: Zondervan Books, 1987), 6.
9. Earl Henslin, et al., *Secrets of Your Family Tree: Healing for Adult Children of Dysfunctional Families*, 38-39 (regarding the time it takes for the deep wounds of trauma and shame to heal, and how at times we or others push ourselves to be through with the process too quickly).

10. If you struggle with forgiveness, a very good book in my Reading List is *When Forgiveness Doesn't Make Sense* by Robert Jeffress. Appendix VII also provides an interesting study of "Forgiveness Therapy for Female Survivors of Abuse."
11. See Appendix VII: "The Use of Forgiveness Therapy with Female Survivors of Abuse."
12. Maurice E. Wagner, *The Sensation of Being Somebody: Building an Adequate Self-Concept*, (Grand Rapids: Zondervan Publishing House, 1975), 116-18.

Chapter 4

1. Frances Ridley Havergal, "Upon Thy Word I Rest," in *Springs in the Valley*, ed. Mrs. Charles E. Cowman, (Los Angeles: The Oriental Missionary Society, 1945), 122.
2. You can find many translations to compare with yours on https://www.biblegateway.com. But personally, I would not substitute this for your own personal copy of God's Word.
3. Brother Lawrence, *The Practice of the Presence of God*, ed. Donald E. Demaray, (Grand Rapids: Baker Book House, 1975), 86.
4. David Timms, *Sacred Waiting: Waiting on God in a World That Waits for Nothing*, (Minneapolis: Bethany House Publishers, 2009), 92.
5. According to many experts on the subject, there are five stages of grief and loss. They can be

experienced in any order depending on the loss and the individual. They are as follows:

1) Denial and isolation
2) Anger
3) Bargaining
4) Depression
5) Acceptance

6. My comments from Nehemiah were inspired from an excellent sermon given by my worship pastor Kevin Kruse. "The Joy of the Lord," Sermon, Laurelwood Baptist Church, Vancouver, WA, June 23, 2019.
7. Note on Psalm 69: Mire is a translation of what would be a *wadi* or a stream bed in the Middle East. *Wadis* are very dangerous. More people in the Middle East die from being in *wadis* at the wrong time than from dehydration in the deserts. A flash flood can come without warning, in a matter of seconds. If a person is in a *wadi* during such a time, he can drown instantaneously. When the water dries up, the mud becomes like a thick mire, almost like concrete, and the person is stuck. He will need to be rescued before another flash flood comes and he cannot move. See also Job 6:15-17 and Psalm 40:2.
8. Quote by J. R. Miller (1840-1912). "Quote by J.R. Miller: 'Christ is building His kingdom with earth's broken things,'" Goodreads, last accessed July 13, 2019, https://www.goodreads.com/quotes/333341-christ-is-building-his-kingdom-with-earth-s-broken-things-men.

9. Note on Isaiah 40: Charles Spurgeon, "May 14, P.M." in *Morning & Evening*, (Peabody: Hendrickson Publishers, 1995), 271. Please see Recommended Reading List.
10. Earl D. Radmacher, Ronald B. Allen, and H. Wayne House, eds., "Abba, Father" and "14:36 Abba," in *New King James Study Bible*, 2nd ed. (Nashville: Thomas Nelson, Inc., 2007), 1581. Earl D. Radmacher, Ronald B. Allen, and H. Wayne House, eds., "8:15 Abba," in *New King James Study Bible*, 2nd ed. (Nashville: Thomas Nelson, Inc., 2007), 1778. Section designations are notes correlating with Mark 14:36 and Romans 8:15.
11. Regarding tears in Psalm 56:8: Charles R. Swindoll, *Growing Strong in the Seasons of Life*, (Grand Rapids: Zondervan Publishing House, 1983), 164.

Chapter 5

1. A.W. Tozer, The Knowledge of the Holy, (San Francisco: Harper, 1961), 87-88.
2. Ernst W. Olson, 1925. Tom Fettke, ed., The Hymnal for Worship & Celebration, (Waco: Word Music, 1986), Hymn 44. These words of a hymn that promises amazing life and hope are from a woman who lived in great pain and anguish. "Children of the Heavenly Father" was written under the influence of incredible grace amid heart-wrenching pain. Karolina Wihelmina

Sandell-Berg, "Children of the Heavenly Father," 1855, trans..

3. Annie Clark, "My Beloved," in Springs in the Valley, ed. Mrs. Charles E. Cowman, (Los Angeles: The Oriental Missionary Society, 1945), 242-43. 4.
4. "Yahweh" is the Hebrew name for God, translated "LORD" in the Old Testament, because the Jews held this name in such high regard they would not pronounce or write it. But many today agree, and I agree with them, that God revealed His name to be known and loved, and therefore spoken, not hidden (Deut. 29:29). So we speak it. For many years it was mistakenly transliterated "Jehovah." It originates from Exodus 3, when God appeared to Moses at the burning bush and told Moses that His name was "I AM THAT I AM," meaning He always existed and always will exist.

For further information on this topic, please read the last chapter of William F. Kerr's excellent book, God, What is He Like?, the last chapter, titled, "What's In A Name?" in which he discusses the origin and use of the excellent name of Yahweh.

5. *"Sheol"* is mentioned in many of the Psalms in this book. It refers to the grave or the abode of the dead in Old Testament theology.
6. A.W. Tozer, *The Root of the Righteous*, (Harrisburg: Christian Publications, Inc., 1955), 13-16.

7. J.H.S., "God of the Impossible," in *Springs in the Valley*, ed. Mrs. Charles E. Cowman, (Los Angeles: The Oriental Missionary Society, 1945), 132.

Chapter 6

1. I didn't feel an overwhelming sense of support from my family when I first let them know I was going to see a counselor. As a group they gave me mixed responses. I had hoped for their approval, especially my mother's. Some responded as she did, but others had their own opinions. Some were very supportive. But I couldn't base my decision on their opinions. This was something I had to do because it was right and healthy for me.
2. My siblings have been very supportive of my writing on this subject and all have said they are looking forward to reading this book. Unfortunately, I have become acquainted with other families who are not so supportive of their family members who have been traumatized by incest.
3. Taken from *Growing Strong in the Seasons of Life* by Charles R. Swindoll. Copyright © 1983, 1994, 2007 by Charles R. Swindoll, Inc. Used by permission of Zondervan. www.zondervan.com
4. Dan B. Allender, The Wounded Heart: Hope for Adult Victims of Childhood Sexual Abuse, (Colorado Springs: NavPress, 1990), 26-28.

Please see Recommended Reading List for details and other helpful resources. "The victim reasons that God is like her abusive father or her preoccupied mother (since children are designed to learn their earliest lessons about God from their parents)."

5. Joyce Landorf, *Irregular People*, 145-46. Italics added. This quote illustrates how the stress of abuse that is not addressed by the healing process can destroy our physical and emotional health. See Recommended Reading List and Bibliography for information on how to obtain this book.
6. Dave Carder, et al., *Secrets of Your Family Tree*, 15.

Chapter 7

1. Earl Henslin, *Secrets of Your Family Tree*, 40-41. See Recommended Reading List.
2. Miry clay is so thick it is like concrete that is beginning to harden. See Chapter 4, Endnote 7 for what will happen if a person gets stuck in miry clay.
3. *Wadi* – See Chapter 4, Endnote 7.

Appendix V

What We Know About Child Sexual Abuse[1]

Child sexual abuse includes a wide range of sexual behaviors that take place between a child and an older person. These behaviors are meant to arouse the older person in a sexual way. In general, no thought is given to what effect the behavior may have on the child. For the most part, the abuser does not care about the reactions or choices of the child.

Child sexual abuse often involves body contact. This could include sexual kissing, touching, and oral, anal, or vaginal sex. Not all sexual abuse involves body contact, though. Showing private parts ("flashing"), forcing children to watch pornography,

---

[1] A Cry For Freedom. "What We Know about Child Sexual Abuse." Published June 23, 2018. http://acryforfreedom.org/2018/06/what-we-know-about-child-sexual-abuse/.

verbal pressure for sex, and exploiting children as prostitutes or for pornography can be sexual abuse as well. Researchers estimate that in our country about one out of six boys and one out of four girls are sexually abused.

Under the child sexual abuse laws, the abuser must be older than the victim in most cases. Some states require the abuser to be at least five years older.

WHO COMMITS CHILD SEXUAL ABUSE?

Most often, sexual abusers know the child they abuse, but are not family. For example, the abuser might be a friend of the family, babysitter, or neighbor. About 6 out of 10 abusers fall into that group.

About 3 out of 10 of those who sexually abuse children are family members of the child. This includes fathers, uncles, or cousins.

The abuser is a stranger in only about 1 out of 10 child sexual abuse cases.

Abusers are men in most cases, whether the victim is a boy or a girl.

Women are the abusers in about 14% of cases reported against boys and about 6% of cases reported against girls.

Child pornographers and other abusers who are strangers may make contact with children using the Internet.

WHAT ARE THE EFFECTS OF CHILDHOOD SEXUAL ABUSE?

It is not always easy to tell whether a child has been sexually abused. Sexual abuse often occurs in secret, and there is not always physical proof of the abuse. For these reasons, child sexual abuse can be hard to detect.

Some child sexual abuse survivors may show symptoms of PTSD. They may behave in a nervous, upset way. Survivors may have bad dreams. They may act out aspects of the abuse in their play. They might show other fears and worries. Young children may lose skills they once learned and act younger than they are. For example, an abused child might start wetting the bed or sucking his or her thumb. Some sexual abuse survivors show out-of-place sexual behaviors that are not expected in a child. They may act seductive or they may not maintain safe limits with others. Children, especially boys, might "act out" with behavior problems. This could include being cruel to others and running away. Other children "act in" by becoming depressed. They may withdraw from friends or family. Older children or teens might try to hurt or even kill themselves.

Sexual abuse can be very confusing for children. For a child, it often involves being used or hurt by a trusted adult. The child might learn that the only way to get attention or love is to give something sexual or give up their self-respect. Some children believe the abuse is their fault somehow. They may think the abuser chose them because they must have wanted it or because there is something wrong with them. If the abuser was of the same sex, children (and parents) might wonder if that means they are "gay."

Almost every child sexual abuse victim describes the abuse as negative. Most children know it is wrong. They usually have feelings of fear, shock, anger, and disgust. A small number of abused children might not realize it is wrong, though. These children tend to be very young or have mental delays. Also some victims might enjoy the attention, closeness, or physical contact with the abuser. This is more likely if these basic needs are not met by a caregiver. All told, these reactions make the abuse very hard and confusing for children.

If childhood sexual abuse is not treated, long-term symptoms can go on through adulthood. These may include:

- PTSD and anxiety.
- Depression and thoughts of suicide.
- Sexual anxiety and disorders, including having too many or unsafe sexual partners.
- Difficulty setting safe limits with others (e.g., saying no to people) and relationship problems.
- Poor body image and low self-esteem.
- Unhealthy behaviors, such as alcohol, drugs, self-harm, or eating problems. These behaviors are often used to try to hide painful emotions related to the abuse.

If you were sexually abused as a child and have some of these symptoms, it is important for you to get help.

WHAT CAN CAREGIVERS DO TO HELP KEEP CHILDREN SAFE?

Although caregivers cannot protect their children 100% of the time, it is important to get to know the people that come around your child. You can find out whether someone has been charged with sexual abuse and find out where sexual abusers live in your area by going to the website FamilyWatchdog.com.

Most importantly, provide a safe, caring setting so children feel able to talk to you about sexual abuse.

OTHER TIPS TO KEEP YOUR CHILDREN SAFE INCLUDE:

Talk to others who know the people with whom your child comes in contact.

Talk to your children about the difference between safe touching and unsafe touching.

Tell the child that if someone tries to touch his or her body in their private areas or do things that make the child feel unsafe, he should say NO to the person. He needs to tell you or a trusted adult about it right away.

Let children know that their bodies are private and that they have the right not to allow others to touch their bodies in an unsafe way.

Let them know that they do not have to do EVERYTHING the babysitter, family member, or group leader tells them to do.

Alert your children that abusers may use the Internet. Watch over your child on the Internet.

WHAT SHOULD YOU DO IF YOU THINK YOUR CHILD HAS BEEN SEXUALLY ABUSED?

If a child says she or he has been abused, try to stay calm. Reassure the child that what happened is not her fault, that you believe her, that you are proud of her for telling you (or another person), and that you are there to keep her safe. Take your child to a mental health and medical professional right away. Many cities have child advocacy centers where a child and her family can get help. These centers interview children and family members in a sensitive, warm place. They can help you report the abuse to legal authorities. They can help you find a medical examiner and therapist skilled in child sexual abuse. The National Children's Alliance website has more information and a listing of centers.

Children can recover from sexual abuse and go on to live good lives. The best predictor of recovery is support and love from their main caregiver. As a caregiver, you might also consider getting help for yourself. It is often very hard to accept that a child has been sexually abused. You will not be supporting your child, though, if you respond in certain unhelpful ways. For example, you will not be able to provide support if you are overwhelmed with your own emotions. Don't downplay the abuse ("it wasn't that bad"), but also try not to have extreme fears related to the abuse ("my child will never be safe again"). It will not help children if you force them to talk, or if you blame the child. Getting therapy for yourself can help you deal with your own feelings about the abuse. Then you might be better able to provide support to your child.

RECOMMENDED BOOKS FOR CHILD SEXUAL ABUSE

My Body Is Private by Linda Walvoord Girard and Rodney Pate (1992)

Please Tell!: A Child's Story About Sexual Abuse by Jessie Ottenweller (1991)

Something Happened to Me by Phyllis E. Sweet (1985)

It Happens to Boys Too by Jane Satullo and Russell Bradway (1987)

The Courage to Heal: A Guide for Women Survivors of Child Sexual Abuse (4th edition) by Ellen Bass and Laura Davis (2008)

Wounded Boys Heroic Men: A Man's Guide to Recovering from Child Abuse by Daniel Jay Sonkin and Lenore E. A. Walker (1998)

Appendix VI

Endometriosis Linked To Childhood Abuse[2]

Diane Mapes

Fred Hutch News Service

New Fred Hutch collaboration highlights yet another poor health outcome associated with adverse childhood experiences

July 17, 2018 • By Diane Mapes / Fred Hutch News Service

[2] Mapes, Diane. "Endometriosis linked to childhood abuse." *Fred Hutch News Service*. Last modified July 17, 2018. https://www.fredhutch.org/en/news/center-news/2018/07/endometriosis-linked-to-childhood-abuse.html.

Endometriosis, a painful condition that affects one in 10 reproductive-age women in the U.S., has been linked to childhood physical and sexual abuse, according to findings published today in the journal Human Reproduction.

Epidemiologist Dr. Holly Harris of Fred Hutchinson Cancer Research Center, lead author of the study, called the association between abuse and endometriosis "particularly strong," since women reporting severe to chronic abuse had a 79 percent higher risk of developing the condition.

"Both physical and sexual abuse were associated with endometriosis risk," she said. "And it's a strong association. There's also a dose response, meaning the risk increases with increasing severity and type of abuse."

Harris stressed that this absolutely does not mean that every woman who suffers from endometriosis — that's about 200 million women worldwide — was physically or sexually abused as a child. Rather, it demonstrates that both abuse and endometriosis are far too common. And while this study does not prove that abuse drives endometriosis (Harris said science is still trying to figure out the exact physiological mechanism), the study does add to the growing body of evidence linking adverse childhood experiences with poor health outcomes.

"We don't want people to think that if you have endometriosis it means you were abused," she said. "That's not true. But abuse in early childhood and adolescence is highly prevalent. In our study population of U.S. women, over a third of all women reported some type of abuse. If anything, this study highlights both abuse and endometriosis as prevalent conditions affecting women. It's not just a women's issue, though — it's actually something that everyone should be aware of.

"We need more research and more knowledge for health care providers and for women and men, in general. Many women and men have some type of history of abuse and that can have many health impacts throughout life."

Fred Hutch epidemiologist Dr. Holly Harris Fred Hutch file photo

A common and painful condition

Endometriosis is a common condition that usually affects women in their 20s and 30s. Although there's a hereditary component and a few known risk factors (starting your period early, lean body size), science hasn't provided a clear reason as to what triggers it. The condition starts when tissue from or similar to the endometrium, which normally lines a woman's uterus, starts growing outside of that area, attaching itself to the ovaries, fallopian tubes, bowel, bladder or other parts of the body.

The endometrium doesn't realize it's outside the uterus, of course, so it carries on as it always has: thickening and then breaking down, shedding and bleeding with every menstrual cycle. But while women usually expel the broken-down endometrium during their period, there's no place for displaced endometrium to go when it's growing outside of the uterus.

And that's a problem. Over time, the extra tissue within the pelvic region creates cysts, scar tissue and adhesions that can lead to chronic pain, excessive bleeding, pain with sexual intercourse, pain with urination or elimination, and, for up to half of women with the condition, infertility.

"Endometriosis has a lot of consequences," said Harris, who's conducted a number of studies on the disease and its potential associations with diet, dietary supplements and other inflammatory conditions.

"It affects quality of life, it causes loss of work. And on average it takes around seven years from first symptoms to actual diagnosis," said senior author Dr. Stacey Missmer of Harvard and Michigan State universities. "That's seven years of suffering, of physicians lacking knowledge of endometriosis and not taking the pain seriously or maybe not having the correct tools for diagnosis, since there are currently no noninvasive diagnostic tests for endometriosis."

Endometriosis research is underfunded, according to Harris, which means it's understudied.

"The amount of money that endometriosis gets in the context of other conditions is very small, considering how common it is and its large impact," she said. "Especially when you look at altered life goals, days of work lost, and the impact on the individual and national level."

Harris, who has a strong interest in women's health issues, said childhood abuse has previously been linked with chronic pelvic pain as well as uterine fibroids. According to the Centers for Disease Control and Prevention, research has also found associations between adverse childhood events (like physical and/or sexual abuse) and autoimmune disease, cancer, chronic obstructive pulmonary disease, frequent headaches, heart disease and many other physical and mental health issues.

Considering this research, as well as the associations that have been found between endometriosis and cardiovascular disease and certain subtypes of ovarian cancer, Harris said "it was natural for our team of scientists and clinicians to ask if there was an association with abuse and endometriosis."

Fred Hutch lead author Dr. Holly Harris emphasized that the pain is not in the women's heads, nor is it necessarily due to an injury caused by early sexual abuse.

Rather, the pain is a physiologic response that's driven by the stress and trauma of abuse — either sexual or physical.

"The stress response activates all these systems and causes you to be more sensitive to pain," she said.

Child abuse and endometriosis

For their study, Harris, Missmer and colleagues from Harvard Medical School and the Harvard T.H. Chan School of Public Health in Boston, among other institutions, used data from the Nurses' Health Study

II, or NHSII. An ongoing women's health study established in 1989, the NHSII queried nurses aged 25 to 42 about their lifestyle, demographics and disease history over the course of more than 20 years; some of the questions covered endometriosis as well as childhood, adolescent and adult abuse.

The researchers evaluated data from the study's original cohort of 116,429 women and found 60,595 premenopausal participants who'd answered questions regarding childhood abuse. Of those, 12,699 (around 21 percent) reported having experienced some level of both child/adolescent physical and sexual abuse.

The team then began looking for an overlap between those who'd reported childhood physical and/or sexual abuse and the 3,394 women (from the same pool of 60,595) who'd received a diagnosis of endometriosis via a laparoscopically-confirmed examination or surgery, which provides the most definitive diagnosis.

They discovered a 79 percent higher risk of endometriosis for women reporting severe-chronic abuse of multiple types compared to those reporting no physical or sexual abuse. Abuse was defined as "mild" when a child was kicked, bitten, or punched or hit with something once; "moderate" if they were hit with something more than once or physically attacked once in some other way; or "severe" if they were kicked, bitten, or punched or physically attacked more than once, or choked or burned ever. Sexual abuse was defined as mild (sexual touching); moderate (forced sexual activity during either childhood or adolescence); or severe (forced sexual activity during both childhood and adolescence).

Examining the association

Understanding exactly what's behind the association between child abuse and endometriosis is "the million-dollar question for all abuse discoveries," Harris said.

But there are nuances to the data that shed a bit of light.

About one-third of women with endometriosis are diagnosed when they want to have a child but can't. They may not be in pain but undergo an infertility evaluation to figure out what's preventing the pregnancy and then discover they have the condition. Other times, women are unable to control the pain with standard treatments such as oral contraceptives, so they undergo a laparoscopic surgery during which they are found to have endometriosis.

The bottom line: some women have painful endometriosis and some women don't. And in this study, the women with painful endometriosis were more likely to have experienced abuse.

"We saw stronger associations among women whose endometriosis was most likely diagnosed as a result of pain symptoms," said Harris. "So maybe the abuse during childhood and adolescence is working through a pain pathway. We know that abuse is associated with chronic pelvic pain; potentially there's a stress response to the trauma that activates these systems and causes you to be more sensitive to pain."

Harris emphasized that the pain is not in the women's heads, nor is it necessarily due to an injury caused by early sexual abuse. Rather, the pain is a physiologic response that's driven by the stress and trauma of abuse — either sexual or physical.

"The stress response activates all these systems and causes you to be more sensitive to pain," she said.

Harris said more research needs to be done to explore the underlying biological mechanisms of this potential pain pathway (she hopes to do more research in the realm of diet and endometriosis symptom relief, as well), but believes this newly published study provides yet more evidence that "early life abuse has health impacts across the course of your lifetime."

"There is building evidence for impact on multiple long-term health outcomes," she said. "This is just one of them. That's the larger picture."

Funding for this study came from the National Institute of Child Health and Human Development and the Atlanta Clinical and Translational Science Institute. The Nurses' Health Study II is supported by a grant from the National Cancer Institute.

Appendix VII

The Use of Forgiveness Therapy with Female Survivors of Abuse

Suzanne Freedman [1] **and Robert D Enright** [2*]
Review Article Open Access

[1] Department of Educational Psychology and Foundations, University of Northern Iowa, Iowa, USA

[2] Department of Educational Psychology, University of Wisconsin and Board Member, International Forgiveness Institute, Inc., Madison, Wisconsin, USA

***Corresponding Author:**
Robert D Enright
Department of Educational Psychology

University of Wisconsin and Board Member, International Forgiveness Institute, Inc., Madison, Wisconsin, USA
Tel: +1 608-262-0835
E-mail: renright@wisc.edu
Received Date: April 28, 2017; **Accepted Date:** May 08, 2017; **Published Date:** May 25, 2017

Citation: Freedman S, Enright RD (2017) The Use of Forgiveness Therapy with Female Survivors of Abuse. J Women's Health Care 6:369. doi: 10.4172/2167-0420.1000369

Abstract

Three intervention studies focusing on the psychology of forgiveness for women who have been abused are reviewed. All three incorporated the process model of forgiveness, used randomized assignment to experimental and control groups, and examined effectiveness through pre-test, post-test, and follow-up assessments. All three were conducted by different interveners. Results show that forgiveness is an effective way of restoring psychological health following abuse as well as increasing forgiveness toward the offender. For example, in Freedman and Enright's study with incest survivors, the experimental group showed a significantly greater reduction in anxiety, state anxiety, trait anxiety, and depression, and a greater increase in forgiving the perpetrator, and in hope. Similar results were found in Reed and Enright's study with women who experienced spousal emotional abuse. Participants who received Forgiveness Therapy, compared to an alternative therapy, demonstrated a statistically significantly greater increase in forgiving the former abusive partner, in self-esteem, in environmental mastery (everyday decisions), and in finding meaning in suffering (moral decisions), and a statistically significantly greater reduction in trait anxiety, in depression, and in post-traumatic stress symptoms. Lee and Enright's study with women with fibromyalgia, who experienced parental abuse in childhood, additionally shows that forgiveness, can help alleviate physical symptoms as well as psychological symptoms. Specifically, the forgiveness intervention participants had greater improvements in forgiveness and overall fibromyalgia health from pretest to the post-test, and in forgiveness and state anger from the pretest to the follow-up test than the fibromyalgia health intervention participants.

Introduction

The idea of forgiveness for women who have experienced emotional, physical and/or sexual abuse is often met with surprise, skepticism, and even horror. In our view, the opposition to forgiveness in this context is based more on a misunderstanding of what forgiveness is rather than on what forgiveness actually is. For example, some people are concerned that if a woman forgives a perpetrator, then she will go back into the abusive relationship [1].

Others think that if she forgives, this will suppress her anger or show that she is weak and not worthy of respect [2]. In contrast to such criticisms, research on forgiveness therapy illustrates that a self-chosen decision to forgive a perpetrator can be effective in restoring positive psychological health for women who have experienced past abuse [3-6].

The purpose of this article is to review the research conducted on the effects of forgiving for women who have experienced emotional, physical, and/or sexual abuse as well as discuss the implications of forgiveness therapy or education for women who have experienced abuse of any kind. Specifically, three studies that focus on forgiveness therapy with female survivors of abuse will be reviewed. Prior to reviewing this research, the definition of forgiveness as discussed in the literature will be given as well as briefly describing the model of forgiveness used in the research studies reviewed.

Forgiveness Defined

When discussing the topic of forgiveness for female survivors of abuse, it is important to be clear about what exactly is meant by forgiveness, specifically what forgiveness is and is not. Forgiveness is a complicated term that is often misunderstood by individuals in the general population as well as academics, helping professionals, and religious leaders [7]. According to Enright [8] and North [9], forgiving others encompasses two parts. First there is a willingness to abandon one's right to resentment, negative judgment, and negative behavior toward one who acted unjustly. Second, forgiving involves the voluntary fostering of the undeserved qualities of compassion, generosity, and sometimes even love toward the one who offended [8,9]. Forgiveness also can be more simply defined as a decrease in negative thoughts, feelings and behaviors toward an offender and perhaps, over time, a gradual increase in more positive thoughts, feelings and sometimes even behaviors toward an offender can occur [1,10]. It is important to highlight, especially to female survivors of abuse, that forgiveness does not mean that you deny or excuse the offender of the wrongdoing or deny and ignore one's feelings of *pain*.

As Smedes [11] states, we forgive in contexts of deep, personal, and unfair hurt. The injury might be psychological, emotional, physical or moral. When one forgives, she admits that the injury occurred and that she was hurt. One also recognizes that what was done to her was wrong as she works through her feelings of pain, anger, and resentment. Admitting that the past abuse occurred and working through one's negative feelings is not easy. It is often easier to deny, ignore, or displace the pain resulting from one's past physical, emotional, and/or abuse.

Although as stated by Arnold-Ratliff [12] in a discussion on both the difficulty and the importance of admitting to and dealing with hurt feelings, "*You realize that when you refuse to feel pain, you wind up feeling it forever; you finance it, setting up an installment plan to buy decades of chronic anguish.*" Admitting that the abuse happened and dealing with one's negative feelings is one of the first steps in the forgiveness journey [8,13].

What Forgiveness is Not...

Forgiveness often is confused with reconciling, forgetting, pardoning, and/or accepting [14,15] even though it is different than all of those terms. Some people criticize forgiveness because they think that advocating forgiveness leads to further abuse or hurt. Safety is the first and most important consideration. Thus, a survivor of any type of abuse would not be encouraged to forgive her abuser until she was safe and removed from the abusive environment [6]. When one forgives, she does not give up her right to a just solution; forgiveness and justice occurs together [13]. Forgiveness is one person's response; reconciliation is a coming together in trust by two or more people [16].

For example, a woman can be abused by her partner, leave him, forgive him, but not reconcile with him. Forgiveness can include a willingness to reconcile or waiting in the hope that the abuser changes his behavior and/or apologizes. Forgiveness is something the injured can do on her own without any response from the abuser. Reconciliation is dependent on a change in the offender's behavior and oftentimes includes an admittance of wrongdoing and/or an apology. The following quote by a survivor of domestic abuse clarifies well the difference between forgiving and other concepts including reconciliation, "Upon forgiving, I have not forgotten what happened. In remembering I make different choices in my intimate relationships. I do not condone what was done to me. It was morally wrong and undeserved. This forgiveness is not pardon, for I do not excuse his behavior or pretend it never occurred. My process of forgiveness was not reconciliation. In fact, mine was the opposite. It is a fracture that will never be mended [17].

The Process Model of Forgiveness

Several models of forgiveness are described in the literature [18,19]. Enright and the Human Development Study Group [20] developed one of the most comprehensive models of interpersonal forgiveness and to date it is the only forgiveness model that has been tested successfully with one-on-one interventions between the intervener and the participant [19] and the one that focuses on abused women. It consists of four phases and 20-units (initially included 17-units) and is the basis for the Forgiveness Therapy and research studies discussed in this paper.

In brief, the first phase is the Uncovering phase (units 1-8) and deals with the awareness of one's deep hurt and feelings associated with the abuse, such as anger, shame and guilt, and cognitive rehearsal or replaying the event in one's mind over a long period of time. The decision phase (units 9 to 11) is next in which the injured person recognizes the way she has been coping is no longer effective and begins to explore forgiveness as an option for healing before making the commitment to forgive. This includes exploring what forgiveness is and is not. Although one makes the commitment to forgive, this does not mean she feels forgiving at that time. The Work phase (units 12-15) is where the injured actively engages in processes such as reframing who the offender is, which includes broadening one's view of the offender as well as recognizing the inherent worth of all individuals, including the abuser, developing empathy and compassion for one's abuser (which takes time and patience), and accepting and absorbing the pain of her injury rather than passing it onto others. As stated by one of the incest survivor's in Freedman and Enright's [3] study 17 years following the forgiveness intervention,

"*There is not a day that goes by where I don't think about how much my participation in your group changed my life and my attitude. Forgiveness is not just an act-it's a way of life. My strongest beliefs are not necessarily religious ones, but ones rooted in Mother*

Theresa's idea that 'we cannot hate someone whose story we know.' Part of what I learned from you was that opening myself to more about what may have happened to my father in his own childhood made it possible for me to understand that he, too, may have been a victim of abuse" [7].

This phase includes some of the most difficult units in the process model and leads to the outcome or discovery phase (units 16 to 20) in which the injured finds meaning in her suffering and the forgiveness process, realizes that she has needed others' forgiveness in the past, that she is not alone in her pain and that she may have a new purpose in life because of her experience. The forgiver also realizes that as she gives the gift of forgiveness to the offender, she is healed as experienced by decreased negative feelings and thoughts towards the offender and perhaps, increased positive feelings and thoughts toward the offender.

It is important to note that forgiving takes time. This is especially true in situations of deep hurt, such as physical, sexual and/or emotional abuse [17]. Previous research conducted on Forgiveness Therapy illustrates that the longer the duration of the counseling or education, the stronger the results [18,19].

According to Worthington, et al. [21], "*Anything done to promote forgiveness has little impact unless substantial time is spent at helping participants think through and emotionally experience their forgiveness*".

Research on Forgiveness Therapy and Intervention with Female Survivors of Abuse

Three studies of women suffering abuse of different kinds are reviewed here. All incorporated the process model of forgiveness, were randomized trials, and employed one-on-one interventions between interventionists and the participants.

Forgiveness Intervention with Incest Survivors

Freedman and Enright [3] conducted an individual educational intervention using forgiveness as the goal with 12 incest survivors from a Midwestern community. This research was the first study to empirically examine the role of forgiveness as a treatment for incest survivors and the first to identify a relationship between forgiving and improved psychological health [3]. The average age of the 12 participants was 36 years with a range of 24 to 54 years. All participants were Caucasian and the average education was 15 years with a range of 12-19 years. For six of the participants (50%) their perpetrator was their natural father; for 8% their stepfather; for 16% their brother; for 16% their grandfather, and for 8% an uncle [3].

The design of the study was a yoked, randomized experimental and control group design in which pairs of participants were matched as closely as possible on nature of abuse, abuser, age abuse began, duration of abuse, current age of the survivor, SES status, and education level. One participant from each yoked pair was randomly selected to be in the experimental group (receive the forgiveness intervention first) and the other participant to be in the control group (receive the forgiveness education after one's yoked partner completed her forgiveness education). Freedman and Enright's [3] study was unique in that there was no specific ending point for participants and the intervention lasted as long as it took for the participants to forgive. Because the intervention was individual, experimental subjects met weekly with the first author for 60 minutes until they had progressed through all 17 units in the process model [20].

At the time of this study, the model included 17 units rather than 20. Each experimental participant was given a manual that described each unit in the process model and offered examples applicable to incest survivors. When a participant had experienced all 17 units and reported that she had forgiven she was given the Self-Report Forgiveness Measure [3], which included three definitions of forgiveness taken from the literature and five questions the survivor responded to regarding her feelings and thoughts toward the abuser in relation to the definitions of forgiveness. If the participant stated she had forgiven and her responses were logical and rational, her forgiveness was considered genuine.

Although Freedman and Enright [3] acknowledge the benefits of group therapy for incest survivors, they explain that the, "*...advantages of individual sessions for this specific intervention outweighed the advantages of group therapy. Because each participant* *continued with the intervention to criterion, each participant had differing amount of time within the intervention*" and were able to spend as much time as necessary on a specific unit. As stated by Freedman and Enright [3], one survivor who felt particularly guilty and ashamed about the abuse was able to spend four weeks discussing her feelings related to this unit.

Once the experimental participant had completed her individual intervention, she and her matched control participant were given the dependent measures and then the yoked control participant began the intervention and followed the same procedure as the original experimental participant. The average length of the intervention was 14.3 months (range of 10 to 16 months), illustrating that forgiveness is not a quick fix for deep hurts. Both the therapist or educator and client must be willing to invest the necessary time it takes to work through all the units in the forgiveness model.

Results illustrated that post intervention participants were more forgiving toward their abusers, had decreased anxiety and depression and increased hope for the future as well as greater self-esteem compared to those who had not experienced the forgiveness education and themselves pre-intervention [3]. In addition, experimental participants were assessed again when their matched control participant completed the intervention and they had maintained their change patterns on all dependent scales illustrating that there was no washout effect 14-months post-intervention. To show the effectiveness of this approach, the participants not only improved in psychological depression but also that depression was reduced to normal levels which were maintained 14 months after treatment ended.

Forgiveness Therapy with Emotionally-Abused Women

In a similar study Reed and Enright [6] examined the use of forgiveness therapy on depression, anxiety, and post-traumatic stress with women who experienced spousal emotional abuse and compared it to an active control group who received a different treatment. They hypothesized that Forgiveness Therapy may be more effective than other treatments because it focuses on decreasing resentment and feelings of revenge towards one's abusive ex-partner as well as the development of goodwill toward the abuser. Reed and Enright [6], emphasize that Forgiveness Therapy does not encourage nor require reconciliation, a frequent criticism of forgiveness in the literature [22, 23].

Forgiveness Therapy allows women who have been abused to choose a moral response to injustice and deep hurt which is both empowering and effective in decreasing the negative psychological outcomes of emotional abuse as one is validated for their anger and other negative feelings and then helped to move beyond them [6].

Participants in Reed and Enright's study included 20 psychologically abused women, ranging in age from 32 to 54 years (with a mean age of 45) in a Midwestern city who had been divorced or permanently separated for at least two years from their abusive spouse or romantic partner. Five (25%) of the participants had remarried and 15 (75%) had not remarried or started a new relationship with a live-in partner. The psychological abuse reported included criticizing; ridiculing; jealous control; purposeful ignoring; threats of abandonment; threats of personal harm; and threats of harm to property or pets. Six participants (30%) also disclosed experiences of sexual abuse.

As in Freedman and Enright's [3] study, a matched, yoked and randomized experimental and control group design was used. Ten pairs were formed from the 20 participants and matched as closely as possible on age, duration of abusive relationship, and time since permanent separation or divorce. Participants were randomly assigned to either the Forgiveness Therapy (FT) group in which they received one hour weekly individual sessions based on Enright's 20-unit forgiveness model or the control group in which they received one hour individual sessions of an alternative treatment (AT) focused on current life concerns, validating survivors' anger, strategies for making healthy choices, and interpersonal relationship skills. Participants in both groups received a treatment manual that included a protocol on FT or the AT. The Forgiveness Therapy was criterion based, as in Freedman and Enright's [3] study, and was completed when each participant reported that she had forgiven her abuser. The matched control participant ended the therapy at that time as well and the mean treatment time for all pairs was 7.95 months with a range of five to 12 months.

Gain scores from pretest to post-test on all dependent variables for the two treatment groups were analyzed using matched-pair t-tests. Results illustrated that Forgiveness Therapy participants demonstrated a statistically significantly greater increase in forgiving the former abusive partner, in self-esteem, in environmental mastery, and in finding meaning in suffering and illustrated a statistically significantly greater reduction in trait anxiety, in depression, and in post-traumatic stress symptoms compared to the participants in the control group who experienced the alternative treatment. Follow-up assessment for the Forgiveness Therapy participants also indicates that there was maintenance of gains from post-test to follow-up. This research is significant as it is the first study to demonstrate that Forgiveness Therapy is effective as a treatment for women who have experienced spousal psychological abuse and were experiencing long-term negative consequences. This study also illustrated that Forgiveness Therapy is significantly more effective in improving psychological health than an alternative treatment recommended in the literature for emotionally- abused women [6]. This study also attempted to control confounds that were present in previous research such as equal treatment duration for the two conditions, presentation of only psychological abuse, and complete separation from the abusing spouse for at least two years before the start of treatment.

Reed and Enright [6] hypothesized specific benefits of the Forgiveness Therapy to survivors of spousal psychological abuse that may not be present in other forms of therapy. These include a specific focus on decreasing resentment towards the abuser as well as the validation of one's anger, the acknowledgement that the survivor is a person of worth and the abuse does not change that worth, and that the survivor is also a person of courage because of her willingness to relinquish her resentment and recognize that her abuser is also a person of worth [6].

The Forgiveness Therapy also was found to be instrumental in helping survivors of spousal psychological abuse engage in relevant social justice issues and causes with positive energy as well as find new purpose in helping others who are in pain or are experiencing injustice. This is important to point out because Forgiveness Therapy and education has been criticized in the past because of the assumption that it prevents female survivors of abuse from assuming an activist role against such abuse and injustices [22].

Forgiveness Intervention for Women with Fibromyalgia

The third study illustrating forgiveness as an effective form of treatment with female abuse survivors was conducted by Lee and Enright [5]. This research compared the efficacy of a forgiveness intervention based on Enright's [8] process model with a fibromyalgia health intervention, focusing on healthy lifestyles and diets, and sleep and stress management, on women with fibromyalgia (FM) who had experienced physical, or sexual abuse, and emotional or physical neglect in childhood by one of their parents. Previous research on forgiveness illustrates that forgiveness is effective in improving physical as well as mental health [24,25]. The participants in Lee and Enright's study were 11 women diagnosed with FM for 1 to 20 years (M=8.91) and ranging in age from 21 to 68 years old (M=43.55). Participants were all volunteers recruited from newspaper advertisements as well as flyers and mass e-mails.

Screening measures were used to identify 16 participants (dropped to 11 by the end of the study) who completed the pretests and then were randomly assigned to either the forgiveness or a FM health intervention. As in the Freedman and Enright [3] and the Reed and Enright [6] studies, participants engaged in individual sessions, although the limit was set at 24 sessions for both groups. Sessions occurred once weekly for one hour with the same intervener. The treatment manual for the participants who received the forgiveness intervention was Enright's [8] book, Forgiveness Is a Choice. Participants (N=5) in the FM health intervention received a 290-page manual consisting of 32 book chapters selected from 15 books, three journal articles, and one outline resource as well as a 10-page syllabus including learning objectives and summaries of all sessions developed by the first author. The intervener had extensive knowledge in both the forgiveness process and the FM [5].

What is unique about this study is that the FM intervention participants completed weekly quizzes to assess their understanding of the readings and both the FM and forgiveness intervention participants completed final tests in FM and forgiveness. According to Lee and Enright [5] the weekly quizzes and final tests were important motivators for participants to read their materials before each session and know that the intervener was intent on helping them learn as much as possible about FM healthy practices and forgiveness. Results illustrate that the forgiveness group participants showed greater improvements in forgiveness, overall FM health, and state anger compared to participants in the FM health group. A follow-up assessment occurred 12 weeks following the intervention and results showed greater reduction of state anger in the forgiveness group. Lee and Enright [5] hypothesize that forgiving parents also may have gradually reduced the forgiveness participants' situational anger [5].

Subjective comments from the forgiveness intervention participants lend additional evidence to the effectiveness of the forgiveness intervention for these women who had FM and experienced some type of parental abuse. Forgiveness intervention participants found the intervention therapeutic, they benefited from learning to view their parents with respect, the forgiveness process appeared to positively impact their FM health, and they appreciated learning about forgiveness as a way to cope with both their past abuse and FM. Learning to forgive for the participants, who experienced both some form of parental abuse as well as FM, not only changed participants' views of their abuser but also impacted their physical and mental health.

Clinical Implications for Psychological Depression across the Three Studies

From a clinical perspective, the women in the Forgiveness Therapy condition across all three studies went from clinically depressed (mild to moderate depression) to non-depressed at the follow-up testing time. The well-established Beck Depression Inventory served as the dependent variable in each study. The results, seen in **Figure 1**, are important because depression can be difficult to ameliorate and the reported findings occurred not just directly after the intervention but at follow-up when the participants were without the forgiveness treatment for 14 months in Freedman and Enright [3], 3 months in Lee and Enright [5], 8.3 months in Reed and Enright (**Figure 1**) [6].

Figure 1: Cut-off scores for BDI-II [0-13: Minimal depression; 14-19: Mild depression; 20-28: Moderate depression; 29-63: severe depression].

Discussion

Research illustrates the potential effectiveness of Forgiveness Therapy and intervention for women who have experienced sexual abuse and incest, spousal emotional abuse, and some type of childhood abuse from a parent. These three studies were similar in that the intervention was individual for all participants, each study used some type of written manual or guide and for two of the three studies, and individuals were able to spend as much time as necessary in working through the forgiveness model. These factors may be an important part of Forgiveness Therapy and intervention in addition to the specific forgiveness content.

The power of forgiveness to impact the survivors' psychological and physical health was illustrated in all research reviewed. As a moral response to injustice and deep hurt, forgiveness focuses on more than just decreasing anger and increasing self-esteem. Forgiveness includes a focus on the paradoxes of extending mercy and good will toward those who were not merciful to the participants. This approach enables female survivors of abuse to see their offenders as human beings who deserve respect despite their hurtful actions. According to Enright and Fitzgibbons [1,10], Forgiveness Therapy helps clients better understand their offenders as well as make a morally good response toward those offenders. As Freedman and Zarifkar [17] emphasize, "*The role of the therapist is critical in educating clients about the forgiveness process as well as supporting clients in their decision to forgive and during their forgiveness journey*."

In an article discussing patient empowerment and the use of care managers in the treatment of 1160 patients living with cardiovascular disease, diabetes, heart failure, and/or at risk of cardiovascular disease in Italy, it was shown that partnerships and collaboration of all health professionals as well as having a care manager for each patient not only improved patients' disease-related health but also empowered and motivated patients to be more proactive regarding their health behavior [26]. This model could be applied to Forgiveness Therapy in a way that could help women who have experienced some type of abuse recognize that forgiveness can be an important component of their healing and provide them with support during their forgiveness journey.

If more medical professionals are aware of Forgiveness Therapy as an option for healing, women who might potentially benefit from forgiving could be targeted early in their treatment by their primary care physician or a care manager. The primary care physician can refer women with a past history of abuse to a professional serving as a "forgiveness" care manager. This "forgiveness" care manager could help women, who have been abused, become educated about forgiveness and support them on their journey as necessary. Women with more complicated issues and past abuse experiences could be referred to a mental health professional with expertise in Forgiveness Therapy. This mental health professional as well as the care manager and primary physician can all support the client during her journey toward forgiveness. The processes in the forgiveness model would be applied to forgiving the specific offender as well as being discussed and highlighted as a way to live a more forgiving life [14]. As in Ciccone et al. [26] research, clients can be empowered to recognize their anger and do something about it before it becomes unhealthy as well as motivated, for example, to use the idea of reframing (seeing the worth in others, including those who abuse) to develop more compassion and empathy when interacting with others or to accept and absorb their pain rather than pass it on to someone else.

Not only does Forgiveness Therapy change one's psychology for the better but also the results reviewed here are strong enough for mental health professionals to begin thinking about incorporating this form of therapy into their practices as stated above. We say this because, for example, depression not only can be reduced but also actually can fall to normal levels in women experiencing the serious injustice of incest and other forms of abuse. It is rare for any kind of treatment to show such effects. By our providing more information about Forgiveness Therapy and the forgiveness process in this article, it is our hope that professionals in the mental health field both recognize and use forgiveness as an effective form of therapy for female survivors of abuse. It further is our hope that more primary care physicians will recognize women who have been abused and who could benefit from Forgiveness Therapy and refer them to appropriate mental health professionals. We encourage more researchers to enter this new and potentially healing area of work so that more replications occur in the published literature. Such efforts could go a long way in alleviating the suffering of too many women who experience injustice.

References

1. Enright RD, Fitzgibbons R (2015) Forgiveness therapy. APA Books, Washington DC.
2. Lamb S (2002) Introduction: Reasons to be cautious about the use of forgiveness in psychotherapy. In: Lamb S, Murphy. Before forgiving: Cautionary views of forgiveness in psychotherapy, Oxford: Oxford University Press pp: 3-14.
3. Freedman SR, Enright RD (1996) Forgiveness as an intervention goal with incest survivors. J Consult Clin Psychol 64: 983-992.
4. Freedman S (2008) Forgiveness education with at-risk adolescent: A case-study analysis. In: Malcolm W, Decourville N, Belicki K. Women's reflections on the complexities of forgiveness, New York, NY: Routledge pp: 93-119.
5. Lee YR, Enright RD (2014) A forgiveness intervention for women with fibromyalgia who were abused in childhood: A Pilot Study. Spiritual Clin Pract 1: 203-217.
6. Reed G, Enright RD (2006) The effects of forgiveness therapy on depression, anxiety, and post-traumatic stress for women after spousal emotional abuse. J Consulting and Clin Psychol 74: 920-929.

7. Freedman S, Chang W (2010) An analysis of a sample of the general population›s understanding of forgiveness: Implications for mental health counselors. J Mental Health Counseling 32: 5-34.
8. Enright RD (2001) Forgiveness is a choice. APA Books, Washington, DC.
9. North J (1987) Wrong doing and forgiveness. Philosophy 62: 499-508.
10. Enright RD, Fitzgibbons R (2000) Helping clients forgive: An empirical guide for resolving anger and restoring hope. APA Books, Washington, DC.
11. Smedes L (1984) Forgive and Forget. Harper and Row, San Francisco.
12. Ratliff KA (2015) Do I feel my feelings? O' The Oprah Magazine 16: 94.
13. Enright RD (2015) 8 keys to forgiveness. Norton, New York.
14. Enright RD (2012) The forgiving life: A Pathway to Overcoming Resentment and Creating a Legacy of Love. APA Books, Washington, DC.
15. Enright RD, Freedman S, Rique J (1998) The psychology of interpersonal forgiveness. In: Enright RD, North J. Exploring forgiveness. Madison, WI: University of Wisconsin Press pp: 46-62.
16. Freedman S (1998) Forgiveness and reconciliation: The importance of understanding

how they differ. Counseling and Values 42: 200-216.

17. Freedman S, Zarifkar (2015) The psychology of interpersonal forgiveness and guidelines for forgiveness therapy: What therapists need to know to help their clients forgive. Spirituality in Clinical Practice 3: 45-58.
18. Baskin TW, Enright RD (2004) Intervention studies on forgiveness: A meta-analysis. J Counseling Development 82: 79-90.
19. Wade NG, Hoyt WT, Kidwell JEM, Worthington EL (2014) Efficacy of psychotherapeutic interventions to promote forgiveness: A meta-analysis. J Consulting Clin Psychol 82: 154-170.
20. Enright RD, The Human Development Study Group (1991) The moral development of forgiveness. Handbook of moral behavior and development, Hillsdale, NJ: Erlbaum 1: 123-151.
21. Worthington EL, Kurusu TA, Collins W, Berry JW, Ripley JS, et al. (2000) Forgiving usually takes time: A lesson learned by studying interventions to promote forgiveness. J Psychology Theology 28: 3-20.
22. Lamb S (2006) Forgiveness, women, and responsibility to the group. J Human Rights 4: 45-60.
23. Arenofsky J (2011) Swept up in forgiveness. Herizons Magazine 2: 2-35.

24. Witvliet CVO, McCullough ME (2007) Forgiveness and health: A review and theoretical exploration of emotion pathways. In: Altruism and health: Perspectives from empirical research Oxford university press, New York pp: 259-276.
25. Worthington EL, Scherer M (2004) Forgiveness is an emotion-focused coping strategy that can reduce health risks and promote health resilience: Theory, review, and hypotheses. Psychol Health 19: 385-405.
26. Ciccone MM, Aquilino A, Cortese F, Scicchitano P, Sassara M, et al. (2010) Feasibility and effectiveness of a disease and care management model in the primary health care system for patients with heart failure and diabetes. Vasc Heath Risk Manag 6: 297-305.

Appendix VIII

Scripture Index

Introduction – Foreword:

Old Testament

Deuteronomy 26:18 xv
Job 10:12-13 xiv
Psalm 25 vii
Psalm 40:1-14 viii
Psalm 55 vii
Psalm 86 vii
Psalm 139 vii
Malachi 3:16-17 xv

New Testament

Romans 5:8 xiv
2 Corinthians 4:7 xv

Chapter 1

Old Testament

Leviticus 18:6 22
Leviticus 18:7-18 23
Ezekiel 22:10-11, 25, ... 23-24
Ezekiel 22:26, 30-31 24

New Testament

John 9:1-3 22
John 11:3-4 25
John 11:36-43 26
John 11:44 27
John 15:5 29
2 Corinthians 5:17 18
Revelation 3:20 18

Chapter 2

Old Testament
Psalm 102:6-7 49
Psalm 139 47
Isaiah 53:3-5 47

New Testament
Hebrews 4:15 47

Chapter 3

Old Testament
Psalm 119:28 75
Isaiah 51:12 NKJV 107

New Testament
2 Corinthians 4:3-4 118
2 Corinthians 5:17 115

Chapter 4

Old Testament
Exodus 23:20 186
Exodus 33:18-20 214
Deuteronomy 6:24 149
Deuteronomy 33:26-27 154
Joshua 1:8 151
Nehemiah 8:10-11 166
Job 10:1 164
Job 10:8-11 164
Job 10:12-13 163
Job 16:16-17, 20 161
Psalm 3:3 157
Psalm 6:8-10 229
Psalm 12:5 201
Psalm 18:1-4, 6, 16-19 178-179
Psalm 22:24 209
Psalm 23:1-6 246

Psalm 25:16-20 211
Psalm 34:18 182
Psalm 55:1-8, 16-19, 22 190-191
Psalm 55:6-8 192
Psalm 56:8, 10-11 231
Psalm 61:1-4 188
Psalm 62:5-8 241
Psalm 68:5-6a 216
Psalm 69:1-4, 13-19 175-176
Psalm 103:13-14 218
Psalm 141:1-2 173
Psalm 142:1-3, 7 173
Psalm 143:1-2, 4-12 NLT 203-204
Psalm 143:5 206
Psalm 147:3-6 181
Isaiah 30:18-19 193
Isaiah 40:11 197
Isaiah 40:28-31 196
Isaiah 41:9b-10, 13 195
Isaiah 42:3 184
Isaiah 43:1-5 171
Isaiah 49:15-16 199
Isaiah 53:3-5 182-183
Isaiah 57:15 158
Isaiah 58:8-10 213
Isaiah 63:9 159
Jeremiah 29:11 220
Lamentations 3:25, 31-33 222

New Testament

Matthew 7:7-11 239
Matthew 11:28-30 244
John 10:10 156
John 11:4 NKJV 224
John 15:5 NKJV 223
Romans 8:15 217
Romans 8:26 228
Romans 8:31-32, 37-39 233
2 Corinthians 12:9-10 169
Galatians 5:22-23 167
Ephesians 3:14-17, 19-21 242
Ephesians 6:10-13 235
Philippians 1:6 237
Philippians 4:13 170
2 Timothy 1:7 223
2 Timothy 2:13 205

Hebrews 4:15-16 153
James 5:11 226
1 John 4:4 NKJV 189

Chapter 5

Old Testament

Psalm 25:1-9 269
Psalm 25:10-20 270
Psalm 25:16-20 272
Psalm 25:20-22 271
Psalm 25:22 274
Psalm 55:1-8 283
Psalm 55:9-19 284
Psalm 55:22-23 285
Psalm 59:10 253
Psalm 86:1-4 277
Psalm 86:5-8 278
Psalm 86:9-10 279
Psalm 86:11-13 280
Psalm 86:14 281
Psalm 86:15-16 282
Psalm 139:1-6 255
Psalm 139:1 256
Psalm 139:2 259
Psalm 139:3 260
Psalm 139:4-5 261
Psalm 139:6 262
Psalm 139:7-10 263-264
Psalm 139:11-12 264
Psalm 139:13-15 265
Psalm 139:16 266

New Testament

1 Corinthians 2:9-12 256-257
1 John 1:9 258

Chapter 6

Old Testament

Exodus 20:12 356
Deuteronomy 6:24 341
Proverbs 4:23 361
Proverbs 11:14 310
Proverbs 15:22 310
Proverbs 19:20 310
Isaiah 26:3-4 NKJV 360
Isaiah 55:8-9 364-365

New Testament
John 17:3 348
Romans 8:18 361
Hebrews 11:1, 3 341-342
Hebrews 12:1-3 342
Hebrews 12:15 325
James 5:13-16 309

Chapter 7

Old Testament
Psalm 6:8 368
Psalm 30:2 369
Psalm 40:1 368
Psalm 40:2 371
Psalm 40:3 372
Psalm 40:5 374-375
Psalm 40:6, 11 376
Psalm 40:13-14 377
Psalm 146:2 367

New Testament
Matthew 7:7-8 369
Mark 9:23 367
John 8:44 373

Epilogue

New Testament
Romans 10:9-10 390
1 John 1:9 389

Appendices

Old Testament
Deuteronomy 29:29 410
Job 6:15-17 408
Psalm 40:2 408
Psalm 56:8 409
Psalm 69 408
Isaiah 40 409

New Testament
Mark 14:36 409
Romans 8:15 409

Appendix IX

Index of Words

(Pages with Scripture are indicated in boldface type.)

-A-

Abandonment: 58, 61, 222, 323, 327. 442

Abba: **217**, 393, 404

Abundant Life: 348

Acceptance: viii, 58, 63-65, 383, 408

Accountability: 307

Ache: 229

Affection: 57, 63, 245, 329

Affliction: 31, **159**, 181, 201, **209, 211**

Affirmation: 329

Allender, Dr. Dan B.: 216, 391, 399, 411

Amy Carmichael: 98, 391, 406

Anger: vi, 40, 56, 64-65, 70, 81, 102, 119, 127, 130, **190**, **282**, 312, 323-324, 354-355, 380, 406

Anti-depressant: 371, 375, 388

Approval: 58, 63, 65, 68-69, 78, 119, 137, 329-330, 411

Ashamed: 9, 46, 120, 145, **211**, **229**, 305, 334, 336, **377**, 440

Attention: 2, 8, 28, 64, 68, 75-77, 328-329, 335 384, 415-416

-B-

Balm: 161, 207

Beautiful: xxix, xxx, 2-3, 15, 30, 32, 64-66, 96, 107-108, 115, 132, 135, 157, 188, 206, 210, 224, 241, 332, 404

Betrayal: xxv, xxvi, 20-21, 56, 102, 182

Bipolar Disorder: 20, 67, 108, 119, 127, 336, 405

Blame: 4, 9, 59, 81, 95, 304, 328, 419

Bondage: 287, 348, 350

Book(s): xi, xiv, xv, xvi, xxi, xxii, xxiii, xxv, xxvi, xxvii, xxx, 5-6, 10-11, 12-14, 22, 41, 61-62, 71, 82, 85-86, 102-103, 135, 140, **151**, 161, 163-166, 179, 186, 207, 231-232, 243, 249, 253, **262**, **266**, 271, 286, 311, 312,, 314, 317, 319, 324-325, 343, 364, 378, **381**, 387, 396, 410-412, 419, 445

Bottle: xxiii, 112, 144, **231**-232, 381

Broken: 16, 19, 21, 29, 30, 32, 41, 49, 87, 90, 98, 109, 114, 119, 125, 149, 156, 158, 167, 181-182, 185, 211, 305, 311, 326, 354, 359, 362, 378, 393, 404, 408, 423

Broken-hearted: **181-182**

Brother Lawrence: 159, 391, 399, 401

-C-

Carder, Dave, M.A.: vi, viii, 83, 339, 391, 399, 405-405, 412

Character: xiv, xxi, 53, 79, 107, 117, 153, 160, 176, 184, 220, 226, 236, 271, 286, 315-316, 322, 363, 373-376

Chemical Imbalance: 371-372

Children:	vii, xiv, 32, 44, 52, 64, 68, 80, 87, 102, 108-109, 121-123, 138, 162, 180, **182**, **189**, 216, 218, 239, 268, **270**, 302, 333, 334-338, 332-336, 357, 387, 389, 391-393, 395-396, 405-407, 407-708, 412-419 417
Christian:	xi, xxii, 13 17, 57, 81, 100, 103-104, 106, 112, 115-117, 285, 286-288, 300-302, 306, 337, 347, 354, 358-359, 361, 387-388, 397
Church:	xix, xx, xxi, xxvi, 13-14, 17, 41, 52-53, 88, 106-107, 112-113, 116, 118, 120-121, 128, 174, 206-207, 242-243, 247, 301, **309**, 320, 343, 347, 358, 390, 392, 396-397, 408
Churchill, Sir Winston:	226
Clothes:	16, 64, 100, 120, 124, 133, 329, 397
Communication:	228
Compliance:	65, 136-137, 330
Confidence:	53, 71, 87, **153**, 165, 198, 237-238, 262, 287, 313, 320, 335
Contempt:	4, 154, 334
Coping:	viii, 322, 326, 341, 344, 349, 357, 360, 454 452
Counseling (Counsel):	xi, xii, 6, 10-11, 42, 46-47, 41, 51, 58, 82, 91, 99, 121, 122, 132, 135, 142, 144, 151, 163, 173, 204, 249, 295, 296-299, 301-303, 306-308, **310**, 312, 314-315, 318-320, 322-324, 330, 358, 379, 387-388, 437
Covenant:	197, **270**, 288
Creator:	3, 40, 156, 158, 161, 164, **171**-172, 181, **196**, 218, 267, 388
Crime:	4, 45, 393
Cross:	xiii, xix, xxx, 17-18, 20, 31, 43, 114, 162, 182, 199, 273, 275, 288, **342**, 289
Crying:	31, 85, 90, 99, **175**-176, 312
Cuddling:	329
Cycle(s):	viii, 69, 84, 139, 322,423

-D-

Damaged:	v, 33, 199, 249, 285, 357, 401
Deception:	45, 373
Defenseless:	157, 328, 335, 384
Denial:	14, 122-123, 125, 305-306, 349, 408
Depression:	xi, xii, xvi, xvii, 2-3, 6, 8-10, 12, 14, 18, 29, 33, 41, 54, 56, 62-63, 65, 81, 88, 127, 144, 151, 161, 163, 169, 173-174, 176, 189, 198, 199, 205, 213-214, 215, 218, 231, 242, 253, 263, 364, 275, 277, 279, 281, 310, 312, 321-324, 328, 330, 355, 357, 369, 371, 373, 375, 377, 385-388, 396, 408, 416, 431, 440-441, 443, 447, 450-451
Desperate:	30, 51, 58, 62, 68, 206, 272, 301-302, 358, 262
Despise:	33, 103, 182, 209, 336
Destroy(ed):	81, 87, 156, **164,** 191, **204**, 235, 326, 333, 335-336, 355
Devastating:	2, **201**, 214
Diagnose(is):	139-140, 336, 372, 424, 426
Dignity:	8, 60, 71, 134, 157, 266
Disability:	6
Drinking:	7, 78, 93, 332-333, 336
Drug-Abuse:	3, 5
Dysfunction:	111-112, 119, 121-122, 300, 396
Dysfunctional:	86, 102, 108-109, 122, 305, 362, 391, 399, 405-406

-E-

Eating Disorder:	141, 349
Emotions:	5-6, 17, 28, 33, 41-42, 60-62, 79, 80-81, 94-95, 103, 110-111, 113, 128, 131, 145, 173-174, 226, 232, 258, 262-263, 279, 303, 309, 312, 315, 319, 322, 324, 354, 360, 371, 380-381, 386, 401, 416, 419
Encouragement:	44, 151-152, 213, 220, 234, 350, 358, 381
Endometriosis:	ix, 69, 86, 129, 139, 140, 224, 406, 421, 422-428

Escape: 10, 111-112, 116, 191-192, 264, **283**, 287, 322, 328, 344, 388

-F-

Faithful(ness): xvii, xxii, 155, 162, **167**, 192, 197, **203, 205**, 220, 258, 286, 374, **389**, 404

Family: xvii, 2, 4-5, 9, 12-13, 24, 34, 40, 45, 48, 51-52, 55, 59, 60, 63, 66, 68, 70, 77, 83, 85, 87, 97, 102, 108-109, 111, 116-117, 120-121, 123-126, 130, 138-139, 199, 206, 216, 237, **242**, 260, 298-308, 312-313, 331-334, 331-334, 336, 339, 356-357, 362, 370, 383-384, 389, 391, 395-396, 399, 405-406, 411-412, 414-415, 418

Father-daughter: 9, 295

Fatherhood: 218, 356

Fear(ful): **xv**, xix, 2, 16, 22, 28, 47, 58-62, 66, 70, 91, 94, 98, 110, 115, 122, **149**, 154-157, 164, **171**, 189-**190**, **195**, 201, 204-205, **217-218**, 220, **223**, 250, 256, 261, 265, **270**, 275, **280**, **283**, 285, 288, 298, 283, 285, 288, 298, 301, 305, 314, 323, 328-330, 334, 343, 345, 347, **372**, 383, 415-416, 419

Feelings: viii, xi, xii, 3, 29, 39, 40-41, 58, 65, 70-71, 79, 80-82, 84-85, 101-102, 104, 124, 128, 130, 134, 136-137, 142, 145, 174, 176-177, 189, 192, 218, 221, 227, 260, 299, 303, 307-308, 310-312, 314, 317, 319, 322-323, 327-328, 330-331, 335, 336, 346, 353, 360, 374, 388-389, 416, 419, 433-434, 436-437, 439-441, 450

Forget: xix, xx, xxiii, 5, 32-34, 51, 54, 88, **199**-200, 295, 303-304, 352, 363, 434, 452

Foreknowledge: xiii

Foundation: 150

Fragrance: 156

Friends: xii, xiv, xvii, xix, xx, xxii, 2, 9, 16-17, 19, **25**, 40-41, 45, 48, 52, 55, 88, 100-103, 106-107, 109, 113, 116, 120, 123-124, 133-134, 143, 204, 207, **270**, 285, 300, 302, 304, 306-308, 310-315, 318, 320, 324, 330, 334-335, 343, 346-347, 359, 364, 377, 379-381, 380-381, 383, 388-390, 396, 403, 414-415

Frightening: 7, 68, 93, 119, 254

Fulfillment: viii, xiv, 320-321

-G-

Grace: xvii, 73, 79, 102, **153**, 159, **169**, 170, 193, 195, 211, 214, 218, 220-221, 229, 238, 268, 273, 277-278, 282, **325**, 332, 338, 409

Grieving: 32, 163, 168, 187, 259, 313, 403

Groaning: **201, 228**

Guilt: xxx, 4,45,58,65, 81, 84-85, 92, 104, 129, 174, 191, 220, 301, 303, 324, 328, 336, 357, 355, 400, 436, 440

-H-

Hatred: 4, **211, 283**, 328, 355

Havergal, Frances Ridley: vii, 150, 392, 407

Healing: vii, viii, xvi, xxvi, 6, 10-11, 16-18, 31, 62, 72, 81, 86, 90, 103, 114, 130, 142, 144-145, 149, 151, 154, 156, 161, 170, 174, 193, 195-196, 199, 207, 215, 223, 226, 232, 235, 239, 245, 261, 278, 280, 285-286, 288, 294, 296, 298, 304, 308-309, 312, 318, 330-331, 337, 354, 367-368, 370, 372, 374-376, 367-368, 370, 372, 374-376, 378, 387, 388, 391, 396, 399, 401, 405-406, 412, 436, 449-450

Health: vi, xiv, 6, 12, 31, 110, 129, 138-140, 163, 174, 318, 320, 341, 412, 418, 418, 421-426, 428, 430-432, 436, 443-450, 452, 454

Heavenly Father: vii, viii, xx, xxiii, 13, 20-21, 46, 127, 142, 146, 153, 156, 186-187, 189, 192, 201, 204-205, 215, 224, 226, **239**, 245, 259-260, 265, 268, 272, 282, 322, 379, 388, 393, 409-410

Henslin, Earl, Dr.: viii, 102, 370, 391, 399, 406, 412

High Priest: 47, **153**, 197, 348

Holy: 22, **24**, 31-32, 79, 116, 153, **158, 166**-167, **171**, **216**, 228, **237**-238, 243, 268, 363-364, 370, 379-380, 382, 389, 394, 401, 409

Hope: xvi, xxvi, 13, 17, 30-31, 37, 71, 79, 86, 90, 99, 101, 111, 113-114, 156, 162-165, 169, 204, 213, **220**, 231, 237, **241**, **269**, **271**-272, 291, 296, 314, 340-341, 391, 396, 399-409, 411, 431, 435, 440, 450, 452

Hopelessness: 92

Hormone(s): 140

Horror: xxv, 6, **190**, 432

Human Trafficking: 5

Hurt: vi, xv, xvi, 2, 6, 9, 15, 29, 33, 39-40, 63, 70, 79-82, 84, 86, 88, 99-104, 113, 117, 119-121, 126, 130, 142, 146, 154, 158-159, 162, 180, 184, 186, 188, 205, 210, 229-230, 234-235, 249, 261, 281, 301, 303, 305, 317, 322-323, 329, 334-335, 338, 353-356, **377**, 381-384, 401, 415, 433-434, 436-437, 440-441, 448

Husband: xvi, xxii, xxiii, xxvii, 3, 23, 51, 82, 108, 123, 313, 332, 350, 375, 395-397

-I-

Immune: 248, 425

Incest: vii, viii, xi, xii, xii, xxiii, 4-11, 14, 17, 21-24, 28, 39-42, 46, 54, 57-64, 66, 68-70, 86, 91, 96, 100-102, 104-105, 108-111, 113-116, 119, 121, 124, 127-129, 134, 139, 141, 151 153-154, 156-157, 161, 163, 166, 173, 176, 180, 186, 191, 201, 220, 222, 224, 234-235, 244-245, 249, 271-272, 277, 285, 286, 295-296, 298-300, 303-305, 315, 317, 319, 321, 324, 328-330, 332-333, 359, 361-362, 368, 382, 395-396, 406, 411, 431, 436, 438-439, 448, 450-451

Incomprehensible: 375

Inflammation: 140

Impossible: vii, 49, 87, 128, 169-170, 214, 228, 244, 288, 291, 348, 375, 392, 411

Independent: 84-85, 136, 257, 350

Insecurity(ies): xxx, 54-55, 60, 62, 88, 136, 154, 156, 191, 234, 329, 343-345, 374-375, 384, 396

Intimate: 8, 44, 61, 95, 186 195, 231, **255, 260**-261, 263, 266, 380-381, 383, 405, 435

Insight for Living: xxi, xxii, 311

Intense: vi, 8, 16, 75, 87, 92-93, 124, 214, 220, 228, 272

Intercede: **228**

Internet: 11, 141, 359, 414, 418

Intimidating: 119, 121

Isolation (Isolating): 8, 330, 408

-J-

Journaling (Journals): v, vl, vii, viii, xi, xvii, xxi, xxii, 6, 11, 17, 33, 48, 58, 62, 70, 79, 84, 90-92, 99, 132, 142, 144, 151, 152-153, 253, 266, 274, 307, 311-312, 319, 320, 360, 383, 422, 430, 445

-L-

Landorf, Joyce: 85-86, 325, 392, 400, 406, 412

Letter(s): vii, viii, 15, 21, 70, 144, 325, 331, 337-338, 379

Light:	vi, 19, 32, 43, 76, 90, 103, 118, 138, 156, 160, 170, 213-214, 244-245, 264-265, 269, 275, 338, 380, 421, 427
Lonely:	vi, 48, **49**-50, 58, 63, 84-85, 117, **211**, **216**, 275, 315, 349, 358, 383
Loneliness:	vi, 3, 8-9, 19, 39-40, 48-49, 58, 60-61, 69-70, 75, 86, 88, 92-93, 191, 211, 381
Loss:	viii, xv, 8, 45, 88, 93, 102, 161, 163, 166, 168-169, 179, 189, 229-230, 259, 276, 287, 313, 320, 383, 404, 407-408, 424

-M-

Majestic:	36
Man of Sorrows:	33, 47, **182**, 209
Manic Depressive Disorder:	08, 405
Married:	xxx, 1, 23, 51-52, 64, 298, 301-303, 320, 332, 335, 379, 382, 395, 396-397, 400, 442
Martyr Complex:	87, 352
Maturity (immaturity):	343, 347
Medications:	7, 12, 20, 66-68, 112, 138, 371-372, 375-375, 386, 388
Megalomania:	5, 403
Memories:	vi, xvi, 2, 5-6, 28, 41, 54, 62, 88, 91-92, 154, 161, 199, 206, 302, 331-334, 383
Mentors:	xi, xix, xx, 17, 79, 206-207, 300-302, 306, 226, 308, 396, 398
Mercy:	20, 79, 88, 142, **153**, 159, **170**, 176, 180, **203**, 211, 214, 226-227, 229, **253**, **270-273**, 288, 448
Missildine, M.D., W. Hugh:	10, 82, 392, 400, 403, 405
Molested:	2-4, 130, 357
Mononucleosis:	248
Mom:	59, 66, 77-78, 84, 108, 118, 127, 331-322, 335
Monroe, Marilyn:	3-4, 40, 391, 403

Mother: 1, 2-3, 15, 48, 51-52, 64-68, 84, 105, 108, 120-124, 126, 133-135, 139, 216, 298-299, 300-301, 303-304, 328, 332-333, 345-346, 352, 356-357, 396, 412, 436

Music: xxi, 41, 97, 113, 185, 195, 206, 241, 301, 320, 358, 393

-N-

Naked: 22-23, 45, 46-47, 71, 214, 334

Negative: 28, 54, 80, 128, 132, 302, 320, 334, 341, 353, 396, 416, 433-434, 437, 441, 443

Neglect: 68, 75, 77, 356, 367, 445

Neurotransmitters: 371

Nightmare(s): xxx, 6, 10, 30, 62, 91, 154, 258, 377

Numb(ing): 2, 10, 84, 142, 161, 297

-P-

Pace: 196

Pain: v, vi, viii, xiv, xxv, xxvi, xxvii, xxx, xxxi, 2-3, 7, 14, 16, 18, 21, 24, 28, 31, 33-34, 36-37, 39, 41, 43, 44-45, 47, 57, 66-70, 73, 75, 79-80, 86-88, 91-92, 98, 100-101, 110, 113, 115, 117, 120-121, 124, 128, 138-141, 144-145, 153, 153-155, 158-162, 164, 169-170, 182, 184, 192, 194, 199, 201, 209-211, 220, 222, 224, 232, 234, 237, 244-245, 249-250, 261, 264, 270, 272-273, 276, 279, 295-296, 298, 302, 305-309, 312-313, 316, 318, 320, 322-323, 325-327, 333-334, 336, 353, 357-360, 363, 368, 373, 380-382, 396, 400, 405-406, 409, 416, 422-425, 427-428, 433-434, 436-437, 444, 450

Passive: 335

Peers: 315

Performance: 58, 79, 88, 101, 317, 376

Perpetrator: 12, 70, 131, 312-313, 315, 431-432, 438

Physical: xv, 11-12, 57, 92-93, 96, 109-110, 129, 132, 138, 145, 160, 174, 224, 247, 249-250, 295, 298-301, 313, 322, 326, 328-330, 338, 346, 357, 371, 381, 412, 415-416, 422, 425-426, 428, 431-434, 437, 445, 447-448

Post-Traumatic Stress 6, 58, 119, 154, 234, 376, 415-416, 431, 443, 451

Disorder (PTSD)

Power(ful): **xv,** 10, **4**, 19-20, 37, 40, 57, 59, 73, 78-80, 98, 100, 106, 110, 114, 116, 119, 126, 142, 153-154, 156-157, 159, 168-**169**, 179, 181, **196**, 220, **223**, 226, 229, 233, 235, 242-243, 256, 261-262, 267, 272, 277, 286, 291, 295, 301, **309**, 329, 336, 344, 353, 389, 403, 448

Prison: 78, 127, 131, **173-174**, 213, 231, 272, 324, 337

Promiscuity: 3

Prostitution: 4-5

Protection: 155, 157, 166, 249, 261-262, 347

Pretend: 51, 94, 100-101, 304, 435

Privilege: 5, 80-81, 207, 355, 362

Profound: 4, 9, 315, 358

Punishment: 45, 328, 354

Purpose: xv, 21-22, 24, 28, 41, 116, 126, 145, 158, 160, 165, 222, 225, 268, 323, 345, 359, 380, 432, 437, 440, 442, 444

Psychiatrist: 371, 388

-R-

Rage: 40, 323-324, 338, 364

Rape(d): 2-3, 4, 70-71, 95, 312, 319, 328, 393, 405

Reading: ix, 14, 82, 102, 118, 135, 152, 208-209, 253, 273, 312, 319, 364, 399, 405, 411-412

Reconciliation: 131, 432-433, 439, 450

Recovery: vii, 6, 11-12, 28, 86, 91-92, 145, 165, 169, 171, 180, 187, 189, 196, 212-**213**, 215, 223, 226-227, 235, 237, 239, 242, 244, 261, 295-298, 308-309, 318-319, 322, 338, 354, 358-359, 361-362, 418

Redemptive: xxv, 28-29, 156, 165

Rejection: 2-3, 52, 58, 70, 85, 101, 103, 117, 119, 120, 191, 195, 222, 305, 321, 330, 383-384

Relationship: xxx, 11, 13, 16, 28-29, 44, 52, 54, 59, 66, 84, 88, 97, 102, 108, 115, 136-137, 153, 181, 192, 207-208, 217, 241-242, 257, 286, 296-297, 314-317, 321-322, 333-334, 337, 347, 362, 383, 416, 432, 435, 438, 442

Remember(ing): 14, 17, 22, 30, 33, 58, 62-64, 75-76, 81, 83, 88, 93, 102, 106-108, 117, 121, 126, 131, 145, **164**, 168, 180, 188, 194, **203**, 205-**206**, 207-209, 226, 247, **269**, 289, 305, 308, 310-312, 313-314, 317-318, 320, 324, 331, 333, 344-346, 351, 354, 368, 435

Respect(ful): 3, 8-9, 12, 45, 48, 55-56, 60, 65-66, 70, 77, 80, 106, 122, 125, 130, 134, 163, 176, 301-302, 307, 329, 334, 336-337, 341, 353, 415, 432, 446, 448

Restless: vi, 48, **190**-191, **380**

Resources: 11, 33, 136-137, 357, **373**, 412

Restricted: 119, 125, 133, 334, 430

Risk: xii-xiii, xiv, 169, 245, 297, 340, 346, 348, 350, 422-423, 426, 449, 451, 454

Role Models: 112-113, 120-121, 206, 300-301, 347

-S-

Sadomasochism: 4

Salvation: 150, **178**-179, **241**, **390**

Satan: 46, 105, 117, 154-156, 235, 344, **373**

Scared: vi, 48, 55, 60, 64, 95, 105, 110, 139, 216, 354

Scriptures: vii, ix, xvii, xx, 21, 152, 153, 160, 236, 253, 262, 264, 363-364, 376

Secret:	xii, xvi, 39-40, 60-61, 70, 83, 94-95, 113, 186, 191, 258, **265**, 304, 328, 377-378, 391, 399, 405-406, 412, 415
Secrecy:	9, 12, 304
Security:	xxx, 34, 55, 60, 62, 78, 88, 136-137, 156, 163, 191, 201, 321, 329, 339, 343-344, 372, 374-375, 384, 396
Self-Esteem:	vi, 15-16, 87, 132, 157, 259, 416
Self-Hatred:	4
Self-Preservation:	349
Sex Addiction:	4
Sexual Abuse:	v, ix, 2-3, 4-5, 8, 13, 29, 31, 39, 86, 122, 140, 242, 316, 391, 393, 399, 403, 413-419, 422-425, 428, 432, 442, 445, 448
Shame:	vi, xxx, 3-4, 9, 21, 29, 44-47, 46-47, 102-103, 120, 145, 154, **176, 211, 229**, 271, 276, 304-307, 332, 334, 336-337, **342, 377**, 406, 436, 440
Shepherd (Good):	v, 19, 36-37, 47, **196, 245**-246, 248-249, 269, 380
Sibling(s):	24, 63-64, 83, 108, 126, 129, 139, 303, 354, 394, 409
Slavery:	**216**
Sorrow:	xxvi, 33, 37, **47**, 162, **182-183**, 185, **209**, 224-225, 228, 268
Spinal Fluid:	371
Spontaneous:	122, 230, 299, 340, 348, 350
Spurgeon, Charles H.	197, 394, 409
St. John of the Cross:	162
Suffer:	xiv, xxii, xxvii, 6, 11, 21-22, 28, 58, 67, 78, 109, 115, 119-120, 123, 127, 158, 164-165, 174, 182, 187, 193, 199, 209, 214, 218, 222, 224, 232-**233**, 244, 267, 271, 335-336, **361**, 376-377, 400, 404, 406, 422, 424, 431, 437-438, 443, 451
Suppressed Memories:	6, 54
Suppression:	8, 39-41, 191, 314
Suicide:	xiii, 2, 8, 14, 111-112, 114, 121-122, 126, 154, 156, 192, 248, 362, 387, 416

Suicidal: xiii, 8, 12, 29, 100, 297, 363, 387, 396

Survive: 19, 40, 69, 89, 297, 338, 340-341, 343-344, 248, 350

Survival Mode: viii, 340-341, 343, 348-349, 350

Survival Mode Overload: viii, 343, 348-349, 351

Survivor: ix, xvii, 5-7, 10, 29, 151, 153, 166, 176, 226, 296, 339, 344, 407, 415, 419, 429-436, 438-440, 442, 444, 448, 450-451

Swindoll, Charles R. xxi, 232, 311, 401, 409, 411

-T-

Taylor, J. Hudson: 61

Tears: vi, viii, xvi, xxv, 16, 21, 39, 42, 80, 90, 99-100, 117, 125, 142-145, 152, 154, 161, 189, 195, 226-232, 242, 244, 249, 296, 308, 312, 323, 353, 358, 363, 368, 381, 387, 390, 396, 409

Ten Boom, Betsie: v, 35

Ten Boom, Corrie: v, 35, 394, 404

Tenderness: 232, 258, 266, 337

Thorn: vi, 73, 98, 393, 405

Thrive: 19

Timid: 335

Timidity: **223**

"To Do" List: 349

Tormented: 4

Tozer, A. W.: vii, 258, 286-287, 364, 394, 401, 409-410

Transform: 169, 266, 378

Trauma: v, vi, xii, xvii, xxx, 2-3, 5, 7-10, 12, 22, 31, 39, 42, 44, 51-52, 54, 58, 62, 69, 75, 88, 91, 96, 101-102, 115, 121, 128, 140, 173, 199, 201, 218, 224, 229, 234, 258, 260-261, 267, 271, 277, 295-296, 305, 308, 310, 319, 324, 337, 339, 361-362, 364, 376, 382, 406, 425, 428

Traumatic: 6, 8-9, 13, 58, 68, 95-96, 119, 154, 199, 224, 234, 259, 362, 376, 431, 441, 443, 451

Treasure: xiv, xv, xvi, 23-24, 145-146

Trophy: 169, 195

Trust: xii, xiii, xxiii, xxvi, 9, 13-14, 19, 20-21, 29-30, 41, 46, 56, 59-60, 70, 72, 77-78, 97, 102-103, 109, 116, 130-132, 153, 156, 170, 176, **178**, 181, 184, 186, 191, 194, 200, 201-**203**, 204-205, 210, 213, 217, 222, **231**, 235, **241**, 245, 249, 255, 262, **269**, 278, 280-281, 285-286, 288, 297, 303, 313-316, 337, 346, 348, 350-351, 354, 356-358, **360**, **372**, 376, 379, 390, 434

Turmoil: 8, 128-129, 300, 357

-U-

Unapproachable: 158

Unchangeable: 336, 379

Unique: 55, 81, 113, 157, 355, 439, 446

-V-

Victim: vii, 4-7, 11-13, 29-31, 39-40, 42, 45-46, 102, 153, 158, 163, 166, 176, 184, 204, 222-223, 235, 242, 249, 271-272, 277, 285, 296, 298, 304-306, 315-316, 319, 324, 339-340, 344, 362, 391, 393, 399, 403, 411-412, 414, 416, 437

Vindicate: 211

Violate(d): 14, 21, 23, 54, 56, 60, 70, 114, 126, 144, 156, 171, 187, 223, 232, 234-235, 281, 286, 304, 331

Voice: xxi, 18, 26-27, 48, 57, 95, 129, 173, 178, 190, 207, 229, 247, 275-276, 278, 284, 304, 317, 368

Volatile: 119, 127

Vulgar: 120, 334

Vulnerable: xii, 7, 14, 78, 94, 157, 224, 329

-W-

Wagner, Maurice: 135, 394, 407

Wandering: **231, 381**

Wasted:	xxi, 49, 138, 231
Weeping:	**25, 161, 229, 368**, 381
Wept:	**25**, 230
Western Conservative Baptist Seminary:	xii, xx, 206, 247, 320-321, 324, 361
Wholeness:	63, 87, 142, 156, 161, 249
Wisdom:	xiii, 16, 130, 142, 160, 245, 249, 351
Withdrawal:	8, 40-41, 65, 92, 191, 330
Word of God:	29, 112, 144, 166, 236, 309, **342**, 360

CPSIA information can be obtained
at www.ICGtesting.com
Printed in the USA
FSHW020825140520
69983FS

9 781545 670262